SUITABLE STRANGERS

IRISH CULTURE, MEMORY, PLACE
Oona Frawley, Ray Cashman, Guy Beiner, *editors*

SUITABLE STRANGERS

The Hungarian Revolution, a Hunger Strike, and Ireland's First Refugee Camp

Vera Sheridan

INDIANA UNIVERSITY PRESS

This book is a publication of

Indiana University Press
Office of Scholarly Publishing
Herman B Wells Library 350
1320 East 10th Street
Bloomington, Indiana 47405 USA

iupress.org

© 2023 by Vera Sheridan

All rights reserved

No part of this book may be reproduced or utilized in any form or by any means, electronic or mechanical, including photocopying and recording, or by any information storage and retrieval system, without permission in writing from the publisher. The paper used in this publication meets the minimum requirements of the American National Standard for Information Sciences—Permanence of Paper for Printed Library Materials, ANSI Z39.48-1992.

Manufactured in the United States of America

First printing 2023

Cataloging is available from the Library of Congress

978-0-253-06460-8 (hardback)
978-0-253-06461-5 (paperback)
978-0-253-06462-2 (e-book)

*To my family: Ian, Aisling and Andrew and
Liadh and Lara, and Neil.*

*In loving memory of David Jolley, who died too soon;
my parents, Éva and Imre; and my grandparents
Mária and György, who loved children and
"lost" theirs to the West.*

CONTENTS

Acknowledgments ix

A Note on Hungarian Names xi

List of Sources xiii

List of Abbreviations xv

PART ONE

1. Defining the Context 3
2. Finding Suitable Refugees 33
3. Camp Life 59
4. The Hunger Strike 97

PART TWO

5. The Lives of Children 123
6. Domestic Problems, International Solutions, Departures 154

PART THREE

7. Comparisons, Legacies, and Conclusion 185

Bibliography 213

Index 223

ACKNOWLEDGMENTS

No book stands alone, so I would like to thank Jennika Baines, PhD, Acquisitions Editor; and Sophia Hebert, Assistant Acquisitions Editor, Indiana University Press.

An interdisciplinary book like this relies on help from a great many sources, and I would like to thank the following:

> Aisling Sheridan for supplying distracting reading
> Anna Letoha for her hospitality
> Ariane Gill for information on medicines
> Barbara Carrick, Our Lady's Hospital, Crumlin
> Councillor Mannix Flynn
> Chris Mullen for making me laugh out loud
> Derek and Carole Leinster for helping to find Elizabeth
> Des Ryan, local historian, Limerick
> Dr. Mel Duffy for sound advice
> Elizabeth Chikány
> Gary Filerman
> Gillian Doel, Art Therapist
> Hajnal Collins
> Hazel Wright Ian Sheridan for innumerable dinners
> Isabelle Vonèche Cardia for her collegiality
> Joe Malone, publican and local history raconteur, Limerick
> John Murphy
> John Thompson for sourcing UK newspapers
> Luke Kearns
> Lynda Mannick
> Mark Coehn
> Mark Collins
> Michael Headen
> Mike Maguire, Limerick City Library
> Neil Sheridan for his sense of humor
> Olga Murphy
> Ronit Lentin for her generosity
> Rosemary and Elizabeth Kearney
> Sean Curtin
> Sharon Bolger, *Wicklow Voice*

Sister Angela and the Mercy Provincial Archive Centre of the Convent of Mercy for their hospitality

Sister Immaculata for granting access to her archive material and for our meeting in Limerick

The Mercy nuns in Limerick for their hospitality

William O'Neill, Limerick City Archives

A NOTE ON HUNGARIAN NAMES

Speakers of Hungarian will notice a certain amount of inconsistency in the spelling of Hungarian names, which requires some explanation, as it is much more than a lack of awareness of Hungarian usage, such as the standard practice of using a surname followed by first name. The full range of diacritics required for proper Hungarian spelling were absent in the Irish media and in the Irish archival material of the 1950s, with one exception: a newspaper headline that used Hungarian, *köszönöm szépen*, for "thank you." In addition, there appeared to be no regard for accuracy when taking down Hungarian names so that some looked vaguely Hungarian but were not in fact spelled correctly. An example is Rezzo, discovered in a newspaper article as Resto (not used in this study). In Hungarian, the name is Rezső; I added the correction for this, as Rezzo would be too strange for a Hungarian reader.

In general, I have used the spellings I came across; otherwise, it would be difficult to see who exactly is referred to in official documents. The range of documentation extends from letters from UNHCR to communication from local branches of the Irish Red Cross. There is one specific exception—namely, Dr. Szövérffy, a scholar who migrated to the United States and would be known by his proper name. There is one terrible misspelling of his name in chapter 3 with a correction in brackets, as otherwise the reference would have been incomprehensible. There are also Hungarian letter writers who signed their names with the correct Hungarian spelling, and I have kept these. In addition, some people might have gone along with the new spelling of their name once they saw it in Ireland or might have translated their first name into the English version or made some attempt to anglicize it—for example, Charles for Károly. Overall, this creates a certain amount of unevenness of spelling that, while it is unavoidable, necessitated elucidation as well as causing some amusement in the narrative.

SOURCES

Archives

Houses of the Oireachtas, Dáil Éireann Debates

Department of Education Industrial School and Reformatory Archive

District Court records

Dublin City Library and Archives

Garda Museum and Archives

General Register Office (GRO), Research Room

Irish Newspaper Archives

Irish Times Digital Archives

Limerick Library and Local History Archive

Military Archives of the Defence Forces

National Archives of Ireland

National Library of Ireland

Representative Church Body Library

Mercy Congregational Archives, Sister Immaculata Collection

Hungary:

Open Society Archives

Newspapers

Irish:

Anglo-Celt

Clare People

Connacht Tribune

Evening Herald
Irish Examiner
Irish Independent
Irish Pictorial
Irish Press
Irish Times
Kilkenny People
Limerick Leader
Longford Leader
Nenagh Guardian
Sligo Champion
Tuam Herald
Wicklow Voice

UK:
Daily Telegraph

Austria:
Die Presse

Organizational Magazines:
The Church of Ireland Gazette
Red Cross World

ABBREVIATIONS

BCAR: British Council for Aid to Refugees

C3: security section of An Garda Síochána

CCC: Canadian Council of Churches

CRS: Catholic Relief Services

DP: displaced person

ESB: Electricity Supply Board

HMS: Her Majesty's Ship

ICEM: Intergovernmental Committee for European Migration

ICRC: International Committee Red Cross

IRC: Irish Red Cross

IRO: International Refugee Organisation

ITDA: *Irish Times* Digital Archive

LÉ: *Long Éireann*, Irish ship

LRCS: League of Red Cross Societies

LWF: Lutheran World Federation

NAI: National Archives of Ireland

NATO: North Atlantic Treaty Organization

NCO: noncommissioned officer

NCWC: National Catholic Welfare Conference

NGO: nongovernment organization

NLI: National Library of Ireland

PCFHRR: President's Committee for Hungarian Refugee Relief

RCBL: Representative Church Body Library

RRP: Refugee Relief Program

SICMA: Sister Immaculata Collection, Mercy Archive

TD: Teachta Dála, an elected representative who sits in the Daíl, the lower chamber of the Houses of the Oireachtas, the Irish parliament, with the Senate and senators comprising the upper house.

UN: United Nations

UNHCR: United Nations High Commission for Refugees

UNRRA: United Nations Relief and Rehabilitation Administration

USEP: United States Escapee Program

USSR: Union of Soviet Socialist Republics

PART I

Part 1. Captured Soviet tank in Budapest street. Source: HU OSA 412 Gary Filerman Collection on Hungarian Refugees of 1956, Vera and Donald Blinken Open Society Archives at Central European University.

1

DEFINING THE CONTEXT

> Only fame will eventually answer the repeated complaint of refugees of all social strata that "nobody here knows who I am"; and it is true that the chances of the famous refugee are improved just as a dog with a name has a better chance to survive than a stray dog who is just a dog in general.
> —Hannah Arendt, *The Origins of Totalitarianism*

> Few though the numbers we welcome may seem, an immense amount of joy and well-being surely lies before those who escape to us—who escaped from the most miserable experiences conceivable to normal life and a home among kindly people in a country unscarred by war.
> —Dorothy McArdle, *"The Iron Cage"*

Sociohistorical Overview

The 1956 Hungarian Revolution began on October 23, and it was brief and bloody. Soviet troops (re)invaded on November 4, 1956, and the revolution was virtually over a week later.[1] Imre Nagy's government fell, and he and other prominent figures, like Pál Maléter, the revolution's military leader, were imprisoned and executed in 1958 as part of the retribution that followed. The new government, with the Soviet-appointed János Kádár at its head, ordered the executions of 229 people; some 22,000 people were sentenced and 13,000 interned. Thousands more were dismissed from their workplaces and placed under police supervision. Retribution ceased only with the amnesty of 1963, although many people in Hungary would continue to endure decades of discrimination.[2] The United Nations investigation into the events of 1956 found that Soviet Russia had committed human rights violations with its deportations of Hungarians to the USSR.[3] Some

200,000 people fled, mainly into Austria; 18,000 went to Yugoslavia. As a new member of the United Nations, Ireland heeded the call to ease Austria's refugee burden as thousands escaped across its borders. Initially, the Irish government considered taking a small number of refugees and thought of offering asylum to 250 Hungarians.[4] Later, government ministers publicly offered to take 1,000 refugees, but eventually 548 arrived in Ireland to live in Knockalisheen camp, which had been prepared for their reception. The camp, in rural county Clare, was fortuitously close to Limerick, so the refugees had access to some urban relief from rural isolation. Almost two years after their arrival, a period that had included a very public hunger strike at Knockalisheen, only 61 Hungarians remained in Ireland, with 25 still waiting to move to another country.[5] The rest had relocated primarily to Canada, but some also traveled to new homes in Australia, the United States, Argentina, the United Kingdom, Israel, and Switzerland.[6]

The reception of the Hungarians, Ireland's first major foray into the world of international refugee resettlement, has never been deemed a success, and arguments have been offered to account for its failure. Contemporaneous analysis by one TD (a Teachta Dála, an elected representative in the Dáil) points toward the outcome as "a big show off to show what we can do." Another took the young state's more nationalist perspective of protecting "one's own" by saying, "We have a lot of people who have not got rashers and eggs for their breakfast but these people have got them."[7] Eilís Ward's political evaluation comes primarily to the same conclusion concerning the status of the venture—that Ireland, as a recent member of the UN, used the occasion to try to bolster its international profile. She believes that bad planning contributed to the situation, as did "a weak interpretation of Ireland's responsibilities under the 1951 Convention." Interdepartmental discussions revealed that there was confusion over the exact status of the Hungarians, though this confusion had no foundation, as all the Hungarians who crossed the border were deemed to be refugees as defined by the Convention Relating to the Status of Refugees of 1951.[8] From a migration perspective, specifically contemporary migration, and with a rapidly changing society in Ireland, Fanning locates the response to the Hungarian refugees in exclusionary state practices and racism. He also takes the view that government hoped to augment Ireland's newfound international standing. In addition, there was intercultural exploration: Katalin Pálmai Bánki interviewed Hungarians who arrived in the 1940s and 1950s and detailed their adaptation to Irish life. The study referred to their motivation and actions and the difficulties they encountered during this cross-cultural process. These differing perspectives point to the necessity of considering a fuller and more nuanced interpretation of events than has previously been the case. This extant literature has focused on adult experiences without any examination of the effects on the lives of the children who comprised approximately half the number of refugees who arrived, as well as children subsequently born in Ireland. The question of daily life in Knockalisheen, which the Hungarians endured for almost two years, has not been addressed despite the fact that camp life, with its daily routines, created moments of significant friction and misunderstanding for both administrators and refugees. There are no references to fond memories of Ireland by those who left or even feelings of gratitude expressed by those who departed or remained. Additionally, there has been no exploration of particular precedents incorporated into state policy regarding the Hungarian refugees.[9]

Likewise, this resonance exists in the contemporaneous geopolitical context of the Cold War. As bipolarization emerged between East and West, Cold War politics had already begun to shape the international political sphere. Concerns around communism, communist infiltration, and subversion played out in national arenas, where local social and cultural interpretations of its dangers, or benefits, influenced domestic spaces. In tandem with these preoccupations concerning refugees and communism, European countries, some of which had signed the Convention on the Status of Refugees of 1951, also had to confront the question of what to do with the people escaping from behind the Iron Curtain. There was a steady stream of refugees from East to West Germany, for instance; the international press reported stories of spectacular and ingenious escapes that turned some fleeing individuals into temporary celebrities. These human-interest stories roused emotional sympathy and linked the domestic "inside" and the international "outside" aspect of the Cold War, where the presentation and manipulation of such stories drew the foreign element into the domestic sphere and into popular understanding.[10] In Ireland during the 1950s, national television had not yet emerged, and national radio did not broadcast throughout the day. Consequently, newspapers, magazines, and the popular Catholic press predominated as sources of news. The narratives of great escapes received considerable press coverage through syndicated columns bought by the major Irish presses for their readers. The reading public consumed articles written by well-known American journalists such as the *Herald Tribune*'s foreign correspondent Don Cook and Pulitzer Prize–winning war correspondent Marguerite Higgins.[11] Irish newspaper readers became increasingly familiar with the international context of the Cold War and Cold War refugees. They were aware of Soviet disinformation, interpreted as "the diabolical cunning of the rulers of the Kremlin," that would allegedly contribute to the ultimate destruction of the West. Such contextual considerations further indicate that there is room for a fuller inquiry into the case of the 1956 Hungarian refugees in Ireland.[12]

Situating the Study

Refugee research is often policy driven and focused on contemporary events in contrast to the historical. Though Elie points toward studies of large-scale refugee movements, international organizations, and the international refugee regime, scholars have called for a turn to history in relation to the multidisciplinary field of refugee and forced migration studies.[13] There also remains a marked absence of the *presence* of refugees in forced migration and history; refugee voices are characterized by their absence, or by being forgotten, in the historical record so that "denial of refugee histories is part of the process of denying refugee realities today."[14] A significant contributor to this state of affairs is the omission of refugees from the story of the nation and its people, despite the fact that the formation of a state results from identifying who can and cannot belong and, as a consequence, who may be forced to move.[15] Instead, the frame of reference is "taken-for-granted ways of thinking about identity and territory" contained in a "sedentarist analytical bias" of a sedentary nation-state with its population held snugly inside, in contrast to globalization and transnational realities.[16] More recently, historians have been called on to look beyond the perspective of the nation-state and studies of specialized histories of discrete movements of refugees.[17] Gatrell has proposed a history of "refugeedom" that "incorporates the social and cultural history of refugees within shifting systems of power" and can act as a corrective, inclusive of the discourses that frame responses to refugees.[18] In their responses to refugees, states may well turn to their tradition of hospitality to strangers and generous welcomes—a discourse that depicts the state as benevolent and refugees as being worthy of munificence, for which they must exhibit gratitude but never criticism of state practices. Critiques of these popular national discourses of welcome and hospitality may irritate national self-image but contribute to a reevaluation of the historical record.[19] Such reevaluation links to memory, to collective and individual imagining, as with the envisioning of the Irish Famine and Irish emigration. This envisioning of the national self-image is subject to shifts in both collective and individual memory, either as aspects of the grand historical narrative fade in memory or as a particular aspect is rediscovered or reemphasized over others.[20] Links between memory and migration not only include hospitality but can veer toward nationalism, such as "looking after our own" or protectionism in objections to employing displaced persons (DP) after the Second World War instead of Irish workers. Memory can also lapse, as with Ireland's strong but forgotten contribution to postwar aid efforts in Europe, or incorporate affinities in novel interpretations of Irish experiences of the Famine and emigration as a symbol of solidarity with refugees. These examples demonstrate that the interpretation of memory is variable and can be simultaneously negative and positive or lost over time.

Gatrell turns to a maritime metaphor in reference to the displacements of people that have led to perilous journeys across the Mediterranean in order to look beyond the "boundedness of the modern nation state." "Thinking through oceans" offers a path to interrogate "the meanings attached to population displacement and thinking about cultural and social linkages across time and space."[21] Refugees also have something to say about their trajectories, which may relate to others who had already taken the same path, such as prior Hungarian migrations to the United States.[22] Refugees may also have commentary about how they are depicted as helpless masses or as imbued with the state of "the refugee experience" when there is no single experience but a multiplicity thereof. This slipperiness of "the refugee experience" makes it resistant to essentialism where aspects of political and historical processes become inscribed "in the bodies and psyches of the people who are undergoing them."[23] Marfleet considers that history contributes to the story of human movement by helping us understand how contemporary movements relate to past ones and the response of institutional actors to these past movements; by tracing the evolution of discourses about refugees; and, finally, by uncovering how they influence refugee and asylum policies. If the refugee is "everywhere and nowhere" in the national narrative, and if through their absence they are portrayed by others as abject, as apathetic, or as the scrounging migrant, then it becomes imperative to write them into history. If refugees become the subject of inquiry, then so must their lived experience, a difficulty for historians if history has repeatedly omitted them.[24] Marfleet turns to the movements using Thompson's "history from below," where there is evidence of history made by ordinary people previously marginalized and absent in the grand narrative of the nation. Refugees do leave traces of their lives, for instance, in the historical records of the state, nongovernmental organizations, and the media. As a consequence, refugee voices remain filtered by interpreters, their actions understood according to legal or other criteria in a specific cultural context and the prejudices of individuals in contact with them. They are also present in records that states or international organizations prefer to hold secret, particularly if refugees become entangled in the darker narrative of the nation, which itself has to wait for discovery.

In addition, the writer of a history is not absent from its interpretation; addressing referential reflexivity—the relationship between the researcher and the researched—not only aids understanding writer positioning and potential biases but also how a multiplicity of authors understand their actions and situations.[25] From a historical perspective, the multiplicity of authors refers, for example, to the writers of official documents as well as the journalists who record the utterances of officials or refugees, all situated in their sociocultural context; these voices contributed to the strands of heteroglossia that coalesce to form the milieu of the histories of refugees.[26] I acknowledge my own position of being a 1956 Hungarian refugee as a child, smuggled out of Hungary and lucky enough to reunite with my mother in Austria. There we spent time in our first refugee camp, a converted youth hostel in Admont, where there was a sense of some adventure in contrast to the much larger camp of Traiskirchen. We journeyed to England across land and water, where I looked in terror at the gray, heaving waters of the North Sea. We landed on February 6, 1957, and settled first in the Hednesford refugee camp.[27] Refugees, however, when allowed, become settled citizens whose passports, like mine, permit innumerable, uncontroversial, legitimate border crossings across land and sea. Consequently, I add my voice in dialogic tension to those emanating from the other texts included in this history. I also use the term *refugee* here specifically to refer to the 1956 Hungarians as, initially in their case, the convention of 1951 provided this status to all. Second, I also use the term to apply to people seeking safe harbor or short-term sanctuary, in relation to such temporary encounters in Ireland occurring after the Second World War.

Despite the calls to move away from discrete histories to focus on wider comparisons, in-depth studies can contribute to the emerging field of refugee history, as such a study recognizes "the importance of paying attention to the specificities of a particular historical moment."²⁸ An in-depth study becomes a "necessary prerequisite" to the kind of historical approach advocated by Gatrell.²⁹ Furthermore, an in-depth study still resides in the international context of refugee movements. Consequently, this multi-sited study includes the international dimension in relation to the central focus on the Irish context, examining camp life during the two years that a significant number of Hungarians resided in Knockalisheen camp in Ireland. There is no archive of Hungarian refugee oral histories in Ireland, although references arise to specific individuals who remained there, often in relation to commemorations. Yet the 1956 Hungarian refugees in Ireland have left traces of themselves in, for instance, personal testimony, surviving letters, newspaper reports or other media, official government documents, and NGO and religious order records. This study uses these sources and interviews, all of which contribute to a reinterpretation of events that situates the story of the 1956 Hungarian refugees in Ireland in its social, cultural, and historical context. The arrival and subsequent departure of the Hungarians remain at the margins of what is considered to be Irish history even though the historical record reveals profound effects on some of the Hungarians who encountered Irish society and the sociocultural norms of the 1950s. The foregrounding of the Hungarian refugees' experience challenges their marginalization and turns to creating a "history of refugees which is embedded in rather than sitting adjacent to established histories."³⁰ In turn, their lack of inclusion in the historical narrative ignores their disruption of the narrative of the nation, their relationship to prior movements of refugees, and Irish responses to them.³¹

The historian J. J. Lee referred to the 1950s in Ireland as a period of malaise, and Diarmaid Ferriter records such negative labeling of this period with terms such as *stagnation* and *drift*.³² This sense of stagnation did not lift with election results that shuffled the parties in and out of government in the mid-'50s. In 1954, the election result produced an interparty government led by Taoiseach John Costello consisting of Fine Gael, Labour, and Clann na Talmhan with the support of Clann na Poblachta. In March 1957, Clann na Poblachta withdrew its support and forced an election resulting in a change of government with Fianna Fáil at the helm, led by seventy-four-year-old Éamon de Valera.³³ Regardless of these changes, economic stagnation, unemployment, emigration, and rural depopulation contributed to a bleak picture of 1950s Ireland. R. F. Foster writes that by 1956 "it appeared that, despite the injections of post-war aid, the Irish economy was unfit to cope with the strains of independence."[34] Seventy-eight thousand unemployed in 1957, and a net population loss of fifty-four thousand in the same year, contributed to such pessimism that years of inertia and crisis became linked to "a sense of the country living in the stagnant sidestreams of history."[35] Contemporaneous assessment of this period lamented the "lost momentum" of ideas that, fifty years previously, had produced a renaissance in politics, literature, and the language movement. Roland Burke Savage, editor of *Studies*, the Jesuit-founded quarterly, felt that Ireland enjoyed the "stagnant peace of a backwater."[36] However, the decade also produced T. K. Whitaker's economic report in 1958, which helped Irish society transform and turn away from the policy of protectionist tariffs employed to safeguard local industry and an identity drawn from an idealized rural past. Ireland changed into a country that successfully became a member of the UN after the Second World War. By so doing, Ireland regained an international presence it had enjoyed previously as a member of the League of Nations. Continuing with this trend of looking outward, Ireland made its first application to join the European Economic Community some three years later as it forged a route to prosperity in the 1960s.[37]

That is not to say that Irish society changed overnight. Ireland in the 1950s remained deeply conservative, and the power of the Roman Catholic Church was substantial, embodied and embedded in the long reign of Dublin's Archbishop John Charles McQuaid. The position of women and children was not always a happy one and involved personal, family, and public silences around people whose actions did not fit the mores of the time. Poverty reduced children to inmates of industrial schools as an "invidious Irish snobbery" had little sympathy for destitution despite a pretense to a classless society.[38] Petty crime became a route to reformatories, with neither industrial school nor reformatory free from the everyday violence of corporal punishment despite the campaigning efforts of a few. Some of these institutions became involved in decades of psychological and sexual abuse of children in their care. The Commission to Inquire into Child Abuse, established in 1999, developed a five-volume report as it investigated such abuse as far back as the 1940s.[39] Society hid unmarried pregnant women in mother and baby homes so they gave birth to their children in secret.[40] The subsequent adoptions of such children could be made in unusual circumstances, such as the falsification of legal documents or sending babies to the US without the knowledge of their mothers. The effects of this historical situation continue to reverberate in Irish society and are of direct concern to this study of 1956 Hungarians in Ireland. A heavily criticized report on mother and baby homes, published in 2021, contributes to these reverberations.[41] Garvin sums up the social and cultural world of 1950s Ireland as suiting the majority of people, defining this as two-thirds of the population, leaving one-third to experience the unseemly, even ugly side of society at the time, exemplified by the use of coercive incarceration across a range of institutions.[42] Ferriter concluded that state and church colluded to hide and keep secret the "shame" of women and children "whose behaviour or existence challenged the notion of the Irish as more chaste, pious and respectable than people elsewhere."[43]

Postwar Refugees in Ireland

Neutral Ireland, on the periphery of Europe, did not remain immune to the human costs of war during 1939–45, or the Emergency, as it was called in Ireland. Clair Wills, for example, detailed bodies washing up on the western seaboard long after the occurrence of battles at sea.[44] Likewise, following the mass displacement of millions of people during the Second World War throughout Europe came the effort to repatriate or resettle them.[45] Among the many children displaced by war or surviving the death camps were five Jewish children, Bergen-Belsen concentration camp survivors who accompanied Dr. Robert Collis, a pediatrician, back to Ireland, where he later adopted two of the children.[46] Groups of children came temporarily for respite, including the children of Operation Shamrock in 1946 and a hundred Jewish orphans in 1948. Operation Shamrock lasted three years and involved over four hundred children, arriving in groups in Ireland from 1946 to 1949 for a lengthy period of respite. The children came from families where both parents were alive but the fathers were missing, or they were orphans; some came with siblings. Herbert Remmel, however, came because of his special family status: his father, labeled a communist, was persecuted in Nazi Germany. Most of the children came from the Rhine-Ruhr area, which had been heavily bombed by the Allies. The Rhineland was a Catholic area of Germany, and the German branch of Caritas, the global Catholic charity, became involved in selecting most of the children sent to stay with foster families in Ireland. The majority of the children integrated into Irish life though their prolonged stay, which created problems for their return, particularly where deep bonds had been forged with their Irish foster parents, who were grief stricken at their departure; after three years, the younger children had forgotten their German and spoke only English. As a consequence, reintegration into family life was not always smooth and sometimes involved negotiating new sets of relationships, such as a formerly missing father or new siblings. A few children were unable to settle back in Germany and returned to live permanently in Ireland.[47]

Initially, the Department of Justice had rejected a request to bring the one hundred Jewish children to Ireland, infamously on anti-Semitic grounds. The taoiseach reversed the decision following a meeting with the Chief Rabbi of Palestine, Dr. Herzog, which guaranteed the care and maintenance of the children as well as their eventual departure from Ireland. Clonyn Castle in the village of Delvin, county Westmeath became the respite center for this group of Jewish children following its purchase by a Manchester businessman, Jacob Levy. The Chief Rabbi's Religious Emergency Council, a London-based organization, employed a large number of workmen for over a year to renovate the castle, which was situated on more than one hundred acres and had more than seventy rooms. Despite this local employment opportunity, there was a feeble attempt to burn down Clonyn Castle on March 26, 1948. The gardaí stated that "while numbers of the local people do not like the proposal to house Jewish children in the Castle, there is not . . . any local agitation against the admission of the children." Regardless, someone had used force to enter the castle to sprinkle a small amount of petrol on the floors of five rooms; fortunately, the half-hearted attempt to commit arson succeeded only in scorching the wood.[48]

Postwar, the United Nations Relief and Rehabilitation Administration (UNRRA) had repatriated millions of people, even using force to return people to countries under Soviet control. The International Refugee Organization (IRO), UNRRA's successor agency, had the task of resettling people who still refused to meekly return home as the very nature of home had changed, at times utterly, as with the complete disappearance of locales within their communities.[49] With the realization that the DP camps would not empty easily, countries slowly began to accept DPs for resettlement, not because of a humanitarian change of heart but due to the need for labor. The IRO realized that postwar worker shortages could provide an opening for resettling the DPs by matching their skills with the economic needs of a particular country; in this way, they resettled over a million people from 1947 to 1951. However, after enjoying initial success, during which the young, fit, and strong left the camps for new homes in other European countries or migrated further afield to Canada or Australia, by 1950 the IRO was struggling to resettle the DP population. Though a few governments had absorbed some of their number on humanitarian grounds, many people still resided in DP camps in Europe, such as the elderly and the disabled.[50] As the pope had promised to help with the resettlement of DPs, Archbishop McQuaid brought this interest on the part of the Roman Catholic Church to the attention of the Irish government.[51]

The first displaced person to come to Ireland was thirty-four-year-old Stella Askalanzi. She was Greek by birth and Albanian by marriage, and her Jewish husband had been killed in 1943; since then she had lived in several camps and in one of them obtained an IRO certificate as a domestic and laundry worker, as did many such displaced women; they relocated to countries experiencing the worldwide shortage of domestic workers in large institutions such as hospitals or in homes with young children.[52] Through the auspices of the IRO, 145 refugees had arrived in Ireland by 1952, including children orphaned by the war or whose parents could not be traced. Of ten children who arrived from Italy's Bagnoli Displaced Persons Camp near Naples, five young girls, from fourteen to sixteen years of age, went on to complete a two-year domestic training course with the Sisters of Mercy in Dublin; like the IRO certificate, this course would provide a route to employment.[53] The Irish government had requested that the Irish Red Cross (IRC) care for the refugees once the IRO disbanded, and, in consultation with the trade unions, the IRC sourced employment for skilled workers such as electricians, architect's assistants, bricklayers, bakers, and dress designers. By 1953, the Irish government could report in the questionnaire sent by the consultative assembly of the Council of Europe that Ireland had absorbed one thousand refugees, defined as "a person who for reasons of race, religion, nationality or political opinion is unable or unwilling to return to the territory from which he came." Two hundred forty-two of the one thousand refugees had already naturalized as Irish citizens; the government view was that while they had been "absorbed into the national economy since the end of the war . . . it is impossible to give any firm estimate of the number who could be absorbed into the future. . . . the Government are willing to admit refugees for whom employment at standard wages is available, in the absence of objections from trade unions, but the number which can be absorbed must necessarily be small as Ireland is an emigration country. In recent years nearly 20,000 persons (or 6% of the State's population) have emigrated each year."[54] As in many other countries, the Irish response to DPs and others classed as refugees was an opening and potential shutting of doors based on a blend of economic self-interest and humanitarianism.[55] At the same time, a figure was conveyed officially to UNHCR, proposing an additional one thousand Hungarian refugees for resettlement in Ireland—not a fanciful number but one that represented policy continuity based on the previous movement of refugees into Ireland who settled seamlessly and became naturalized citizens.

Setting Sail for Canada

Of significant relevance to the reception and treatment of the 1956 Hungarians in Ireland is the saga of the *Victory*, a ship that landed in Ireland in 1949 while en route to Canada. Once again, geography did not save Ireland from a combination of Second World War combined with Cold War repercussions. Consequently, and unexpectedly, Ireland became caught up with people desperate enough to reach Canada by setting sail from Sweden in overcrowded boats; the passengers were mostly refugees from the Baltic states. They had already crossed the Baltic Sea in two groups, the first in 1940 to escape from the Soviet invasion, which was closely followed by a German takeover; the second exodus was to get away from the Soviet advance near the end of the war. The main impetus for setting sail from the relative safety of Sweden was a palpable fear of the USSR and its proximity to Sweden, where the possibility of further conflict could leave the country vulnerable to potential Soviet expansion. Additionally, in the complex history of the Baltic states there were people who had taken up arms against the USSR and so had aided the German Reich. Soviet demands to return "Soviet citizens" to their countries of origin in the Baltic states and the pressure placed on Sweden had resulted in deportations, which had resulted in terrible acts of suicide during transportation. Some Estonians were forcibly returned in 1946 due to their service to the German army. Consequently, uncertainties and fears outweighed good treatment in Sweden, and some refugees were prepared to risk it all to start new lives in Canada. They took a chance in retrofitted ships that had been built originally for action during the Second World War. These ships, some of which encountered difficulties during the voyage from Sweden, found safe haven in various ports in Ireland.[56]

In early August 1949, the *Gladstone*, carrying 26 passengers, pulled into Sligo for provisions; two weeks later, it reached the Canadian port of Halifax. The previous year, the *Walnut*, a seven-hundred-ton former minesweeper carrying 365 people, including 70 children and extended families, had also found refuge in Sligo. The grossly overcrowded ship, designed to carry a small number of naval personnel, had arrived on November 24, 1948, and stayed for over a week, during which time the vessel took on provisions and one hundred tons of coal. The local branch of the IRC ascertained that the people on board were in good health as they had their own doctor. However, the pilot who had boarded the craft had found scant medical supplies; acting on his report, the IRC sourced donations of glucose, vitamins, and bandages. As the passengers had not washed properly on board the crowded vessel, Sligo residents opened their homes to offer meals and the luxury of a hot bath. There were several people who spoke English, including one who had been an interpreter for the British Forces in Germany; on the Irish side, the secretary of the Catholic Young Men's Society spoke German. From such communication, the staff reporters for the *Sligo Champion* were surprised to find that the works of Irish writers were known to some among this group of travelers. Among the diversity of the *Walnut*'s passengers, some had Canadian dollars, which they exchanged for small items along with fruit, sweets, and souvenir postcards. The Saint Vincent de Paul Society sponsored a concert, the highlight of this joint gathering of Sligo's citizens and the refugees. A spokesman thanked the people of Sligo for their "unexpected kindness" and they, in turn, thronged the quay to watch the *Walnut* depart. Among a few left behind was a young woman who had undergone surgery for appendicitis. She was relieved when Radió Éireann broadcast the news of the ship's safe arrival in Canada and was happy to convalesce while waiting for the IRC to secure her passage.[57]

The thirty-seven passengers on the *Volo* fishing boat were not as fortunate in their choice of craft. They had sailed from Gothenburg and had already stopped in the Scilly Isles prior to arriving in Cobh with engine trouble. They remained in Ireland for about a month and received aid from the IRC as, during this time, their supplies had run low. After departing from Cobh, the ship had to pull into Valentia due to adverse weather conditions. Subsequently, the *Volo* sailed to Dublin, where its passengers hoped to stay until the following spring, when they intended to resume their voyage to Canada.[58] Other ships arrived with greater numbers of passengers and more severe problems to resolve. The *Sarabande*, an ex-minesweeper, arrived in Cork with 253 displaced persons on board, 60 of whom were children. The ship arrived at the end of July 1949 needing time-consuming repairs to its boiler. Once again, the IRC aided the stranded passengers. City

Medical Officer of Health Dr. Saunders examined some of them at city hall and said they were constantly telling him how thankful they were for the gifts from the people of Cork. They were particularly surprised by the level of poverty, which did not deter Cork citizens from bringing food parcels for the children on the ship. The *Sarabande* duly set sail and arrived in Halifax, where the Canadian authorities immediately interned passengers for ten weeks before eventually allowing them entry into Canada. These temporary landings and departures, however, serve as a prelude to the longer saga of the *Victory* and its passengers, almost one hundred of them children, which arrived in Cork at the end of September 1949.[59]

The Victory Voyagers at Rockgrove

Like previous ships, the *Victory* was held in joint ownership; a group of Estonians had created a company to purchase former British landing craft, refit them into passenger ships, and carry Baltic-state displaced persons already residing in Sweden to their preferred destinations. The *Victory* left Gothenburg at night, was pursued by a police launch before leaving Swedish waters, and ran aground shortly after. The ship finally reached Ireland, where it was discovered that it had no safety certificate and its lifesaving equipment was "seriously deficient." The verdict of the Department of Industry and Commerce was that the ship could easily sink in the Atlantic with significant loss of life. The *Victory*'s hull could not have withstood the heavy seas as the vessel's construction was similar to that of a pleasure boat used in Dublin Bay during the summer. The ship was also so overcrowded that some passengers slept on deck, and if the *Victory* had continued on its journey they could easily have been swept overboard. The Irish government had no option but to detain the ship as Ireland was a signatory to the International Convention for the Safety of Life at Sea, which had been signed into domestic law. Such was the concern about the condition of the ship that the department had instructed the local surveyor of the Department of Industry and Commerce to serve a detention order on the *Victory* even though this action could not have prevented the vessel from leaving following repairs. Once more, the IRC came to the rescue for passengers who were in urgent need of food and medicine and, following their hasty removal from the *Victory*, created an instant accommodation crisis. The secretary of the IRC contacted the minister for defense, who immediately offered the use of Rockgrove, an evacuated military camp in county Cork, to house the refugees. The IRC stepped in to provide food, fuel, and other necessities for the running of the camp at a cost of forty pounds a day.⁶⁰

The IRC, having come to the initial aid of the passengers and crew of the *Victory*, referred the matter to the taoiseach, contending that the situation had become a government issue regarding the status of the *Victory*'s passengers. The question arose whether they should be "treated as refugees whilst their credentials and money credits are being examined and investigated."⁶¹ Consequently, the case of the *Victory* was put on the agenda for a government meeting set for October 18, 1949, with the Department of Justice and the Department of Industry and Commerce each submitting a detailed memorandum to the government. The main concern of the discussion points was that if the *Victory* was not permitted to leave then the "authorities here will be faced with the problem of disposing of the aliens." The Canadian high commissioner's office had already warned that there would be no entry to Canada without visas but that visas could be issued in Ireland. From the perspective of the Department of Justice, there were two objectives to accomplish—namely, "induce as many as possible of the aliens to leave the state" and reduce the cost of their maintenance by trying to get them to take up employment. Work permits could be available for as long as they remained in the state; those with means could pay for their maintenance at Rockgrove. Passengers with visas could leave, with either the IRC or the state paying their fares to Canada or to other countries interested in providing visas for displaced persons from the Baltic states. The Department of Justice further recommended that the Department of External Affairs should try to persuade the Swedish government not to permit any additional departures of unseaworthy ships. Alternatively, there was a suggestion that the Irish government could charter a ship to send the *Victory*'s passengers back to Sweden, though this course of action was not recommended as Sweden could refuse readmittance, and "sending them back to a country from which they fled on account of terror of the Russians would be an inhuman act." The Department of Justice contextualized their stance with the admission that "this country has taken in fewer displaced persons than nearly any other country in Western Europe." This was partly due to geography, as only a few had managed to make their way to Ireland, but with the aspiration that numbers would not increase as "our total alien population (2,000 approximately over 16 years of age) is comparatively small. In the circumstances the Minister suggests that we should adopt a charitable attitude to these refugees, notwithstanding the fact that this may encourage other refugee ships to call here." The department embraced the hope that most of the "aliens" would leave and would cost the state as little as possible, and the state could remain charitable while accomplishing the two former aims of speedy departure and drawing as little as possible on the public purse.[62]

The government's contribution to being "charitable" was to postpone decision-making and leave the IRC to manage the situation at Rockgrove camp. This neatly sidestepped the two aims, which were clearly irreconcilable with a charitable stance. Disregarding the Department of Justice's view that the case of the *Victory* was an urgent matter, the government referred it instead to a cabinet committee for consideration, comprising the ministers for the Departments of External Affairs, Justice, Defense and Industry and Commerce.[63] Minister for External Affairs Seán MacBride dealt with the pressing matter of visas for entry to Canada by contacting Canada's acting high commissioner. The Canadian government proposed sending a four-man team from London to Cork to examine the refugees there, an action that met cabinet approval at the end of October, almost four weeks after the arrival of the *Victory*.[64] Subsequently, the situation at Rockgrove was on the agenda for several government meetings, and each time significant decisions were deferred, even as the IRC began to feel the financial cost of maintaining the Rockgrove camp. The IRC contacted the taoiseach once more as the Cork branch had incurred expenditures of £1,000, which the executive had decided to provide with the stipulation that no further funds would be forthcoming. The Cork branch was willing to carry on aiding the people stranded at the Rockgrove camp, as they had previously with the *Sarabande*, though it would run into debt. To alleviate this pressure, the branch secretary suggested placing Rockgrove camp on army rations if the *Victory*'s passengers remained in Ireland after November 16 or 17, 1949.[65] As previously, this immediate matter was resolved with the IRC recouping its expenditure from the Department of Defense, a provision contained in the 1950/51 defense estimate.[66] The interdepartmental conference met twice, first on November 12 and once again on December 12; the government had also met on December 9 but directed again that the interdepartmental committee should examine the Rockgrove situation.

The *Victory* had arrived with 17 crew and 354 passengers, mainly Estonians and Lithuanians; a few passengers with Canadian visas soon booked flights from Shannon to Sydney in Canada. By the beginning of December, 16 people had departed by air, and three births had occurred, leaving 367

Table 1.1. The *Victory*'s passenger numbers, December 1, 1949

Men	147	Number of families	85
Women	132	Number of people in families	290
Children under 16	88	Single people	77
Total	367		

Source: TSCH/3/S11007 B/1. National Archives of Ireland (NAI).

people, mainly families, in Cork (see table 1.1). Seventy people who had been evacuated from the *Victory* had enough money to pay their fare to Canada at a cost of $150 per person; others had a little money, and the rest were penniless. Due to this financial situation, there was the possibility of a large percentage of the *Victory*'s passengers remaining in Ireland. As the majority did not speak English, language and housing were foreseeable problems, but, as they were all under the age of forty, "healthy and robust," they had skills to offer. Seventy-five percent of the men had worked in industry in Sweden, followed by the agricultural sector, while 50 percent of the women had been textile workers and dressmakers. Initially, employment did not appear to be a problem as there was a labor shortage on the Erne hydroelectric and turf schemes. Consequently, from a government perspective, these two programs could absorb large numbers of the people at Rockgrove with their families. There were also employment opportunities for agricultural laborers and domestic services, though these two areas were generally below the level of the *Victory*'s passengers' skills. What did preoccupy government was the cost of either securing passage to Canada or elsewhere or providing public assistance to any who might remain in Ireland. To ascertain the level of wealth carried on board the *Victory*, plainclothes gardaí, accompanied by a chief superintendent, searched the ship, the passengers, and their belongings and discovered that most had access to at least a little money, a fact that might have quashed the rumors concerning vast amounts of bullion and currency on board. Of over three hundred passengers, only twenty-six had access to greater financial reserves; otherwise, people had sums of money ranging from $5 to $500 or had credit held in Canadian bank accounts, of which the largest sum was C$200. This exercise occurred due to the suspicion that the voyagers might try to hide their actual financial circumstances by not providing "reliable information" to the authorities.[67]

Two hundred twenty-three people had obtained visas for Canada by the time of the November and December interdepartmental meetings, in which the question of finance was discussed, given that not everyone was in a position to pay for their passage. The view, which had become significantly less charitable than previously, was that the state should pay the transport costs only of people who were penniless and had also been unable to find work. Two reasons were put forward to account for this position. First was the nationalist view that many Irish people would also like their fare paid to Canada. Second, the Department of External Affairs said that those who refused visas for Canada or were unable to pay their fare or possessed no skills should be sent back to Sweden—a course of action that the Department of Justice had rejected previously. The Department of External Affairs also believed this move would prove difficult as Sweden could refuse to take the refugees back, but the effort should be made as it would serve as a deterrent and "discourage an influx of further refugees from Sweden." The Department of Finance noted that the Public Assistance Act, 1939, imposed a duty on the local authority to provide public assistance to the refugees. However, the government decided informally that the local authority should in fact make no such contribution regarding the welfare of the refugees, a decision that needed to be confirmed formally. In addition, while the minister for justice had no objection to reimbursing IRC expenditures for this group of refugees, this generosity did not extend to refugees in general. The IRC was to encourage them to leave and "refuse to maintain any refugee who neglects to leave when he is in a position to do so." They could not stay indefinitely in Ireland and had to find ways to reach Canada on their own, as the *Victory* was not seaworthy. Cabinet minutes following the subsequent government meeting in mid-December confirmed that no action was to be taken regarding state involvement in paying fares to Canada for those who had received visas and that the refugees had to be made aware that they had to be self-sufficient.[68] These less than charitable views held severe financial repercussions for voyager refugees who had to remain in Ireland. Some of the *Victory*'s passengers were unable to obtain visas owing to their medical status, as the Canadian government was extremely selective, for instance, with regard to tubercular infections. Canadian officials refused visas to Canadian scholar Lynda Mannik's grandparents because her grandfather had tuberculosis scarring on his lungs dating from the First World War but requiring no further treatment. Following this rejection, family already residing in Canada raised the funds to pay for legal representation in order to obtain visas for their relatives in Ireland. This was not an immediate process, and Lynda Mannik's grandparents remained in Ireland for two years in precarious circumstances. They lived in a trailer with little food or heating, and her grandfather supported the family by performing odd jobs. As far as Mannik's family is aware, apart from her grandfather's ingenuity in securing labor, they received no public assistance and lived through a particularly harsh time.[69]

Fortuitously, the Lutheran World Federation (LWF) came to the rescue in December 1949, when they sent two of their representatives—David Ostergren from the Lutheran Society of America and Reverend Jack Taul—to Cork. By 1947, with the approval of the IRO, the LWF had become involved in transporting German Lutheran DPs from Europe to America: not only was one in ten Lutherans a refugee but one out of three Lutherans was a DP.[70] The federation had been working with German Lutherans but hoped to include the 260 Lutherans at Rockgrove. The IRO sent one of its ships to Cork as the federation would pay the Lutherans' fares; each would repay this loan over a number of years. For the low fare of thirty pounds per person, the IRO would also provide transport for others who had obtained Canadian visas. At this point, in January 1950, Rockgrove housed 239 remaining refugees. Canada had refused visas to 40 of them, and 190, if issued visas, would be unable to pay their own fares; the offer from the LWF solved this outstanding matter. The IRC offered to help pay the fares of the destitute, particularly "if it helps to clear up an awkward situation." A memorandum prepared by the Department of Justice on January 26, 1950, for a government meeting to be held the following day recommended this course of action and noted that approximately 50 people, all eventually rejected by Canada, would be left at Rockgrove. This small number would "not present a serious problem" as they could seek public assistance, find employment, or even obtain visas for countries other than Canada.[71]

Finally, after almost four months, the case of the *Victory* and its passengers appeared to be resolved with very little input from the government. Fifty-seven people remained in Rockgrove; eighteen found employment almost immediately, most as construction laborers, cabinetmakers, and domestics; there was also a carpenter, an upholsterer, a machinist, a farmhand, an architect, a motor mechanic, and a tailor. They were earning on average seven pounds a week, and the IRC was continuing to subsidize the situation by feeding wives and children in Rockgrove. Unfortunately, matters were not concluded completely satisfactorily; the IRC chief executive officer wrote to the private secretary to the taoiseach in May 1950 that the IRC could not continue to care for the refugees at Rockgrove after June

30, 1950, not because of the considerable financial pressure their upkeep had brought to the organization but because of social problems, as "there is a minority which give considerable trouble." The "trouble" concerned personal life choices that did not jibe with the mores of 1950s Ireland. For example, a man had moved to Dublin and found employment, but his wife refused to join him with her family. Others at Rockgrove refused to accept "necessary medical treatment"; the nature of these treatments and the reasons for refusal are not given, though previously there had been references to tuberculosis and to an unfortunate woman who, supported by her husband, required treatment for a venereal disease. The third complaint, however, appears to be the most egregious, described delicately as "one lady is engaged in a profession not regarded here as an honest livelihood." Due to these displays of misconduct, the IRC stipulated that the refugees had to follow the laws of the land and behave accordingly. What was not clear was whether this was a legal or moral system, though the IRC did refer to the issuing of temporary residence permits, a process of regularization, to draw the refugees toward compliance. Surprisingly, the IRC mentioned in the letter to the private secretary to the taoiseach that these refugees were living on the *Victory* rather than at Rockgrove and urged the taoiseach to act swiftly, as they could not remain on board after the autumn, and there was no housing for them in Cork. The IRC noted that "the present system of indecision results in degeneration of the natural inclination among the majority of the refugees to fend for themselves."[72] In other words, "drift," "malaise," or "stagnation" produced ill effects. The government held a meeting on May 12, 1950, to discuss the letter informally; copies were sent from the Department of the Taoiseach to the Departments of Defense, External Affairs, and Industry and Commerce for consultation "for the necessary action." The minister of the Department of Industry and Commerce was sympathetic to granting employment permits to people with work. However, this action was made with the state of the labor market and the attitude of the trade unions, who might be concerned by any potential employment, in mind. Otherwise, the charitable perspective, but not the obfuscation, had run its course.[73]

Conclusion: Conceptualizing Refugees

Emma Haddad states that a refugee's identity is created by the lack of belonging, by the status of being an outsider and being "between rather than within sovereign states." The voyages depicted in this chapter exemplify, literally and metaphorically, this state of being "between" and not "within." The international sphere of sovereign states is where refugees reside, but whereas political borders harbor citizens, or those on the inside, refugees stand outside borders as "others." From an international relations perspective, Emma Haddad contends, as long as separate states delineated by political borders exist, so too do refugees as they are forced "into the gaps *between* states." Refugees exist in this sphere not as an occasional problem but as an integral part of the international order. From this viewpoint, refugees dwell in the mainstream of events rather than on the periphery, as an adjunct to the unfolding of international incidents. This centrality to the international order of things occurs because borders, like the international order, are not static but rather exist in a dynamic set of relationships where they are porous, contested, and movable with or without agreement. A refugee "is an inevitable if unanticipated part of international society," and, as a consequence, any refugee episode, whether pre- or post the Hungarian refugees of the 1950s, involves a home country, a displaced individual, and a host country.[74] While this trinity is ever present, the international community offers differing responses, if any, to particular movements of refugees that are rooted in specific historical, political, and social contexts. As Liisa Malkki iterates, "What is the state of not being a refugee like? How is it denoted? These questions lead into considerations of citizenship and nationality, origins and nativeness, nationalisms and racisms, and of the concept of identity, ethnicity and culture."[75] A historical perspective allows for the tracing of these entanglements, which emerge in the Irish context, as the young state meets others, not citizens. These others were classified as aliens, in accordance with the Nationality and Citizenship Act and the Aliens Act, 1935, and its later revisions, which created the legal framework for the development of postwar refugee policy. The early stages of this development came in the form of aid donations abroad linked to a general preference for Catholics and Catholic organizations and allied to unemployment and emigration concerns. Others were permitted entry into Ireland but with their future departure planned: children maintained by the Red Cross or private individuals, such as the Jewish orphan children and Operation Shamrock; university students who would move to other countries upon completion of their studies; distinguished individuals such as scientists or other experts and political exiles from certain countries such as Spain and France.[76]

Likewise, the encounters with the refugees on boats were temporary, and, apart from those displaced persons resettled by the IRO or NGOs, most left. Their temporary nature did not provide time for the slower and deeper process of mutual accommodation nor for the recognition of individual foibles, as had begun to emerge with some of the final residents of Rockgrove. Departing refugees were clearly grateful for the unexpected kindness they encountered and surprised by the poverty they saw in Ireland. Those remaining were supposed to be respectable, particularly the women; a married woman's decision to leave her husband for reasons unknown was a scandal ripe for comment, as was the suggestion that one woman was involved in prostitution. While the view was that the refugees had to adapt to or adopt the "Irish way," there was no consideration of the war, the Emergency, and postwar effects on individuals' day-to-day survival. The Baltic states had been invaded three times, once by Germany and twice by Russia; in times of war, women and their bodies are vulnerable, and some women on the ships that docked in Ireland may well have had so-called irregular sexual histories. As these events occurred far from Ireland, such matters would have been difficult to conceive of. Consequently, moral judgments regarding women, their behavior, and their sexual health, which did not conform to convention, would have been ignorant of troubling personal histories. The government had been reluctant about extending public assistance to the refugees on the *Victory*; potential destitution combined with lack of knowledge about the lawful availability of public assistance could easily lead to reenacting previous survival behavior.[77]

Regardless of the social and cultural differences, the local welcomes and kindnesses offered to the passengers of the Viking ships, as the Canadians came to call them, did not go unnoticed. Some of the Polish passengers on the *Victory* had made Polish and Irish flags for their voyage, which they intended to present to the people of Cork; the welcomes other ships had received were known and remained salient in people's lives. The rector of the Church of Ireland St. John's Church in Sligo, Pastor Browne, received several letters of thanks for the hospitality offered by the people of Sligo to the passengers of the *Walnut*. Likewise, Pastor Browne did not forget but wrote about and reflected on his encounter with the *Walnut*'s passengers, stating that the "next time we read of millions of refugees we will think in terms of human beings and not just of figures on paper. We have seen for ourselves they are indeed just like you and me." The *Walnut*'s passengers organized regular reunions—their fiftieth was held at St. Peter's

Lutheran Church in Toronto—which included a celebration of their short stay in Sligo. Similarly, the welcome but short sojourn of the small group of Jewish children in Clonyn Castle was not forgotten; in fact, it became a turning point in their lives.[78]

In contrast to these local welcomes, the government's desire to move the *Victory*'s passengers out of Ireland as soon as possible and at little cost quickly replaced an initial moment of sympathy to their plight. Their unexpected irregularity, turning up unexpectedly in straitened circumstances—the very essence of people seeking international protection—was no doubt unwelcome. The government took as little action as possible; it did not wish to take responsibility for the welfare of outsiders. However, these differences do not present a neat division between society at large and its representatives in relation to the narrative of the hospitality of the nation. In February 1950, an unemployed man threw a brick through the employment exchange in Dun Laoghaire in protest of being unemployed and being unable to provide for his wife and child. His action created a flurry of sympathy, including from the judge who tried him and decided to simply apply the Probation Act rather than impose a heavy sentence for the twenty pounds' worth of damage the brick had caused. The *Longford Leader*'s editorial commented on the number of letters in the press calling "attention to the care and tenderness lavished on the Latvians and Estonians who landed in Cork and the huge sums provided for German and French children brought here as guests while our own children go ragged and hungry." The editorial went on to say that a cynical view would have seen the man posing as a refugee, as he would have obtained work immediately even though he would not have been able to speak English: "it is a cruel fact that inability to speak English is a passport to a job in Dublin." In other words, a patriotic stance would not have allowed such preferential treatment to be meted out to strangers washing up on shore.[79]

These initial encounters raise the question of identity, of who refugees are—a question that taxed the IRC concerning the *Victory*'s passengers and, in the case of the Hungarians, appeared in discussions at the first interdepartmental conference. Official categories or academic perspectives may well be in conflict with how refugees view themselves. Lynda Mannik found that some of the *Walnut*'s passengers were unhappy with her description of them as refugees or, worse, boat people. There was instead a reference to being a traveler or simply going from one place to another, despite the voyage on the *Walnut* not being an ordinary event.[80] Discourses on the subject conceptualize refugees as a problem or burden, yet the voyages, desperate as they were, reveal refugees as entrepreneurs setting up companies with shareholders; they were people willing to take personal and financial risks in pursuit of finding safety and security. With hindsight, the arrangements to transport people across the Atlantic because of an expected war might seem delusional, as that war never came. However, Mr. Enari, one of the displaced Balts on board the *Victory*, referred to a significant level of organization in Sweden and Germany aimed at buying thousands of tons of shipping, some working on short routes around Norway and Sweden and others engaged in longer voyages. With such pre-planning, all shipping could be deployed in the event of an expected further war.[81] Consequently, the delusion was matched, fortunately only to some extent, by unwise investments in inappropriate boats. Not all the ships or small boats that set sail from Sweden arrived at their intended destination, and unknown numbers of lives were lost at sea. Displaced Balts were not the only ones to set sail; in 1948, seven German refugees, while escaping a potentially impending war, lost their engine in the North Sea, hoisted the open boat's one sail to travel nine hundred miles, and eventually, after sailing for twenty-six days and running out of food, arrived on August 22 at the fishing village of Cheekpoint in Waterford.[82]

The irregular nature of being a refugee becomes evident through comparisons of their treatment where timing assumes importance—in other words, when flight occurred. People fleeing from the same state can receive differential treatment as in the pre-and postwar flights from the Baltic states. In Sweden, initial sympathy led to fears of a future influx, even though the Swedish government had assumed the welfare and work permit responsibilities following the closure of the legations representing the Baltic states. However, while hardworking and self-supporting refugees were welcome, they were expected to accept jobs on offer and to leave the better ones for Swedes: the labor market still prioritized Swedish interests, as Ireland's market favored the Irish. Also similarly, Sweden had a family system with a single provider, but refugee women had higher employment rates than the Swedish average. As they were encouraged to work, maternity care, childcare, and the schooling of refugee children all presented challenges to the government. The Swedish state had accepted responsibility for refugees, and as policy evolved it became linked to the emerging welfare state in Sweden.[83] This development changed in the late 1940s, coinciding with an increase in the numbers of refugees arriving from across the Baltic Sea. They were not as welcome as previous groups and were viewed as economic migrants rather than political refugees so that the "influx of these 'refugees' . . . (was) . . . a cause of irritation and worry." Similarly, Irish interdepartmental discussions entertained this fear, which also surfaced in the Canadian administration's deliberations concerning the irregular arrivals from Sweden.[84]

The labeling of refugees as economic migrants and not as "real" refugees, as with the later wave from the Baltic states, bestows differentiated identities, dealt with differently by bureaucratic systems.[85] Contemporary iterations, such as real or deserving asylum seekers, contribute to the labels encountered so far of people categorized as displaced persons, economic migrants, or political refugees. The label of economic migrant bestows a further identity that is different from being a refugee, while "refugeeness" itself is a manifestation of otherness, as evidenced in differences between a citizen, safe and secure within borders, and a refugee squeezed into a space literally or metaphorically outside. Official distrust of the unexpected travelers aiming to sail across the Atlantic led to searches of their bodies, belongings, and temporary shelters to ascertain their financial worth. Just as the IRO served as an international employment agency in order to resettle displaced persons, states have contributed to this economic aspect of the refugee experience by selecting able-bodied, relatively young, skilled individuals or families for their labor potential. Therefore, the conflation of refugee and economic migrant becomes difficult to untangle, as does the notion of deserving refugees who want to work. These conceptions and attitudes are apparent in the saga of the refugees from the Baltic states who passed through Ireland, as are their agency and desperate enterprise to find security. This enterprise occurred not because of overtly bad treatment in Sweden, as that was not the case, but rather because of the hope for a more secure future.[86] The interweaving of these emerging themes of welcome and rejection, of being in between or liminal, whether at sea or in a camp on land, and being a deserving, hardworking refugee / economic migrant / displaced person resonates with the arrival not only of the 1956 Hungarian refugees in Ireland but of others since. Even as humanitarian crises unfold, there continues to be surprise at their occurrence and wrangling over the genuine refugee identity of people seeking international protection and similar issues emerging in the resettlement process. The persistence of surprise and its accompanying themes of protection or otherwise and the sociocultural concerns around resettlement and identity are profoundly evident in contemporary refugee crises. If refugee flows are inevitable, then the arrival of the 1956 Hungarians in Ireland provides the opportunity to examine their reception from the perspective of their centrality to such questions, which reside in a historical context.

This specific historical, social, and political context, national and international, affects the response to the 1956 Hungarians' arrival in Ireland and the unfolding of the "hostipitality"—Derrida's term for the common origins of hospitality and hostility.[87] The difference in the Irish economy in the late 1940s and the shocks encountered in the mid-'50s is salient. There was no official concern regarding the employment of the DPs who had arrived in Ireland previously, as they found work reasonably easily. This contrasts with the offer to take a thousand Hungarian refugees, a number similar to the displaced people/refugees already absorbed by the state. A major factor was the arrival of the Hungarians coinciding with a period of high unemployment, so the target of a thousand Hungarian refugees was never reached. Contributing to the decision to take fewer refugees was the lack of immediate temporary accommodation—Knockalisheen had space for only some five hundred people—and the potential of increasing pressure on the public purse at a time of fiscal crisis. Yet, as Emma Haddad says, there is also a sense of history repeating itself.[88] The IRC and the kindness of strangers combined initially to welcome the Hungarians, as had been the case with the refugees on their way to Canada. Similarly, the government remained at a remove, leaving the long-term day-to-day running of the refugee camp to the Red Cross—although it did, yet again, create interdepartmental conferences. However, first came the search for suitable Hungarian refugees to bring to Ireland. This activity raised questions of nationalism, racism, origins, and identity explored by Malkki.[89]

Notes

The epigraphs are from Hannah Arendt, *The Origins of Totalitarianism* (New York: Harcourt, Brace, Jovanovich), 1973, and Dorothy McArdle, "The Iron Cage," *Irish Press*, October 26, 1950, 6.

1. There is already a significant body of literature on the 1956 Hungarian Revolution. See for instance: Scarlett, *Window onto Hungary*; Békés, Byrne, and Rainer, *1956 Hungarian Revolution*; Granville, *First Domino*; Congdon, Király, and Nagy, *Hungarian Revolution*; Sebestyen, *Twelve Days*; Cox, *Challenging Communism*. For the permeation of Communism into daily life, see Applebaum, *Iron Curtain*. For the Canadian context, see Hidas, "Hungarian Refugee Student Movement" and Hidas, "Hungarian Jewish Refugees."

2. Kőrösi and Molnár, *Carrying a Secret*, 1.

3. United Nations, *Report of the Special Committee*, deportations 123–27, cruel and inhumane treatment 129–36. The UN report noted the difficulty of trying to "establish an

applicable criterion on the basis of the Universal Declaration of Human Rights" due to the conditions in Hungary prior to the 1956 Revolution and after, 136.

4. Department of the Taoiseach to Department of Defence, November 13, 1956. File TSCH/3/S11007 C, National Archives of Ireland (NAI). Henceforth, this full designation is replaced by the file number only. Materials residing in other archives have their designation indicated.

5. Pálmai Bánki, "Crossing Borders," 144.

6. Unlike the traditional countries of immigration, and with the exception of a few Hungarians already living in Ireland, there was no diaspora community to aid the refugees during their stay in Knocklisheen or with integration at a later stage.

7. *Dáil Éireann Debates*, volume 161, no. 6 (May 2, 1957, Private Notice Question Hungarian Refugees, statements by Deputy McQuillan and Deputy Murphy). All debates available on the Houses of the Oireachtas website: https://www.oireachtas.ie.

8. Ward, "Big Show-Off," 140.

9. Fanning, *Racism and Social Change*, 87; Fanning, *Migration*, 167; Pálmai Bánki, "Crossing Borders." For an early work turning to refugee voices in the context of oral history, see Papp, "Hungarians in Ontario."

10. Carruthers, *Cold War Captives*, 21–22.

11. Both Cook and Higgins were veteran reporters and had covered the end of the Second World War. Marguerite Higgins began her war correspondent career by reporting on the liberation of concentration camps and later went on to report the Korean War; her reports from the field earned her the first Pulitzer awarded to a woman for international reporting. Don Cook arrived in Britain in 1945 and reported on significant political events in the postwar period such as the development of the Marshall Plan.

12. "Confusion in the West Aim of New Red Body," *Irish Independent*, April 13, 1949, 6. Irish Newspaper Archive (INA), and henceforth this designation is omitted. Newspapers or periodicals residing in other newspaper archives have their designation indicated.

13. Bakewell, "Researching Refugees," 6; Elie, "Histories," 23. For calls for history, see Marfleet, "Refugees," 137; Gatrell, "Refugees—What's Wrong," 174–84.

14. Marfleet, "Refugees," 137.

15. Kushner, *Remembering Refugees*, 17.

16. Malkki, "Refugees and Exile," 508 and "National Geographic," 25.

17. Gatrell, "Refugees—What's Wrong," 178–79; Frank and Rheinisch, "Refugees and the Nation-State," 478–80.

18. Gatrell, "Refugees—What's Wrong," 179.

19. Kushner, *Remembering Refugees*, 18–22.

20. Kleist and Glynn, *History Memory*, 1–16; Glynn, "Famine Commemorations," 1–2, 173–83.

21. Gatrell, "Refugees—What's Wrong," 172.

22. Puskás, "Hungarian Images," 181–82, 192–96.

23. Malkki, "Refugees and Exile," 511.

24. Marfleet, "Refugees," 137, 145.

25. Schmidt, "I Know What You're Doing," 91–96.

26. For heteroglossia, see Bakhtin, *Dialogic Imagination*, 6. For examples of its use, see DeSantis, "Caught between Two Worlds," 4–7; Sheridan, "Inadvertent Cosmopolitan," 365–69; Gatrell et al., "Reckoning with Refugeedom," 75.

27. For further detail, see Sheridan, "Letters of Love."

28. Taylor, "Their Only Words," 122.

29. Stone, "Refugees Then and Now," 102.
30. Taylor, "Their Only Words," 123–24.
31. Marfleet, "Refugees," 139–43; Gatrell makes a similar argument that he also extends in *Making of the Modern Refugee*, 10–11, 283–96.
32. Lee, *Ireland 1912-1985*, 271–328; Ferriter, *Transformation of Ireland*, 326–27.
33. Lee, *Ireland 1912-1985*, 326–57.
34. Foster, *Modern Ireland*, 578.
35. Brown, *Ireland*, 201.
36. Savage, "Ireland Tomorrow," 3.
37. T. K. Whitaker, then eighty-five years old, was voted Irishman of the Century in 2002. His 1958 study *Economic Development* led to the production of a white paper, "Programme for Economic Expansion," that outlined the potential of the Irish economy to "release a dynamic of progress." Whitaker, *Economic Development*, 48.
38. Ferriter, *Occasions of Sin*, 333.
39. Ryan, *Commission to Inquire*.
40. For women's daily lives and interests, see Clear, "Woman's Life Magazine," 73–78; for the sociocultural context of policy, see Luddy, "Unmarried Mothers," 112–18; for "coercive confinement" across a range of institutions in Ireland such as industrial schools and reformatories, Magdalen homes, county homes for unmarried mothers, and psychiatric hospitals, see O'Sullivan and O'Donnell, "Coercive Confinement," 32–40.
41. Department of Children, Equality, Disability, Integration and Youth, *Mother and Baby Homes*. This commission made no findings with regard to the five hundred institutional survivors who told their stories to the confidential committee, which ran in tandem with the main investigation commission. Only some sixty-four survivor testimonies, told to the investigation commission, were considered for the final report. For critique, see Crowe, "Commission and the Survivors."
42. Garvin, *News*, 17.
43. Ferriter, *Occasions of Sin*, 333.
44. Wills, *That Neutral Island*, 112–13. For an overview of waves of refugees, see Fanning, *Migration*. For German, Czech, and Austrian refugees, see O'Connor, *Irish Government Policy*, and Holfter and Dickel, *Irish Sanctuary*.
45. For numbers of the displaced, see Lowe, *Savage Continent*, 27–28; Judt, *Postwar*, 22–26; for the wider context that "sits before the Cold War," see Shepherd, *Long Road Home*, 3.
46. For the British arrival in Belsen, see Hitchcock, *Bitter Road*, 341–47; for some information on Collis but also for the story of the liberation of Belsen, see Shepherd, *After Daybreak*, 141–43.

> Dr. Robert Collis joined the International Red Cross in 1945 and went to the newly-liberated Belsen where he set up a hospital for sick children, one aspect of his distinguished career. He cared for Zoltan and Edit Zinn and eventually brought them back to Ireland with three other children and adopted Zoltan and Edit. Robert Collis and Han Hogerzeil wrote about their first-hand experience of Belsen in *Straight On*, 44–100 (an account not for the faint-hearted); Zoltan wrote a memoir, including how his two "personal angels of Belsen," found him, *Final Witness*, 98.

47. Molohan, *Germany and Ireland*, 52–66. For memories of the adult children, see Brandis, *Children from Operation Shamrock*, 55–122. Herbert Remmel, who spent much of his sojourn on a farm in Mayo, later wrote a memoir, *Cologne to Ballinlough*, about his time

in rural Ireland and what was already a vanishing way of life. For an appraisal of Remmel's memoir, see O'Driscoll, "'Half Irish.'"

48. Department of Justice, "Admission of 100 Jewish Children from Poland," memorandum, April 28, 1948. TSCH/3/S11007 B/1. See also Keogh, *Jews in Twentieth-Century Ireland*, 209–16.

49. Wyman, *DPs*, 61–85; Lowe, *Savage Continent*, 3–11; Marrus, *Unwanted*, 313–17.

50. See, for instance, the European volunteer worker scheme that brought the Baltic Cygnets to Britain as workers in hospitals and domestic service for the upper classes; Shepherd, *Long Road Home*, 328–32; McDowell, "Workers, Migrants Aliens," 872–76.

> In relation to families with children, the prevailing view was that "the child born damaged or incurably damaged by war was of little interest"—Balint, "Children Left Behind," 155. Consequently, a family's choice would have been stark: remaining at a camp to keep the family intact or leaving disabled children behind in order to resettle elsewhere.

51. Archbishop McQuaid, letter, TSCH/3/S11007 B/1.

52. "Arrival of the First DP," *Irish Press*, September 12, 1950, 5. The "dominance of women" in such schemes form part of an "exceptional period of recruitment" and a period that slipped into a conflation of economic need with the term *DP* or *refugee*. McDowell, "Workers, Migrants Aliens," 865.

53. "More Refugees Arrive Homeless Find New Security," *Irish Press*, October 13, 1951, 1; "Ireland Shelters 145 Refugees," *Irish Press*, October 15, 1952, 7.

54. Questionnaire Council of Europe, TSCH/3/S11007 B/2. Apart from the naturalized citizens, there were 604 registered refugees: 265 Poles, 68 Czechs, 52 Russians, 44 Estonians, 39 Belgians, 31 French, 28 Latvians, 25 Hungarians, 21 Lithuanians, and 12 Yugoslavs; a few Bulgarians, Dutch, and Ukrainians; and 1 Spaniard.

55. See, for instance, an analysis of US policy: Loescher and Scanlon, *Calculated Kindness*, 1–67.

56. Mannik, *Photography, Memory*, 59, 107–11.

> This fear of a Soviet invasion already existed among displaced persons from the Baltic states in camps in Germany; Bakis based his findings concerning DP apathy within this group, who had already experienced the Soviet Invasion of 1941, as part of a "suffering of an almost cosmic kind." Bakis, "So-Called DP-Apathy," 79. See also Wyman, *DPs*, 61–62, 79.

57. "Refuge Ship Reaches Nova Scotia," *Irish Times*, August 20, 1949, 1. Irish Times Digital Archive (ITDA), henceforth ITDA. "Refugee Ship at Sligo before Atlantic Crossing," *Sligo Champion*, November 27, 1948, 1; "Heart-Rending Scenes as Refugee Ship Sailed from Sligo," *Sligo Champion*, December 4, 1948, 7; "Refugee Ship's Safe Voyage," *Sligo Champion*, December 18, 1948, 1.

58. "Refugees Seek New Homes in West," *Irish Times*, July 30, 1948, 3. ITDA. "Fishing Smack Leaves Cobh," *Irish Examiner*, August 20, 1948, 5; Letters, "Refugees' Plight," *Irish Examiner*, October 2, 1948, 6.

59. "Relief for Refugees on ss Sarabande," *Irish Examiner*, August 9, 1949, 4; "Food Gifts for the Refugees," *Irish Examiner*, August 5, 1949, 3.

> For a fuller account of HMS *Sarabande*, see the following Washington History Society article: http://www.washingtonhistorysociety.co.uk/community/washington-history-society-12965/hms-sarabande.

60. Department of Industry and Commerce, memorandum for government, October 17, 1949, TSCH/3/S11007 B/1.
61. Irish Red Cross Society to Taoiseach John Costello, October 7, 1949, TSCH/3/S11007 B/1.
62. Department of Justice, memorandum for government, October 17, 1949, TAOIS/3/S11007 B/1.
63. Cabinet minutes, item 7, October 18, 1949, TSCH/3/S11007 B/1.
64. Canadian Acting High Commissioner to Seán MacBride, October 26, 1949; Cabinet Minutes, October 28, 1949, item 9, TSCH/3/S11007 B/1.
65. Secretary Irish Red Cross, Cork branch, to Taoiseach John Costello, November 7, 1949, TSCH/3/S11007 B/1.
66. Department of Defence, note to Taoiseach John Costello, November 22, 1949, TSCH/3/S11007 B/1.
67. Department of Justice, memorandum to government, October 17 and December 1, 1949, TSCH/3/S11007 B/1.
68. Department of Justice, memorandum to government, December 1 and December 15, 1949, TSCH/3/S11007 B/1; Cabinet minutes, December 16, 1949, item 5, TSCH/3/S11007 B/1.
69. Lynda Mannik kindly shared this part of her family history with me.
70. Wyman, *DPs*, 199.
71. Department of Justice, memorandum to government, December 15, 1949, and January 26, 1950; Irish Red Cross to Taoiseach John Costello, January 3, 1950, TSCH/3/S11007 B/1.
72. Irish Red Cross to Taoiseach John Costello, February 6, 1950; Irish Red Cross to Private Secretary to Taoiseach, May 10, 1950, TSCH/3/S11007 B/1.
73. Note to Taoiseach John Costello, May 11, 1950; Department of Industry and Commerce to Department of the Taoiseach, May 30, 1950, TSCH/3/S11007 B/1.
74. Haddad, *Refugee in International Society*, 7, 5.
75. Malkki, "Refugees and Exile," 515.
76. Ward, "A Big Show-Off," 133, 135.
77. Judgments were also made in the Canadian context with refugee women. Iacovetta, *Gatekeepers*, 233–87.
78. Pastor Browne wrote an article about the *Walnut* and its refugees titled "November 1948—Refugees." Available on the *Walnut* website: http://www.walnutship1948.ca/Sligo.html; "Reunion with the Past—and What Might Have Been," *Irish Times*, May 6, 2000, 10. ITDA.
79. "Dynamic Brick," *Longford Leader*, February 11, 1950, 6.
80. Mannik, *Photography, Memory*, 59–60, 153–54.
81. "Baltic Exodus Planned," *Irish Independent*, October 11, 1949, 5.
82. "Twenty-Six Days at Sea in Open Boat, German Refugees Arrive in Waterford," *Irish Examiner*, August 23, 1948, 5.
83. Köll, "Baltic Refugees," 429–30.
84. Chargé d'Affaires, Irish legation, Stockholm, to Secretary Department of External Affairs, October 21, 1949, TSCH/3/S11007 B/1.
85. For a more detailed exposition of labeling, see Zetter, "Labelling Refugees" and "More Labels."
86. Mannik, *Photography, Memory*, 136.
87. Derrida, "Hostipitality," 15.
88. Haddad, *Refugee in International Society*, 4
89. Malkki, "Refugees and Exile," 515.

2

FINDING SUITABLE REFUGEES

> From the uniforms of border guards, from the flags the red star has been ripped, the hated symbol of Communism is effaced wherever found. As sporadic fighting continues, the red regime offers virtual self-rule and Russian forces begin withdrawals. Shipments of plasma are rushed across the frontier where once the Iron Curtain barred all friendly contact. . . . The human need is clear, yet the political outcome hangs in the balance after a revolt that began with student demonstrations and spread across the country like wildfire.
>
> —*Freedom Road, Hungarian Patriots Force Red Retreat, Universal Studios*

> Those pictures of the Hungarian tragedy must unsettle for the rest of the programme any cinemagoer with a heart. The vivid young faces of the students, rejoicing in the hope of freedom, crowd the Budapest streets, the compulsory Communist literature is burned by young men outside the headquarters of the Secret police, a smiling girl on a window balcony waves a national flag. How many of those young people are alive this Monday morning?
>
> —Benedict Kiely, *"The Heroic Men of Budapest"*

Initial Reactions to the Crisis

The Irish approach to receiving Hungarian refugees began with some confusion in November 1956. The Department of Justice felt slighted over the lack of consultation; the Irish Red Cross debated a plan for the reception of Hungarian refugees without an idea of exactly how many to prepare for. However, a final figure materialized, and UNHCR acknowledged the "most generous offer to accept up to 1,000 refugees into Ireland" and immediately advised "UNHCR Austria of your offer and suggest Irish Legation Berne consult with this office and Migration Committee Geneva concerning transport arrangements." At the same time, the Department of Defense proffered the use of Knockalisheen, a disused army camp like Rockgrove, this time in county Clare, which would require refurbishment.[1] As the Irish Red Cross had built up some expertise in managing expected and unexpected refugee arrivals as well as the day-to-day running of the camp at Rockgrove, it was only natural that the government should direct them to advise the Department of Justice along with John Charles McQuaid, the archbishop of Dublin. The IRC proposed taking family groups, to be housed in a camp for their exclusive use. There had been families, including extended families, on board the *Walnut* and the *Victory* so the assumption of bringing Hungarian refugee families to Ireland had some foundation. This time, however, the suggestion to take such groups originated as a development in Irish policy and rested on the firm conviction that this action would, first, "maintain (the) best Christian ideals of family life" due to "the best possible care and attention given to the moral, spiritual, educational and physical welfare of the family as a unit." Second, problems of resettlement and employment would be reduced "if they can be limited to the bread-winner in each family."[2] The Roman Catholic Church wielded significantly more power than a nongovernmental organization, and in this instance, it appears the Irish Red Cross and the Department of Justice deferred to the higher authority. Unfortunately, the composition of the 1956 Hungarian refugees was different from what was planned or expected: they were not, in general, family groups fleeing advancing armies in wartime but people who had been pushed to act amid the chaos of a revolution. Regardless, events moved swiftly, and there was no time to debate either the advice, its underlying premise that Hungarian refugees en masse upheld Christian ideals of family life, or that families would adhere to the convention of a male "bread-winner" with a wife and children who would serve as the principal liaison with the authorities.

A stream of people was already crossing the border from Hungary into Austria, which had seen the retreat of Soviet troops only the previous year and emerged as a neutral state. This short-lived normality gave way to Vienna once more becoming a city of espionage as nongovernmental organizations and secret service agencies descended to gather intelligence for East and West. Regardless of this volatile background, Austria's borders remained open, and UNHCR clarified the status of the Hungarians pouring across the frontier. The Austrian Federal Ministry for Social Welfare announced that "alle Neuflüchtlinge, die nach dem 23.10. 1956 nach Oesterreich gekommen sind, bis zu einer endgültigen Klärung als Konventionsflüchtlinge betrachtet warden, und daher bei Vermittlung eines Arbeitsplatzes wie Inländer behandelt warden. [All refugees who arrived in Austria after October 23, 1956, have been clarified as being convention refugees and as a consequence can seek employment on the same basis as a citizen.]" With this recognition, all Hungarian refugees were to receive equal treatment and were not to be considered as being in competition or conflict with their hosts.[3] At the same time, the Austrian government was anxious to move as many people out of the country as soon as possible in order to cope with the refugee flow. The initial response from the international community was lukewarm: Britain, for instance, was not concerned with resettling Hungarian refugees. The chancellor of the Exchequer argued that "the United Kingdom was not an immigration country."[4] Other English-speaking countries, traditional migration destinations, were similarly tepid; the government in Ottawa dithered, not over security concerns about communist infiltration but over the costs involved in bringing Hungarians to Canada. In the United States, the Eisenhower administration had to balance the competing claims of the restrictionists and their more humanitarian counterparts in the US Congress. In contrast to governmental indifference or caution, the media celebrated the image of "Freedom Fighters" on the New Year cover of *Time* magazine; Elvis Presley dedicated the song "Peace in the Valley" to "Hungarians and their anti-communism" on the *Ed Sullivan Show* on January 6, 1957; and charities worldwide started collections for the Hungarian refugees. Despite such attention, media depictions did not fully capture the magnitude of the refugee flow and the immediate concerns of the Austrian government and UNHCR.[5]

From Austria to Somewhere in Between

Personal stories attest to the fears, confusion, and grim moments of black comedy that accompanied the crossings into Austria. Olga Murphy, a teenager at the time, had participated in the revolution and as a wanted person had no option but to flee. Near Austria, she traveled with a group who had hopes of crossing the border at nightfall. A farmer guided them to the border, where a water channel divided Hungary from Austria, and warned of Russians ahead before leaving them in the darkness of the countryside. Hiding in the cover of tall marsh grass and trying not to make any noise, the group walked along the banks of the border canal. The canal was fast-flowing, and no one dared enter the rush of black water to attempt a crossing. Regardless of the danger, one man was intent on getting to Austria; his wife would join him once he had crossed safely. In an ill-judged moment of sudden action, he decided to brave the current, but once in the water, he was swept away. The others, realizing they could not cross, continued walking until they could see a bridge ahead patrolled by soldiers; these border guards heard them and began sending flares into the night sky. Each time a flare went up, the would-be refugees fell to the ground to hide in the cover of the grass. Eventually, they saw a soldier coming down the canal in a boat and realized he was Hungarian, as he was swearing loudly and lengthily at the group taking cover in the marsh grass. "We know where you're hiding," he said, "and we've been sending up the flares to bloody well guide you across, not shoot you, you fools. Once you were across, we were going to follow." Turning his boat so it spanned the width of the canal, he guided the group across, including Olga; they reached Austria with no further mishaps, and volunteer guides escorted them to the nearest refugee camp.[6]

The five thousand to six thousand to even over ten thousand refugees pouring across the border into Austria day and night did not equate with the slow scale of evacuation from Austria, which, at first, averaged less than one thousand refugees per day. Care and accommodation for fifty thousand refugees was creating an "intolerable strain on Austrian resources despite assistance already received from abroad." Without increasing departures to other European countries, Austria would not be able to "alleviate [the] tragic situation of new refugees arriving wet, hungry and worn out in increasingly deplorable conditions and in subzero temperatures." UNHCR was looking at a mass evacuation in order to avert a humanitarian crisis and "prevent loss of life."[7] UNHCR reported that the flow of refugees into and out of Austria from October 28, 1956, along with those residing in Austria, remained constant at around seventy thousand, regardless of the numbers that departed (see table 2.1). However, November 29 was a noteworthy day: "Am 29. November haben zum ersten Mal seit dem 23. Oktober mehr Flüchtlinge Oesterreich verlassen (4,950), als nach Oesterreich hereinkamen (4,432)." (For the first time since October 23, more refugees left Austria [4,950] than arrived on November 29 [4,432]).[8] Regardless, the situation had become so disturbing that the Austrian government issued an aide-mémoire for the attention of other states that outlined the stark reality in Austria, which saw no end to the flow of refugees and their "unimaginable need" given the conflict in Hungary.[9]

Table 2.1. Refugee flow tabulated from UNHCR reports

Report number	Date	Numbers residing	Numbers after departures
4	October 28	50,511	42,101
5	November 27	87,525	68,748
6	November 30	100,511	70,392
7	December 4	112,454	74,688
8	December 7	119,029	71,311
9	December 11	128,218	74,605
10	December 14	131,961	70,739
11	December 18	136,901	68,501
12	December 21	147,467	72,007

Source: DFA/6/419/33/11. NAI.

The Austrian government had good reason to be vociferous, as there were 190,000 refugees already present in Austria—almost the same number as those streaming in from Hungary. This group was a combination of DPs remaining from the aftermath of the Second World War and new refugees from the Iron Curtain countries. The 190,000 remained "between sovereigns," and many—the unwanted—spent the remainder of their lives as such; the movement of refugees did not occur as discrete events with tidy beginnings and endings but remained unresolved for decades. There was still a cattle market atmosphere when countries came in search of labor, which led to emptying the DP camps of the young and strong.[10] The aide-mémoire issued by the Austrian government specifically referred to this era: "As in the case of the earlier refugees Austria is also at the present time conscious of the duty imposed on her by humanitarian principles and in the spirit of the Refugee Convention is willing to afford refuge to all refugees. These refugees cross the border bare of all possessions, some of them sick and wounded and with wives and children. Austria takes upon herself a very difficult burden in accepting these refugees." The best way for Ireland or any other country to help was to accept mixed groups of refugees quickly and not try to screen them, as that would not "represent effective support in the present emergency."[11] Families should not be separated, and countries were not to limit their intake to young people and those able to work.[12] This request was particularly pertinent as many of the Hungarian refugees were young adults: a North Atlantic Treaty Organization (NATO) report characterized them as "young, active and very tough." In addition, there were approximately eight thousand students whose studies had been interrupted as well as skilled workers and professionals, so their combined exodus represented a brain drain from Hungary.[13]

To alleviate refugee spur-of-the-moment decision-making, especially in cases where it would be immediately binding, the Intergovernmental Committee for European Migration (ICEM), at the request of the Austrian government, prepared a leaflet for distribution. ICEM assured Hungarians that everything possible was being done to relieve their "desperate and needy situation" and set out the receiving process established in Austria. Hungarian refugees would first pass through a transit camp that would attend to immediate needs. Next, after a few days, people could proceed to a country offering asylum or into better quarters in Austria. There was no coercion, as the leaflet stressed: "Everything is being done to help you to take advantage of the generous invitation of countries outside Austria which have offered you a temporary or permanent home. Every consideration will be given to your selecting either a temporary or permanent home. You are not in any way obliged to accept another temporary or permanent country of resettlement unless you wish." Crucially, the leaflet stated:

> The following countries have offered you either temporary or permanent asylum:
>
> European countries (temporary or permanent asylum):
> Switzerland, France, Belgium, Sweden, United Kingdom, Germany, *Ireland*, Italy.
>
> Overseas Countries (permanent):
> The United States, Canada, Australia, New Zealand, Union of South Africa, Brazil, Colombia, Chile.[14]

Institutional actors, therefore, provided Hungarian refugees the option of a temporary stay in a European country, such as Ireland, before resuming their journey to a final destination. This measure provided respite for refugees in Austria and afforded the Hungarians a decision-making process regarding their choice of country of temporary or permanent resettlement.

The Irish Response Abroad: In Search of Families

Regardless of the specifics of the situation in Austria, an Irish representative had already departed in search of families, though one representative would have had difficulty visiting the more than 250 camps hastily set up

ANNEX 2

INTERGOVERNMENTAL COMMITTEE FOR EUROPEAN MIGRATION

HUNGARIAN REFUGEE PROGRAM.   REPORT NO. 8

TEXT OF THE LEAFLET GIVEN TO THE HUNGARIAN
REFUGEES IN AUSTRIA

1. The Austrian Government and international refugee relief agencies are working night and day to help your desperate and needy situation.

2. The stream of your compatriots is daily increasing, thousands come still every day over the border; please be patient if the machinery dealing with your problem is severely strained.

3. Many of you will first pass through a transient camp where your immediate needs will be cared for.

4. In the immediate future perhaps a matter of a few days you can proceed to one of the countries who have offered you asylum or you will be transferred to better quarters in Austria.

5. If you have relatives or friends willing and able to take care of you, private arrangements can eventually be made if you report to the Caritas or Red Cross office.

6. Everything is being done to help you to take advantage of the generous invitation of countries outside Austria which have offered you a temporary or permanent home.

7. Every consideration will be given to your _selecting_ either a temporary or permanent home.

8. You are not in any way obliged to accept another temporary or permanent country of resettlement unless you wish.

9. Registration teams from the Intergovernmental Committee for European Migration (ICEM) and voluntary agencies are now operating through Austria.

10. These teams are equipped to register you for placement outside Austria whether you are living privately or in a camp.

Fig. 2.1. Statement provided to Hungarian refugees in Austria, page 1. Source: DFA/6/419/33/11. National Archives of Ireland (NAI).

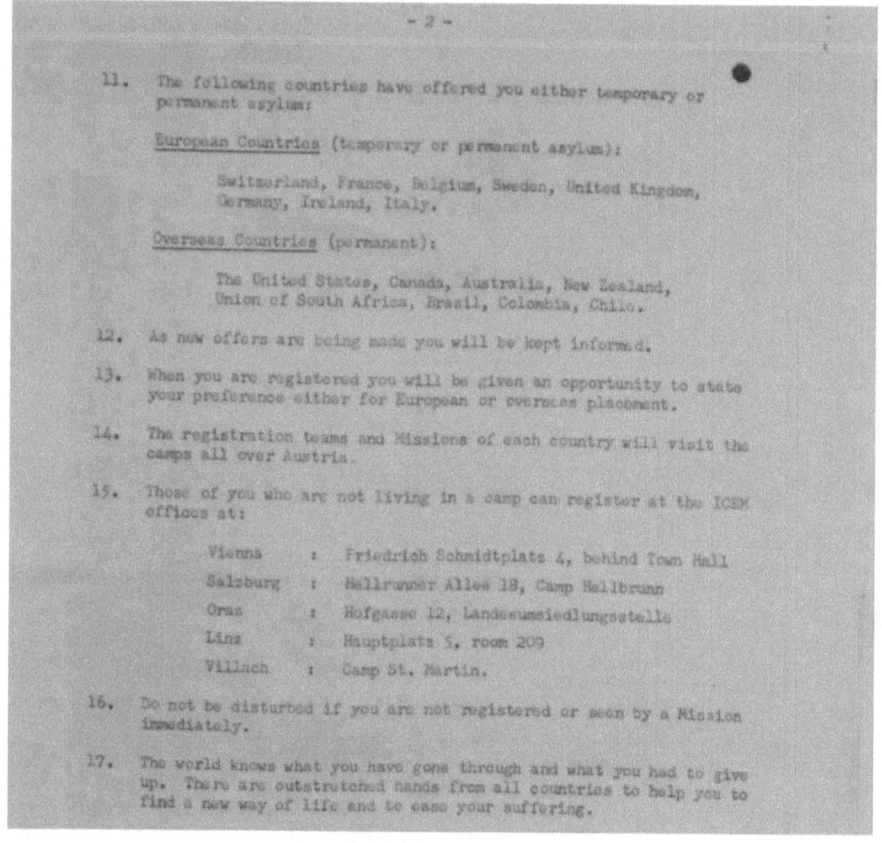

Fig. 2.2. Statement provided to Hungarian refugees in Austria, page 2. Source: DFA/6/419/33/11. NAI.

across the country. To confound matters further, the camps contained very different compositions of refugees. Ninety percent of the refugees in the transit camp in Eisenstadt were single men and women who, fearing deportation to Russia, had fled to Austria. There was a scarcity of conventional, possibly Christian family groups, and the Belgians had abandoned their policy of searching for specific categories of refugees in their first hour. There was pressure on the ground from the Austrians and from the British team already in place, who were willing to aid the single Irish representative but were not in a position to wait indefinitely in one camp as the representative searched for families. The fluidity of the situation and the reliance on telegrams, even as events changed hourly, presented an uneven flow of communication once the Irish representative requested a loosening of the Irish policy regarding families: "Under pressure from Austrian authorities to release special train waiting in Eisenstadt. Total persons in family groups now registered 85. Can you please extend to unmarried people? Shall make every effort secure families." Approval came for the 85 refugees but was not extended to the unmarried or any further commitments. However, by this time, 161 refugees had left Eisenstadt by train, a contingent including 20 single men and 10 family relationships described as "irregular." Two more Irish officials arrived in Austria, one from the Irish Red Cross, and they, too, found an abundance of refugees but few conventional family groups:

> Total influx refugees 28 October until this morning 79,141 of whom 6,096 last 24 hours.... Austrian Government and ICEM most anxious move maximum numbers onwards with minimum delay as position almost out of hand. Austria fears large number young men near border has dangerous possibilities for them. British and French taking trainloads without any screening. We are insisting any further shipments for Ireland meet our requirements. Difficulty is finding children and families with children as great majority are young men fearing deportation fleeing before Soviet infantry. Visited transit camp Eisenstadt today and going Traiskirchen tomorrow with Caritas representatives.... Wholly conjectural as to success as supply will depend largely on border crossings day by day.[15]

This misconception about the composition of the refugees also extended to religion.

Nongovernment organizations, secular and religious, such as the Roman Catholic Caritas, had descended on Austria to work with UNHCR and to demonstrate once more their capacity to play a significant role in a refugee crisis. The majority faith in Hungary was Catholic, and the "Catholic spokesmen purred with pleasure" at witnessing the large movement of Catholic refugees and anticipating "the prospect of being able to greet staunch adherents of the faith."[16] This simplistic religious labeling, however, ignored the long-standing complexities of Hungarian society, where industrialization and urbanization had been accompanied by a loosening of religious adherence: Hungary was no longer a rural society held in thrall by religion. While there was no suggestion of seeking Catholic families only, Hungarian refugees who decided later to remain in Ireland have stressed the importance of being a Catholic Hungarian refugee in order to be allowed to travel there. Anna Letoha thought that she fulfilled the criteria, as she was a practicing Catholic and had a family. Ted Vanya, who continued his journey to Canada, stated that his father-in-law saw a notice pinned to a tree stating that Ireland preferred Catholic families and promising work and assistance to leave Ireland for other countries if desired.[17] Thus, an implication of religious bias lingers, though it is unclear if it was deliberate, a mistranslation, or an unconscious bias emanating from a religious NGO. The Irish government adopted a two-strand strategic approach in response to the situation. First, it softened its stance slightly, expanding the strict definition of the "family group" to account for "irregularity" and include children accompanied by one or both parents or grandparents, or a combination of both.[18] Second, the government clarified its decision to accept children and family groups rather than "able-bodied adult persons" as being due to Ireland's "special circumstances which, in view of our unemployment and emigration problems are entirely different from those of Britain and France."[19] As such, the decision-making transformed into being simultaneously charitable and circumscribed by the pleading of special privilege. In the expectation of bolstering their stance, the Irish representatives had to convey this specific instruction to the Austrian authorities and to ICEM. The Irish mission adhered to its mandate, but promises of employment as contained in the note pinned to a tree, travel to another country for resettlement as indicated on the ICEM memo, and the early combination of inflexibility combined with ambivalence evident in the positioning of Ireland as having special status would all contribute to future government woes regarding its decision to admit Hungarian refugees.[20]

The Irish mission stayed in Austria from November 24 until December 4, 1956, trying to find family groups, which meant going from camp to camp near the border with Hungary, as telephone communication was impossible. A day's search might involve traveling over fifty miles to try to register one family during long working days that could stretch from 8:00 a.m. to 10:00 p.m. The Irish mission operated in five camps—Eisenstadt, Traiskirchen, Spratzern, Judenau, and Kaisersteinbruch; the British operated in Eisenstadt, and the Americans were yet to establish a base in Kaisersteinbruch.[21] A journalist observed the simplicity of British operations, wherein the first stage was a loudspeaker announcement indicating that a train would leave shortly for England. A Hungarian refugee had to submit their name at the office and subsequently prepare for immediate departure. Officials established proof of identity by accepting Hungarian identity cards, drivers' licenses, or factory workers' cards and entered relevant information on a numbered list that was placed in a folder. Consular officials issued collective visas for the group; one included occupations such as carpenter, upholsterer, civil servant, motor mechanic, farmer, technician, printer, apprentice, music teacher, post office official, electrician, lathe operator, shop girl, waiter, and locksmith. This simplified procedure resulted in the acceptance of self-selecting individuals or families in contrast to the Irish team's strictly defined search for families.[22]

However, with the aid of a doctor, an interpreter, and typists provided by ICEM, the Irish mission streamlined its approach. Following the departure of 162 people for Ireland, the next wave were all screened as to category—namely, family group, general suitability, identity, and security. Some families agreed to go to Ireland only if other relatives would be accepted, but this was not agreed to. Others wanted assurance that they would have permission to work; this was also not given. Even as refugees registered, the Irish mission encountered the frustrating situation of losing a group if transport was not available within twenty-four hours, as people either changed their minds or simply decided to travel elsewhere with earlier available transport. The Irish representatives persuaded the Ministry of the Interior to provide a room at Kaisersteinbruck, a large transit camp, which they used as a holding center while waiting for the arrival of aircraft in Vienna.[23] The airlift to Ireland began in November, planned first as two planes with some 30 passengers each and with a further transport of 230 refugees to follow a few days later. A flurry of telegrams confirmed flights such as the plane that left on December 5, 1956, with 34 passengers bound for Shannon.[24] By December 7, 1956, the number of Hungarian refugees booked for travel to Ireland rose to 517. The ICEM paid for the transport but welcomed contributions to cut such costs. Harold Tittman, ICEM's director, was responsible for coordinating assistance to Hungarian refugees, including transport costs, and wrote to the Irish government that ICEM could operate only in emergencies with funding and that just over a million US dollars had been spent in two months on the emergency program. Transport was the largest cost, and ICEM had agreed immediately to assist Ireland following its decision to take a thousand refugees, so there would be no delays. Under the circumstances, Tittman considered it his duty to ask the Irish government to make a contribution to ICEM to assist with the Hungarian Refugee Program. The appeal, however, did not generate a contribution. A memorandum for government detailed the solution to Tittman's request: Ireland was not a member of ICEM, and the minister for external affairs did not intend to pursue a proposal to make a contribution to the organization because there was an alternative solution. Aer Lingus had presented ICEM with a bill of

£4,475 for its costs in transporting the Hungarian refugees to Ireland. The minister concluded that ICEM need not be involved as Aer Lingus could be paid "out of moneys publicly subscribed for aid to Hungarian refugees." The Irish Red Cross would require a formal request from the government, and this process would occur with the Department of Defense, which liaised with the Red Cross. Government would thus be spared extra expense and dealing with ICEM.[25]

The Response at Home: Collecting for Christian Warriors

Deputy Éamon de Valera, in opposition, had already raised the question of Hungary in the Dáil by asking Taoiseach John Costello whether the government proposed to make a special contribution to the Irish Red Cross, so it too could play a part in "relieving suffering in Hungary and in assisting the Hungarian refugees." The taoiseach's reply on November 7 stated that the Irish Red Cross had already engaged in fundraising and gathering supplies. Furthermore, the IRC had already sent consignments to Austria and was in the process of sending further shipments of clothing, food, and medical supplies as well as launching its appeal and national collection. This funding would be "to provide relief for the victims of the aggression in Hungary," and the government would step in with funding if "the generous contributions in kind that the Society is receiving from our people, may prove insufficient." The taoiseach's reply further stated:

> The Minister for External Affairs has already, this afternoon, given expression, in this House, to our feelings of sympathy with the people of Poland and Hungary, of admiration for the matchless courage they have displayed in their unequal struggle for freedom and human rights and of abhorrence of the ruthless measures of suppression to which the people of Hungary have been subjected. I have no doubt whatever, that, by a generous response to the appeal of the Irish Red Cross Society, our people will show their practical sympathy with the Hungarian people in a manner more striking and effective than any action that it would be within the government's power to take.[26]

The response, while strong on condemnation, offered no further involvement apart from providing the IRC with additional funding if necessary.

The Irish Red Cross had been preparing for a national fundraising day for Hungarian refugees by organizing a church gate collection for every parish on Sunday, November 11, 1956; additionally, it created a temporary drop-in depot in the Great Hall at University College Dublin. The *Irish Press* reported almost daily on the surge in activity around the collections and drives for Hungary. Donations from businesses included cheese sent from twelve creameries federated to Golden Vale food products, chocolate from Fry Cadburys, new clothes, and medical supplies from Cavan chemists, Sandoz Products, and Squibb Products. The *Kilkenny People* issued a history and background of Hungary in relation to the Irish Red Cross appeal. The newspaper urged people to give generously, according to their means, in the spirit of "Christian charity" as the uprising was an "anti-Communist fight." The editorial expounded that countries that had "escaped the devastating tyranny of the Kremlin [were] to be ever on their guard against the penetrating influence of the Communist cult" and its false appeal to "national and patriotic instincts." The *Kilkenny People* was confident that the "Irish people abhor Communism" and would demonstrate their sympathy with the Hungarians "in the cause of Christianity." People across the country rose to the occasion and did indeed give generously according to their means, including the money from a child's savings box from a family of six who had been saving to send one of their children to Lourdes.[27]

The outpouring of activity involved other significant organizations apart from the well-publicized IRC collections. The Irish Association of the Sovereign and Military Order of Malta organized relief for the Hungarians following a request from the Order in Rome, which characterized the situation in Hungary as a "movement for independence . . . against the oppression of Godless Communism." Walter Smithwick, of Smithwick's Brewery, wrote to James Lyons, a Limerick chemist, informing him of the call sent to all Knights of Malta in the twenty-six counties of Ireland about the urgent need for warm woolen children's clothing, canned food, and drugs for transport to Austria. The list of suggested drugs was penicillin, sulphatriad, adrenaline, aminophylline, tetracycline, oral and intravenous digoxin, local antiseptic, and morphia. These drugs would be safe to transport in a variety of temperatures and "most useful in practice." The letter detailed the procedure for the collections, including the necessity of providing a receipt for every donation and locating a depot that could be advertised in the local press. Walter Smithwick referred to the Hungarian border with Austria, where the Russians were not permitting aid to enter Hungary so that all goods would arrive by plane in Austria.[28]

Groups of thespians organized plays with proceeds forwarded to the Red Cross; the Irish Ballet Company staged performances in aid of the appeal, University College Dublin Dramatic Society presented Oliver Goldsmith's *She Stoops to Conquer*, the College Players in Limerick contributed the takings from the final performance of the play *Is the Priest at Home?*, and the Ximenes-Vargas company of Spanish dancers gave a performance in aid of Hungarian children. The Jewish community became involved with donations sent either to the IRC or to the Chief Rabbi's Emergency Appeal for Hungarian Relief. There was a variety show in the Abbey Theatre in Dublin, a carnival in Limerick, and a student demonstration in Dublin, all of which raised money. Churches held prayer meetings; the Irish Municipal Trades Union passed a resolution condemning "the savage butchery in Hungary of innocent men, women and children by the Soviet armies"; Sligo Rovers and Evergreen United football clubs wore black armbands for their league of Ireland match while Cobh Ramblers and Glasheen observed a two-minute silence at the Munster Football Association game. There were special collections from Killaloe to Ossory, from the Kilrickle branch of the Irish Countrywomen's Association to the proceeds from the opening of the Leinster junior boxing championships.[29] There were many offers to provide a home for Hungarian orphans. There were even letters to the editor that included romantic, heroic poems about Hungary.[30]

With the revolution quashed by "Godless Communism" following the reentry of Soviet troops in Budapest, a further flurry of articles flourished in the press such as the article on "Hungary's role as defender of Christianity," which had first appeared in the *Register*, an American Catholic weekly. A special correspondent reporting for the *Irish Press* wrote at length about the fate of Cardinal Mindszenty, who had been freed from his prison during the revolution; "on the great onslaught on the activities of the Church" in 1946 in Hungary; and on the removal of schools from the control of the Catholic hierarchy in 1948.[31] The pope's apostolic letter in November 1956 asked for prayers for Hungary, and the bishop of Clonfert responded with a solemn High Mass in Saint Brendan's Cathedral. Simultaneously, the Catholic faithful in the Hungarian city of Győr prayed before the miraculous painting of the Irish Madonna brought to Hungary in the seventeenth century by the bishop of Clonfert. These references of religious solidarity in the press played out in turn across local parishes; Galway city churches observed a day of prayer for Hungary where "large congregations attended the special devotions. The Legion of Mary and Third Order of St. Francis recited a Chain of Rosaries from noon until late evening. There were also large congregations at the Holy Hours and Benedictions of the Holy Sacrament."[32] An array of organizations expressed solidarity with the Hungarian people such as the Galway County Committee of Agriculture, which condemned Russia's "brutal attack" on the country. Carrying Irish and Hungarian flags, five hundred University College Galway students marched in silent solidarity from the college to Eyre Square.[33] The Dublin Trades Union Council passed a resolution to demonstrate solidarity with Hungary, the final wording referring to "the heroic people of Hungary on their gallant stand against the murderous attack by Godless Communist rulers."[34] Dr. Szövérffy, a Catholic academic who had been a lay adviser to Cardinal Mindszenty in Hungary and was working for the Irish Folklore Commission, spoke on Radió Éireann, with local press advertising the broadcast as "Hungary: Europe's bulwark to the East." As part of his speaking and writing activities, Dr. Szövérffy addressed a protest meeting in aid of Hungary in Blackrock College, where he urged people to "help in whatever way they could."[35]

Overall, the level of involvement across society as individuals and communities threw themselves into various forms of assistance to raise funds for Hungarian refugee relief as the revolution was quashed is abundantly evident. The press played a significant role with the historical articles it provided, which offered cultural and specifically religious links with Hungary, including one on Saint Elizabeth of Hungary, a contemporary of St. Francis of Assisi, as well as accounts of events unfolding in Hungary and reactions in Ireland.[36] Michael Headen was age nine at the time of the Hungarian revolution. He was an altar boy at the time and remembered the regular prayer for the conversion of Russia at the end of mass. His father, a school inspector, discussed the events of the revolution with Michael and showed him newspaper articles complete with photos. There was a sense of pride in Ireland taking a quota of Hungarians; it presented Ireland as playing a part on the world stage, and this pride extended to the arrival of the Hungarian refugees and their gratitude to Ireland as reported in the press.[37] This, however, did not mean that the whole of Irish society could be encapsulated in the pious outpourings recorded by the press or heard from the pulpit. In fact, there were sightings of another Ireland, a rebellious Ireland of the young, some of whom went to see Bill Haley's film *Rock Around the Clock* in Mary Street cinema in Dublin. Mayhem ensued inside and out so that Gardaí were called and eventually baton-charged the "500-strong juvenile 'rock-n-roll' riot" to disperse the crowd.[38] The dominance of social conservatism, piousness, and Irish Catholicism did not mean there was no dissent against social conformity, though this predominant view interpreted events in Hungary. Also standing apart from the simplistic perspective of shared religious norms in relation to Hungarian refugees coming to Ireland was the rather lonely voice of the Reverend Professor Dr. O'Doherty of University College Dublin. He indicated some difference between the perception of a homogenized shared culture through referencing Christianity and Catholicism, as he stated that the refugees did not want "pity or grudging charity but an opportunity to work out their welfare in freedom. As hosts, they must understand that the refugees had a different way of life." This perspective was, in general, lost in the outpouring of sympathy toward a perceived pious Hungary and the flood of its suffering Christian refugees arriving in Austria.[39]

Suspending the Irish Effort

The government information bureau issued a press release dated November 21, 1956, intended for the evening and following morning papers and Radió Éireann news: "The arrangements being made by the Government for the reception of Hungarian refugees have now been completed. The first batch of sixty refugees will arrive at Shannon airport towards the end of this week. They will be followed next week by a further two hundred and thirty refugees. They will be received on arrival by representatives of the Irish Red Cross Society and the Department of Defence. For the time being they will be accommodated at Knockalisheen Camp, Co Clare, which will be used as a distribution centre." Just over two weeks later, the government suspended the process. The British embassy received this news following their inquiry about the government's achievements and future intentions for the Hungarian refugees. There was surprise at ICEM, which anticipated another increase in the flow of refugees: further fighting had been expected from December 9 until December 11, 1956, and indeed took place. The numbers forming that wave of refugees would depend on whether the Russians managed to seal the border with Austria. A discussion ensued with ICEM on the suspension of activity, and the organization received grateful thanks for its assistance. There was relief at not having to discuss it with the Austrians as there was no explanation to give apart from the fact that Knockalisheen Camp had a capacity for approximately five hundred refugees.[40]

Not everyone, however, was pleased with the apparent speed of events or with the decision-making process, as the Department of Justice made clear: "The Minister for Justice is responsible in law, for the admission and control of aliens. Up to 20th November there has been no consultation whatsoever from any source with the Department of Justice, in relation to the admission of Hungarian refugees and, any information there is has been got from newspaper reports." There were several areas of concern for the Department of Justice. The first related to the composition of the one thousand refugees, as "we have no idea what proportion of this number is to be (1) unaccompanied children, (2) children accompanied by adults, (3) adults." Second, the department wondered about screening on security and health grounds, and suitability for employment. The British team was creating full dossiers to identify the individuals in the family units and young men and women to be admitted to Britain, with some refused entry on security grounds. Medical screening, for example for tuberculosis, was mandatory for the Hungarians, as Ireland would need to have the facilities to treat any illness; the British, having a team of doctors at their disposal, had also refused entry on medical grounds. The main concern, however, related to security, to knowing fully who the refugees were, as "the British investigating teams in Austria are fluent German and French speakers and have little or no language difficulties. The security problems of the British and ourselves are identical and the British immigration team (1 Chief Inspector and 5 Immigration Officers) in Austria would give us on request, any help they can to screen refugees coming to Ireland." The concern with security was palpable, particularly once the Department of External Affairs phoned the Department of Justice about the imminent arrival of two planes at Shannon Airport, each bringing 30 Hungarian refugees, followed by 260 more Hungarians: "Are the Department of Justice to clear the refugees through the Airport without more than a count of heads? Are the immigration formalities to be completed in the camp and will the services of interpreters be available and paid for (if necessary) by Government."[41] The situation, however, was not as dire as the Department of Justice imagined. Plenty of identifying documentation accompanied the refugees going to Ireland, including ICEM registration forms carrying the details of each family. Major General Sweeney, the Irish Red Cross official present in Vienna, also received a nominal roll prepared for each planeload of refugees from the ICEM data; they formed the basis for the passenger manifests. In addition, each family possessed either a group or individual medical certificate, with names taken from their identity documents and bearing a stamp from the Irish legation in Vienna. The stamp was in turn authenticated by an Irish official next to the endorsement "Accepted for Ireland."[42]

Table 2.2. Hungarian refugee numbers, December 8 and 10, 1956

Category	461 refugees with 118 families, December 8, 1956				526 refugees with 138 families, December 10, 1956			
	Male	Female	Children	Religion	Male	Female	Children	Religion
Adults in families	262	199						
Adults					177	126		
Children in families			182					
Single	27	7			35	7		
Lone married	8	2						
Unaccompanied child 12–15 years	8	2	10		8	2	10	
Calvinist				45				
Lutheran				6				
Greek Orthodox				4				
Greek Catholics				2				
Unitarian				1				
Evangelist				1				
Jewish				2				
Roman Catholic				208				416
Unspecified								110
Total		192	269			223		

Source: DFA/6/419/33/11. NAI.

Refugee Numbers: Coming and Going

A number of demographic details present incomplete snapshots of the Hungarians' presence in Ireland as they arrived and departed: by December 8, 1956, there were 461 refugees at the camp, rising to 526 refugees two days later, the majority in family groups (see table 2.2). Among the first group of arrivals, 208 identified as Catholics even if this was not necessarily the case. Of note are the figures for Roman Catholics and the number of people identifying as such two days later. Whether this was the result of a prudent decision to indicate belonging to the greater group is not known. Ascertaining the truth of the matter is no longer possible and has to remain a conundrum. The figures for age groups are quite incomplete but exist for forty-four individuals (see table 2.3). Of these forty-four identified by age,

Table 2.3. Hungarian refugee age profile, December 8, 1956

Age	Men	Women	Total
70	0	1	1
60	0	0	0
50	3	2	5
40	7	3	10
30	9	2	11
20	16	1	17
			44

Source: DFA/6/419/33/11. NAI.

almost half are age twenty or under, so even with the criteria applied by the Irish mission in Austria, some young people, who formed a substantial number of the refugees in Austria, managed to make their way to Ireland.[43]

In this near final tally, the majority of the Hungarians belong to family groups so that the policy of searching for "suitable" families was successfully implemented. Finally, 104 people, including over 20 families, left the destination camp of Knockalisheen almost immediately as they found employment, some because of fortuitous contacts. Others took up offers of accommodation in Cork city and county; Carlow, Drogheda, Limerick city and county; Castleblaney in Monaghan; and Ardee in county Louth, as well as in Dublin. At the same time, by January 18, 1957, families not only had moved from the camp but had left Ireland altogether. Mr. Barth, a Swiss citizen, traveled to Switzerland with his family, and Mr. Somogyi and his wife moved to England to take up employment with the West Auckland Clothing Company in Bishop Auckland, county Durham.[44]

Conclusion: Doors Opening and Closing

At this early juncture, three groups appear in relation to the Hungarians in Ireland: the people who left the camp at Knockalisheen fairly quickly, those departing to other countries, and—the largest group in January 1957—those residing in Knockalisheen Camp. A fourth group would emerge after some months of people leaving Knockalisheen to return to Hungary. The Hungarians who left the camp early benefited from local networks and found themselves the recipients of all kinds of help from local contacts like Dr. Szövérffy, a Hungarian who had been living and working in Ireland for several years. Dr. Szövérffy was an adviser to Cardinal Mindszenty in Hungary, and the Roman Catholic Church would have opened doors for him when he came to Ireland. Dr. Szövérffy worked at the Irish Folklore Commission based in University College Dublin and had become an Irish citizen in 1955. Professor Michael Hayes had suggested a letter of introduction to bring him to the notice of the taoiseach; accordingly, Professor Delargy wrote that Dr. Szövérffy was "a close friend and valued colleague on the staff of the Irish Folklore Commission," where he had worked for four and a half years. Having such connections in Irish society, which operated according to the principle of "not what you know but who you know," was essential and helped the Hungarians settle into Irish society. Anna Letoha stressed the importance of this aspect of Irish social life and the creation of personal networks, which Dr. Szövérffy had already established.[45]

Other individuals were also crucial in helping the Hungarians settle into Irish life, whether by showcasing Hungarian talents or by drawing on personal networks to find them employment. Anna Letoha mentioned the Appleby family, who opened their home to a young Hungarian man over Christmas 1956, after which Mr. Appleby assisted him in finding a job; such Christmas contacts also proved useful to other families. Apart from the well-known Appleby business family, Anna thought that Geraldine Fogarty, who came from a prominent family, "knew everybody" and could make those vital introductions that helped Hungarians succeed. Religious orders contributed to this success, and Anna mentioned Catholic secondary schools waiving fees and opening their doors without charge to Hungarian children, primarily to girls in convent-run secondary schools. As secondary education was not provided freely by the state in the 1950s, this gesture provided significant help to Hungarian families and upward mobility for their children. Anna related how, the moment her family had financial resources, they paid such fees and felt empowered by finally becoming self-reliant and "paying back." In her estimation, those who came with a significant amount of social capital had the wherewithal to reinvent themselves in Ireland just as she had done. A trained teacher, she realized that she would not be able to practice her profession, and after pondering what she enjoyed, she went to Paris to train in design. As the life of a designer was short-lived, she went into marketing, where she pursued a successful career, as did her husband, a telecommunications engineer with the Electricity Supply Board (ESB). She considered that a background in the humanities was of greater individual benefit than a science or technical background, as these areas had not developed in Ireland. As a consequence, there were limited sources of employment opportunities for the majority of arrivals. However, the few who did remain were in a position to take advantage of economic developments that occurred in the 1960s.[46]

Irish people, strong in their support of the refugees at this juncture, continued their generous support, already demonstrated through the Irish Red Cross collection, which raised approximately £150,000, a considerable sum for the time. Members of the defense forces became involved; five officers and fifty-six crew members of the naval corvette the LÉ *Maev* contributed money, averaging seven pounds a week, to support two Hungarian families for six months.[47] The two families had been offered a house, the Moorings, in Rush, rent-free. This generosity was celebrated on board the LÉ *Maev* once the two families were employed and no longer needed to be subsidized. Mr. Takacs, a technician, left Rush for temporary employment elsewhere in Ireland, and Laszlo Lovas, an artist, secured a post teaching pottery in a vocational school. Both families presented gifts to the crew, which was followed by tea and biscuits on board the LÉ *Maev*. The event received press attention and was reported in the *Irish Pictorial* complete with a headline in Hungarian: "Köszönöm szépen!"(Thank you!)[48]

In contrast to public sentiment, charitable donations, and long-term support, the government was simultaneously attempting to learn more about refugee resettlement while indulging in buyer's remorse. Ireland became a member of the United Nations on December 14, 1955.[49] The taoiseach had approved the signing of the Convention Relating to the Status of Refugees, 1951, on May 18, 1956.[50] In December of that year, as a response to the urgent November communiqué from UNHCR, the taoiseach wanted to "have as much information as is available about any action being taken by other countries, either individually, or by international arrangement, to provide assistance in the form of money for the benefit of Hungarian refugees in Austria." Additionally, there was interest in the steps countries had taken to manage the reception and resettlement of Hungarian refugees. In mid-December, the Department of External Affairs contacted Irish legations and embassies in Europe about limits on the number of refugees received and arrangements for "their registration as aliens, maintenance and employment."[51] This request contrasts with communication that same month from the Department of the Taoiseach to External Affairs, requesting "that the Minister for External Affairs should have enquiries made, through the Ambassador in London, as to the possibility of arranging that employment would be found in Britain, in suitable cases, for refugees from Hungary admitted to Ireland."[52] These confusions can be attributed partly to the rapidity of events once Ireland had rejoined the international political sphere, and there was a need to acquire knowledge about implementing planning details. The desire to offload the refugees somewhere else, however, would indicate that beyond the gesture, there was no desire to engage with long-term planning.

Just as the *Victory*'s passengers had departed to their chosen destination, the link to Canada offering a solution remained active. The Department of External Affairs learned that in principle, Canada would be open to taking Hungarian refugees from Ireland, just as it was going to take some already in the UK in April 1957. The Canadian government, therefore, had decided that a refugee's country of first asylum would not be a hindrance to proceeding to Canada. This position agreed with the ICEM leaflet provided to Hungarian refugees about choices regarding temporary and final countries of resettlement. The level of fear and paranoia of people who had been living under the repercussions of high Stalinism and had crossed the border, accompanied at times by spies and professional agitators sent by the regime to foment discontent in the Austrian camps or further afield, could easily be forgotten in the effort to transport people out of Austria. The Canadian ambassador in Vienna understood the presence of this fear and paranoia among the Hungarians retrospectively. As a result, he directed that a group of refugees be sent from Austria to a temporary sojourn in Holland instead of traveling immediately to Canada. The ambassador made this decision so that the group would stay in Holland for the winter and subsequently arrive in Canada during more clement weather in the spring of 1957; this more temperate adjustment to a new life would be beneficial for their resettlement. While this might seem overly solicitous, the Canadian ambassador recounted the story of one group who had arrived in Canada in the winter of 1956. As part of a refueling stopover, the refugees found themselves in a Canadian forest area, which caused them great distress: they mistakenly thought they had been duped and taken to Siberia by a circuitous route. Consequently, the pertinence of the information set out in the ICEM leaflet to Irish interests of moving on the Hungarians was apparent but did not appear to resonate. Instead there was delay, during which time many Hungarians took matters into their own hands and quietly disappeared from Knockalisheen Camp to make their way to England.[53]

Notes

The epigraphs are from *Freedom Road, Hungarian Patriots Force Red Retreat*, October 24, 1956. Universal Studios, available at https://archive.org/details/1956-10-24_Freedom_Road, and Benedict Kiely, "The Heroic Men of Budapest," *Irish Press*, November 12, 1956, 8.

1. "May Bring Hungarian Refugees to Ireland," *Irish Press*, November 7, 1956, 7; "1,000 Refugees," *Irish Press*, November 16, 1956, 5; UNHCR, telegram to Dublin, November 17, 1956, DFA/419/33/11.
2. Department of Defence, memorandum for government, November 9, 1956, 1, TSCH/3/S11007 C.
3. *Koordinierung der Hilfe an die ungarischen Neuflüchtlinge, Mitteilung 4*, November 22, 1956, 5. Geneva: UNHCR. DFA/419/33/11.
4. Kushner, *Remembering Refugees*, 21.
5. Troper, "Canada and Hungarian Refugees," 188; Markowitz, "Humanitarianism versus Restrictionism," 46–59.
6. Olga Murphy received the Gold Cross of Merit of Hungary from the ambassador of Hungary on October 24, 2017, for her participation in the 1956 Revolution in a ceremony in Dublin. Interview with Olga Murphy, October 31, 2017.
7. UNHCR, telegram communique, November 24, 1956, DFA/419/33/11.
8. *Koordinierung der Hilfe an die ungarishen Neuflüchtlinge, Mitteilung 6*, November 30, 1956, Geneva: UNHCR. DFA/419/33/11.
9. Government of the Republic of Austria, aide-mémoire to Irish legation, Berne, November 15, 1956, DFA/419/33/11.
10. For the organization of World Refugee Year, which aimed to resolve the long-standing issue of refugees still residing in camps, see Gatrell, *Free World*.
11. Government of the Republic of Austria, aide-mémoire, to Irish legation, Berne, November 15, 1956, DFA/419/33/11.
12. Josephine McNeill, telegram to Department of External Affairs, November 16, 1956, DFA/419/33/11.
>Seán MacBride, Clann na Poblachta's leader and Minister for External Affairs in the 1950 inter-party government, appointed Josephine McNeill as minister to the Netherlands in 1950. She was the first Irishwoman diplomat to represent Ireland abroad in a ministerial role though never promoted to the title and office of ambassador. Josephine McNeill was the minister plenipotentiary to the Irish legation in Berne from 1956–1960.
13. NATO, *Report on Hungarian Refugees*, 9. For the background on Hungarian students in their words, see Sheridan, "Support and Surveillance."
14. Leaflet given to Hungarian refugees in Austria with text from *Hungarian Refugee Program Report 8*, Annex 2, Intergovernmental Committee for European Migration, December 21, 1956, DFA/419/33/11.
15. There was a flurry of telegrams, some on the same day, between Vienna and Dublin, November 22–25, 1956, DFA/419/33/11.
16. Gatrell, *Free World*, 51.
17. In Austria in 1956, "religious agencies gave special but not exclusive attention to their coreligionists," Niessen, "God Brought the Hungarians," 583. Some Hungarians emphasized

this religious link with regard to coming to Ireland and religious pressure following their arrival; Pálmai Bánki "Crossing Borders," 151, 155. Ted Vanya's story in O'Brien and Dobbs, "Hungarian Refugee Crisis," (unpaginated); interview with Anna Letoha, November 16, 2017.

18. Department of the Taoiseach, November 27, 1956, DFA/419/33/11.

19. Department of the Taoiseach to Department of External Affairs, November 26, 1956, DFA/419/33/11.

20. Dublin to Mr. McCann, Vienna, November 28, 1956, DFA/419/33/11.

21. Mr. McCann, report, December 7, 1956, and Irish legation to the Secretary, Department of External Affairs, December 14, 1956, File DFA/419/33/11.

22. *Daily Telegraph*, November 26, 1956, 5. Newspaper cutting. DFA/419/33/11.

23. Mr. McCann, report, December 7, 1956, DFA/419/33/11.

24. Telegrams from Irish legation, Berne, November 20 and Vienna, December 5, 1956, DFA/419/33/11.

25. Harold Tittman to Dublin, December 10, 1956; "Payment by the Irish Red Cross Society of Expenses Incurred by Aer Lingus in Transporting Hungarian Refugees to Ireland," memorandum, January 31, 1957, DFA/419/33/11.

26. Dáil Éireann Debate, volume 160, no. 5 (November 7, 1956, Private Notice Question, Relief for Hungary, statements by Deputy de Valera and Taoiseach John Costello).

27. "Emergency Depot Set Up by Irish Red Cross," *Irish Times*, November 7, 1956, 4, ITDA. "Ireland Helps Hungarians in Hour of Need," *Irish Press*, November 8, 1956, 7; "Nation behind Red Cross 'Aid Hungary' Drive," *Irish Press*, November 12, 1956, 9; "Hungary's Place in European History," *Kilkenny People*, November 17, 1956, 7; "Aid for Hungary," *Kilkenny People*, November 17, 1956, 5; Cavan News Items, *Anglo-Celt*, November 17, 1956, 12.

> Some people's enthusiasm would have been linked to earlier knowledge about Hungary from Arthur Griffith's book *The Resurrection of Hungary*, first published in 1904. Mayor of Limerick, Mr. G. E. Russell alludes to this connection in his thanks to the people of Limerick for their contributions in response to the Irish Red Cross appeal: "Limerick's Generous Response to Red Cross Appeal," *Limerick Leader*, November 12, 1956, 1. Thomas Kabdebo focused on Griffith and the emergence of nineteenth century nationalism in Ireland and Hungary in his study *Ireland and Hungary*.

28. Lieutenant Ernesto Paternò Castello di Carcaci, the Order of Malta, sent an appeal to its venerable grand priors and national associations, October 29, 1956. Walter Smithwick of Smithwick's Brewery, Kilkenny, to James Lyons, Limerick, November 11, 1956, Des Ryan Collection.

> The drugs were for a range of treatments: adrenaline for cardiac arrest and anaphylaxis or life-threatening allergic reactions, aminophylline for severe asthma, digoxin for irregular heart rhythm, sulphatriad for diarrhea, and the two antibiotics tetracycline and penicillin.

> There was an impasse regarding aid reaching Budapest between the closing of Hungary's airports by Soviet troops on October 31 and the opening of the Austro-Hungarian border following the arrival of an ICRC convoy on November 9, 1956. The convoy proceeded to Budapest after a day's delay and arrived on November 12, 1956. Perret, "ICRC Operations" (unpaginated).

29. "Nation behind 'Aid Hungary' Drive," *Irish Press*, November 12, 1956, 9; "Dublin Gives over £10,000 for Hungary," *Irish Press*, November 14, 1956, 8; "Hungary Relief Fund

Growing," *Irish Press*, November 16, 1956, 5; "Generous Response," *Irish Independent*, November 12, 1956, 12; "Killaloe," From Town to Country Local Correspondent, *Nenagh Guardian*, November 17, 1956, 5; "Relief for Hungary," *Kilkenny People*, November 17, 1956, 1; "Tribute to Hungary," *Connacht Tribune*, December 8, 1956, 7; "Limerick's Generous Response to Red Cross Appeal," *Limerick Leader*, November 12, 1956, 1.

30. Hungary's Orphans," *Irish Press*, November 9, 1956, 6; letter to the editor, *Kilkenny People*, November 12, 1956, 5.

31. "Hungary's Role as Defender of Christianity," *Tuam Herald*, December 15, 1956, 2; "The Darkness Falls Over Hungary," *Irish Press*, November 6, 1956, 4.

32. "Prayers for Hungary," *Connacht Tribune*, November 3, 1956, 19; "Day of Prayer," *Connacht Tribune*, November 24, 1956, 10.

33. "Sympathy with Hungary," *Tuam Herald*, November 24, 1956, 3; "Students' Tribute to Hungary," *Connacht Tribune*, November 24, 1956, 10.

34. "Unions' Sympathy with Hungary," *Irish Press*, November 7, 1956, 8.

35. Peter Boyd, Commentary, *Tuam Herald*, December 15, 1956, 7; "Hungary Proves the Soviet's Failure," *Irish Press*, November 26, 1956, 4.

36. "The First Lady of Hungary," *Irish Press*, November 20, 1956, 6.

37. Michael Headen spent a significant time abroad working with humanitarian organizations. He is the honorary consul for Malawi in the Republic of Ireland. Interview with Michael, June 30, 2021.

38. "Baton Charge after Dublin 'Rock-n-Roll,'" *Irish Press*, November 16, 1956, 5.

39. "Hungary Proves the Soviet's Failure," *Irish Press*, November 26, 1956, 4.

40. Press release, Department of Foreign Affairs to British embassy, December 7, 1956, DFA/419/33/11.

41. "Admission of Hungarian Refugees," memo, November 19, 1956 (though completed later as the document indicates).

42. Mr. McCann to Department of Foreign Affairs, December 13, 1956, DFA/419/33/11.

43. Compiled from Irish Red Cross report on Knockalisheen, December 10, 1956, and from "The Position of the Irish Red Cross, Refugee Camp," report appendix, to Interdepartmental Committee, January 18, 1957, TSCH/3/S11007 D.
    See also *Stateless*, the novel by Mark Collins (2006), where at least one refugee self-identifies as Catholic in order to secure a place to travel to Ireland.

44. Mrs. Barry, "Hungarian Refugees Who Have Left Knockalisheen Camp up to 17 January, 1957," report appendix, to Interdepartmental Committee, January 18, 1957, TSCH/3/S11007 D.

45. Undated letter of introduction from Professor JH Delargy, Irish Folklore Commission, UCD, DFA/419/33/11.
    For further details of Joseph Szövérffy's life, see Pődör, "Joseph Szövérffy," 192–205. National Library of Ireland (NLI), henceforth NLI.

46. An aspect of Irish life that persists today. Interview with Anna Letoha, November 16, 2017.

47. The designation LÉ is given to ships in the Irish Naval Service's fleet in front of the ship's assigned name.

48. "*Köszönöm Szépen!*," *Irish Pictorial*, November 30, 1957, 1, ITDA.

49. Ireland had enjoyed an international presence when it had belonged to the League of Nations. While keen to regain this presence, Ireland had to wait for nine years to pursue

its international policy goals by becoming a member of the UN, as the Soviet Union blocked its first attempt in 1946. These international policy goals were premised on Ireland being a Christian country, anticommunist, and a neutral state that nevertheless stood firmly in the Western democratic bloc as an ally of the United States and Western Europe. The UN provided the opportunity for Ireland's strategy to serve its own interests in the international arena: to forge bilateral relations with other nations, to create close links with Commonwealth countries like Canada, and to continue with established alliances, chief among them Ireland's alliance with the United States. The diplomatic staff assigned to represent Ireland in the UN had a short span of time to integrate into the organization before a series of major events erupted on the international stage, starting with the 1956 Hungarian Revolution. Skelly, *Irish Diplomacy*, 18–51.

50. Letter, Department of the Taoiseach, May 18, 1956, TSCH/3/S11007 C.

51. Department of the Taoiseach to Department of External Affairs, November 26, 1956; enquiry December 15, 1956, from the Department of External Affairs directed to embassies and legations in London, Paris, Bonn, Berne, Brussels, Hague, Stockholm, and Lisbon, DFA/419/33/10/1.

52. Department of the Taoiseach, note to Department of External Affairs, December 6, 1956, file DFA/419/33/11.

53. Irish embassy, Ottawa, telegram to Department of External Affairs, December 11, 1956; Irish legation, Berne to Department of External Affairs, January 23, 1957, DFA/419/33/11.

3

CAMP LIFE

> Traditional Ireland relied for its survival on a human haemorrhage....
> The crisis of "traditional" Ireland in the 1950s threw down the gauntlet to a new generation. It remained to be seen if any were left who could rise to the challenge.
>
> —J. J. Lee, "Continuity and Change in Ireland, 1945–70"

> At least 20 Hungarian refugees—about a quarter of the male population—have absconded from the camp at Knockalisheen and are known to have entered Britain illegally.... The refugees have discovered that no permit is normally necessary to travel between Ireland and Britain; but, while this does not apply to them, they slip through at Fishguard and Holyhead unnoticed. Some are known to have travelled to Belfast to make the crossing. A few have turned up in British refugee camps, but the rest are believed to be working in England.
>
> —*Irish Times*, "Refugees Abscond to Britain from Knockalisheen"

Refugees, Camps, and Apathy

Internationally, prevailing views of refugee camps incorporated the postwar management experiences of the military, NGOs, psychiatrists, psychologists, writers, and visitors. Instead of finding enthusiasm, influential visitors who toured the camps set up across Europe soon after the end of the war found hopelessness, apathy, and dispirited people waiting in their barracks, unable to make decisions or assume responsibilities for themselves. However, while this may have been true at a point when people had the luxury of coming to terms with displacement and much worse, the perspective of DP apathy endured in contrast to the refugees' innovation, creativity, organization, and entrepreneurship, including black marketeering, which flourished in camp communities where people lived for years on end. Official administrations were not the only ones to manage and regulate camp life; people organized themselves, including sourcing accommodation outside a camp despite their DP status or escaping the confines of the camp by withdrawing into alcohol consumption and card playing 'hour after hour, day after day." Camp school systems developed into elaborate organizations, and camps had preschool children and high school or even college students along with clubs and activities; the creation of DP universities was perhaps the most extraordinary achievement of all. Adults too engaged in life-affirming activities such as weddings and births by toasting with alcohol that was often brewed or distilled in the camp; adults also created and served on camp committees and took opportunities for paid work as offered by UNRRA. Sports, dances, theatrical shows, plays, and national holidays provided entertainment while national newspapers were a source of information. Regardless of such activity, terms such as *DP apathy* and *rehabilitation* survived the camps, though the latter was never clearly defined and generally interpreted as a fitness to return to civil society after the length of time spent in camp existence. This image of good refugees who could be rehabilitated was also present in NGO vocabulary and attitudes in Ireland. The Irish Red Cross, for instance, a branch of an international organization that held regular congresses, made many references to rehabilitating the Hungarians despite the fact that they had hardly spent any time in Austrian camps and consequently had, in fact, little time to process the shattering changes in their lives or descend into apathy.[1]

Such thoughts and feelings were absent at Shannon airport, where some three hundred members of the public greeted the first five chartered planeloads of 161 Hungarians arriving from London on the evening of November 25, 1956, after a four-day journey across land and sea. Among the welcome party was Mr. Murphy, the future Irish Red Cross administrator of the refugee camp being prepared at Knockalisheen; an additional sixty Red Cross members; various dignitaries; and the press. Mrs. de Parcher, a Hungarian refugee who had come to Ireland in 1947, acted as translator with Mr. Stephen Remenyi, a naturalized Irish citizen who had been working for Irish Shipping Limited for eleven years. There were immigration formalities but also a hot meal, described as goulash, and a welcome written in Hungarian on the menu. Following this respite, journalists heard stories of freedom fighters, escape, and families torn apart as some could flee while others remained behind. One young woman, Magda, and her husband left without their nine-month-old son, who was left in the care of her mother-in-law. Press reports varied on the number of tears shed; some stated that the refugees shed no tears but that the members of the public did once they saw the refugees coming down the plane gangways with their meager assortment of possessions. They were welcomed as Christians fighting to preserve Catholicism, and it was noted that the youngest member of the group, a four-week-old baby, had not been baptized.[2]

Knockalisheen Camp

The group of 161 refugees traveled to Knockalisheen in four buses and twenty private vehicles for their first night's sleep in a camp expected to hold five hundred refugees. The army had prepared welcoming urns of tea for the travelers, and the Hungarians politely endured the strange Irish habit of drinking tea with milk instead of flavoring it with lemon or perhaps rum when something stronger was required. The following morning, it became clear that the camp, consisting of seventy-two huts, was not completely ready, even if the Red Cross had provided stocks of clothing and other requirements such as razors and blades, baby items, cigarettes, matches, and flashlights. There was no linoleum on the hut floors, and "women and girls washed garments in water boiled in iron pots on the coal and wood stoves standing in the center of each hut for heating purposes. Some refugees sat on blanket-covered mattresses stretched over pallets on the floor to form beds. All this is part of the normal difficulties of a refugee camp and army officers, soldiers and Red Cross personnel did everything to make the refugees' lot as comfortable as possible." It would be difficult to critique the army personnel who had worked to turn an uninhabited army camp, built during the Emergency and described by an IRC official as a wreck, into homely dwellings. They had had little time to prepare but had made the effort to install signposts in Hungarian, which, on the first evening of arrival, were picked out in the beams of specially installed floodlights. Refurbishment was not complete, and the Red Cross was still sourcing items, including a radio, which a Limerick member of the organization eventually forwarded to the camp recreation room. The Singer Company was to send two sewing machines, and a call went out for a barber as there was no one among this group of refugees to cut hair. In other words, camp organization still had to settle into a rhythm approximating daily life as the Hungarians waited for their new life and new future in Ireland.[3]

Fig. 3.1. Huts at Knockalisheen camp. Source: Sean Curtin Collection.

Once Knockalisheen was selected and inspected by the Department of Defense, the official view became that it was clearly not large enough to hold a thousand refugees, and further arrivals were suspended after the first approximately four hundred and fifty refugees had been brought to Ireland.[4] The actual description of the camp at Knockalisheen was somewhat at odds with the ones in the press, partly because it was prepared at a date significantly later than the arrival of the refugees in November 1956. Knockalisheen consisted of fifty wooden huts, some of which were sixty feet by twenty feet in size and others sixty feet by sixteen feet. Huts were partitioned into two, four, or five sections, depending on family size or number of occupants. The huts were lined internally with sheeting and had linoleum floors, and each section had a heating stove where a fire had to be lit and maintained for warmth. There were wash stations in separate buildings, as each hut did not have such facilities, though there was electricity. The main part of the camp also had surfaced roads, but this was not the norm throughout the camp. Olga Murphy, who stayed in Knockalisheen until its closure almost two years later, still remembers constantly cleaning the mud from her shoes in winter. Two huts were set aside for religious services, and a Hungarian Jesuit, Father Kis, and a Presbyterian minister visited the camp to conduct religious services, baptisms, and marriage ceremonies. The Department of Defense had spent £8,307 on the camp, mainly on partitioning the huts, connecting electricity, and installing a sewage system. The facilities were described in military terms: "The electric lighting arrangements are excellent and cooking and dining facilities are well up to the standard of a military non-permanent post. Recreation rooms are available and there are certain recreational facilities available." The camp, therefore, met the standards of the time for a short-term stay and would be adequate for refugees who would move out fairly quickly into their future lives, as was happening with Hungarians who had arrived in other European countries.[5]

The army, An Garda Síochána, the Irish police force, and the Irish Red Cross all had a permanent presence at Knockalisheen Camp, with each performing a range of duties. The Irish Red Cross, mandated to undertake responsibility "for the reception, care and maintenance" of the Hungarians, played the major administrative role.[6] Mr. Murphy, the IRC camp controller, oversaw fourteen paid workers and eight volunteers including an ambulance driver; a storekeeper; a typist/accountant; a head cook and four or sometimes two assistant cooks; two or occasionally one laborer; two nurses; and two interpreters, Mrs. O'Shaughnessy and Miss Kos, joined later by Mrs. O'Brien.[7] The total weekly wage bill amounted to ninety-six pounds and fourteen shillings. An Garda Síochána assigned a superintendent, two sergeants, and seven gardaí to the camp and ran the Aliens Registration Office on-site.[8] Senior gardaí also sent regular reports to the assistant commissioner of C3, the crime and security section of An Garda Síochána involved in intelligence gathering. A series of such reports submitted to C3 and passed on to Mr. Berry in the Department of Justice provide an alternative perspective on events as they unfolded at the camp. For instance, Superintendent Lavan, based in the Clare division of An Garda Síochána, sent a series of reports from December 12 to December 31, 1956, indicating that the gardaí kept a keen watch on the daily life of the camp. An army officer, Captain Brennan, was in charge of army intelligence at the camp and offered yet another perspective on the site's daily activities from those reported by the press, the Irish Red Cross, or interdepartmental discussions and reports.[9]

The army's Twelfth Infantry S Battalion had the greatest number of personnel at the camp with nineteen members on duty: Commandant O'Callaghan, two captains, a lieutenant, five NCOs, and ten privates, comprising a key presence for the running of the camp. The officers attached to the camp included the commandant in charge of the military staff, the company quartermaster supervisor, an engineer, and Mr. McCann, the camp doctor. In addition to the officers, the army personnel included a noncommissioned officer responsible for the orderly room or administration hub where one individual manned the switchboard; a cook and two men worked in the officers' mess; one cook and one helper were in the NCO men's mess; and one store man served the company quartermaster as the army were in charge of provisions.[10] Mr. McCann, the camp doctor, had a full-time role at the camp, but the army later considered withdrawing him and making his position part-time as An Fórsa Cosanta Áitiúil, the local defense force, commenced annual training. The Irish Red Cross chair, Mrs. Tom Barry, took immediate action by contacting General Seán MacEoin regarding conditions at the camp and the health of the Hungarians during their first Irish winter in Knockalisheen:

> You very kindly visited the camp. You realise its situation and also the number of children, expectant mothers amongst the group of refugees. These have not reacted well from a health point of view to Ireland's moist climate. The care of a full time doctor is more essential to our Staff than any other official. Knowing the keen personal interest you have taken in the Refugees, I am now asking you to have Dr McCann left on full time duty. He is an excellent officer and doctor and is much trusted both by the Refugees and the Irish Red Cross Society.

Mr. McCann remained at the camp.[11]

Feeding the large number of people came under the control of the army and to a lesser extent the IRC as "each refugee receives full rations on the same basis as the Army. In addition, milk and food suitable for babies and the sick are supplied. Junior and Red Cross members supply gifts of sweets and fruit from time to time."[12] A sample menu from the second week in March 1957, seen in table 3.1, can be considered representative of meals at the time in Ireland, which, we must remember, was not a wealthy state. Nor was it renowned for its cuisine. The menu would be a far cry from Hungarian cuisine, which, for example, did not have marmalade as part of its breakfast fare, and there is a clear absence of fresh fruit, fresh vegetables, and fresh milk for the large number of children in the camp. At the same time, the sight of Hungarians picking *sóska*, sorrel, growing wild in the fields would have appeared strange to their hosts.[13] Some changes were made from time to time, and two days after the first groups of Hungarian refugees arrived some of the women began helping the army cooks "by giving the food a Hungarian touch."[14] Overall, there was no significant deviation from the general menu.

Table 3.1. Knockalisheen weekly menu, March 10, 1957, to March 16, 1957

Date	Breakfast	Dinner	Tea
Sunday, 3/10/57	Coffee, bread, butter, and marmalade	Soup, beef, potatoes, onions, and rice pudding with dried fruit	Tea, bread, butter, corned beef, and cocoa
Monday, 3/11/57	Coffee, bread, butter, and jam	Soup, boiled bacon, beans, mashed potatoes, and semolina pudding	Tea, bread, butter, jam, and cocoa
Tuesday, 3/12/57	Coffee, bread, butter, and marmalade	Soup, brown stew, mixed veg, mashed potatoes, and rice pudding with dried fruit	Tea, bread, butter, rasher and egg, and cocoa
Wednesday, 3/13/57	Coffee, bread, butter, and marmalade	Veg soup, fried fillet of whiting, onions, mashed potatoes, and farola and semolina pudding	Tea, bread, butter, cheese, and cocoa
Thursday, 3/14/57	Coffee, bread, butter, and marmalade	Soup, boiled beef, carrots, mashed potatoes, and semolina pudding with dried fruit	Tea, bread, butter, rasher, sausage, and cocoa
Friday, 3/15/57 Hungarian National Holiday Special	Coffee, bread, butter, and marmalade	Soup, roast pork, beans, mashed potatoes, and semolina pudding with dried fruit	Tea, bread, butter, rasher and egg, fruitcake, and cocoa
Saturday, 3/16/57	Coffee, bread, butter, and marmalade	Soup, boiled bacon, mixed veg, mashed potatoes, and rice pudding and dried fruit	Tea, bread, butter, and cocoa

Source: TSCH/3/S11007 D. NAI.

Clothes and other items such as soap, polish, and shaving kits had already been allocated, and a clothing store remained open daily so that there was ready access to items as needed. The Hungarians received pocket money—fifteen shillings a week for men, ten shillings a week for women; families who left the camp to reside with Irish families received twenty-five shillings per week per adult and ten shillings per week for each child in addition to the pocket money. Once employment was found, these sums continued to be paid until wages were received; a grant of sixty pounds was also supplied for furniture.[15] What the Hungarians did not know, though it was reported in the press on their arrival, was that the Irish Red Cross considered that the camp would house five hundred refugees for three years. There was no mention of long-term plans extending beyond the confines of Knockalisheen. A positive note, however, was the plan for the Hungarians to hold free and fair elections to create a workers council of refugee representatives.[16]

Camp Life: Quarantine

Each new arrival of refugees began a two-week quarantine period in Knockalisheen; during one such time, two Hungarian refugees, already restless, began to take matters into their own hands concerning their own and their compatriots' long-term future. The two arrived in Dublin at the beginning of December 1956 and went to the Australian embassy. They were identified as Béla Farkas and, rather unusually, Huibe Huiré, which is not a known Hungarian name, though it could be an effort at some sly humor that has not survived transcription by someone unversed in Hungarian pronunciation. At the Australian embassy, the two refugees spoke to a Miss Williams and said that they represented fifteen others in Knockalisheen. Miss Williams asked them to return later and contacted the Department of External Affairs. An official informed her that "the question of the disposal of Hungarian refugees in Ireland was the subject of Government consideration at the moment," and the Australian embassy would be informed of any decision made. Later in the day, the same two men showed up at the American embassy; the embassy phoned the Department of Justice about their arrival. At the Department of Justice, the decision was to follow the men discreetly as the department considered it wise not to make a fuss by apprehending the men to take them back to Knockalisheen. A discreet tail could at least make sure they would not try to abscond to England.[17]

The adventures of these two men continued as a US embassy official took them to the Irish Red Cross office in Westland Row, where someone phoned the Department of External Affairs: the advice was to return them to Knockalisheen. However, this did not happen, first because the IRC, having decided not to engage further with the situation, had closed their doors to the two men. Second, the following day, December 5, 1956, the

Department of Justice informed External Affairs that gardaí were questioning the two men in Dublin Castle. After questioning, four facts emerged: the men did not want to return to the camp; they represented fifty families who were unhappy with the food and conditions in the camp and did not wish to remain there; the Hungarians had been misled and misinformed about the conditions of their reception in Ireland; and, finally, they wanted to go to America. After only a week at Knockalisheen Camp, it was already apparent that the Hungarians were neither meekly grateful nor prepared to stay within its confines as they were refugees, not prisoners. From an official perspective, they were proving to be recalcitrant and not at all ready to be rehabilitated into good refugees.

The immediate situation of what to do with the two men was further complicated by the Irish Red Cross saying that they did not wish to have the men back at the camp, as they were troublemakers. The Department of Justice considered that the two men could not be left to roam at will, as they would no doubt get into some sort of trouble. The solution was a suggestion that the minister of justice issue a residence restriction order under the Aliens Act; the order would return the men to Knockalisheen, where they would stay until allowed to leave. The Department of Justice deemed the situation to be most unsatisfactory and complained that "although these were aliens and in the normal way subject to the control of the D/Justice, the Department seemed to be the last one consulted and their hands were tied."[18]

The department could not act, as there were no instructions from government, despite the appointment of a committee of three ministers to manage the matter of the Hungarian refugees. The Department of External Affairs, considered to be the coordinating department, interpreted their role as merely being a post office. External Affairs would pass on all information relating to the arrival of refugees but would not engage with decision-making. The department adopted this attitude to demonstrate that it was not attempting to usurp the Department of Justice's territory. However, the Department of Justice remained frustrated, and the lines of administrative demarcation remained firm rather than yielding to more flexible approaches to manage a novel and increasingly long-term situation.

Weddings and Holidays

The initial outpouring of support toward Hungary had led to expressions of what the taoiseach called the practical sympathy of Irish people, which resulted in not only money and goods flowing to the Irish Red Cross but also solutions to immediate problems.[19] Three weddings took place at the camp almost immediately, all on the same day. The three brides were able to enjoy a traditional white wedding as recently married Irish women offered to donate their wedding dresses. The year-old romance between two young refugees—Johanna, a twenty-one-year-old typist, and Josef, an eighteen-year-old steelworker—made the papers. On October 27, Josef had visited Johanna to tell her of his intention to join friends to fight the Russians; he also asked Johanna to marry him on his return. Instead, the two fled Hungary, beginning their journey by train to Győr, some thirty miles from the Austrian border, after which they walked a roundabout route for three days to avoid any patrols.[20] The *Evening Herald* featured another bride-to-be, Kathleen, and her disappointment at not having any bridal wear. Barbara Page, the *Women's Saturday Magazine* columnist for the *Evening Herald*, documented the subsequent efforts to make the wedding a special occasion:

> Immediately the offers started coming in, by telephone and by letter, and one of the first offers to come was from a young Dublin woman whose measurements coincided almost exactly with Kathleen's. Over the wire went the vital measurements . . . the reply: please rush down wedding dress . . . Kathleen is delighted to accept. So out to Glasnevin went our special messenger with a car to pick up the wedding dress . . . a ballet length with shoulder length veil and pearl headdress, already packed. It was rushed to catch the afternoon train to Limerick and Kathleen had it by Thursday night. It isn't easy for a young bride to give up her wedding dress to a stranger and I asked Mrs. O'Connor how she felt about letting such a treasured possession go. "When I read of Kathleen's disappointment I felt I just had to give her my dress," she says, "and I have no regrets. . . . I intended to keep it always. . . . But now I am happy that this Hungarian girl is to wear my dress. . . . And this is my wedding gift to her."[21]

Because of this generosity, Kathleen, a twenty-year-old weaver, wore a bridal outfit when she married twenty-one-year-old Andreas, a carpenter; Johanna had a trousseau provided by Mrs. Clancy, wife of the *Evening Herald* staff photographer in Limerick. Twenty-nine-year-old Maria married thirty-year-old László, who had owned a grocery shop in Budapest. Father Kis conducted the ceremonies; people threw confetti at the newlyweds, followed by each bride cutting a slice of the wedding cake that had been sent by an unknown benefactor.[22]

As well as arranging the delivery of the wedding dress, Barbara Page also sent a large box, delivered anonymously to her office and containing bridal lingerie, to Knockalisheen Camp. Unfortunately, the gift spoiled the celebratory mood of the human interest story. Commander Callaghan, the military camp commander, issued a statement to journalists on behalf of the bishop of Limerick: "His Lordship most Rev Dr O'Neill Bishop of Limerick, has asked me to express his deep displeasure at the type of journalism indulged in by sections of the Press on this occasion. He wishes it to be known that the undignified activities of certain members of the press have, in his opinion, constituted a public scandal, and he would be grateful if all were immediately mindful of their duties in this regard." Whether it was the thought of two young unmarried people being together over a few nights or the mention of lingerie is not clarified in the bishop's statement, nor indeed how young people should have behaved as they were fleeing together toward the Austrian border. Such censure, however, formed part of the bishop's remit in the social and cultural life of 1950s Ireland. Conversely, the bishop had nothing to say when one of the brides learned of family news from Hungary: her father had been deported to the Soviet Union.[23]

In contrast to the bishop's high moral tone, Irish families opened their homes to Hungarian refugees for their first Christmas in Ireland; Córas Iompair Éireann, the Irish railway company, offered free travel for Hungarians visiting their Irish hosts.[24] Irish homes were also open to informal arrangements between Hungarian and Irish families such as that between Mrs. McMahon and the Somodi family: she looked after the Somodis' young daughter, Kati, until the family eventually moved to England, where Mr. Somodi, an engineer, obtained employment.[25] Publicity resulted in offers of employment so that Barbara Page could report to her readers that Janos, a hairdresser from Budapest who had symbolically given away the young bride Kathleen at her wedding, took up a hairdressing position in Drogheda, which came with a flat, courtesy of the owners, Mr. and Mrs. Simpson.[26] Martin Hauser also offered employment in those early days. Formerly of Essen, Germany, he had migrated to Ireland at the end of the Second World War after three years spent in the Dachau concentration camp. He rebuilt his life in Ireland, where he was the owner-manager of an artificial jewelry factory in Ennis, county Clare. The piecework entailed stringing beads or pearls; the work could be carried out at the camp and seems to have continued throughout the time the refugees were in Knocklisheen. Mr. Hauser commented, "The people left in the Knocklisheen camp could live independently of the Red Cross subsidy on their earnings from my factory. I realise, however, that it entails long hours of work, but it is all done in the confines of their own quarters. . . . I have been a displaced person for years and I know how they feel." This employment was certainly a lifeline and contributed to efforts to save some money prior to leaving the camp.[27]

Interdepartmental Meetings: Conflict(ing) Reports

Apart from the Irish Red Cross's administrative presence at Knockalisheen, An Garda Síochána and army interdepartmental committee meetings took place in Dublin. Meeting for the first time on December 10, 1956, some two weeks after the arrival of the 548 Hungarians, the committee had senior representatives from the Departments of the Taoiseach, External Affairs, Justice, Defense, Health, Finance, and Social Welfare. There was no representation from the Department of Education despite the presence of so many children at the camp. Mrs. Barry, the Irish Red Cross chair, was keen to clarify whether the committee was a decision-making body and asked that the committee's terms of reference be clarified before discussion of the agenda proceeded. The committee's role was primarily consultative, but it could aid the IRC by reviewing problems and arriving at decisions. The IRC, however, needed urgent decisions as, apparently, at this early juncture, there was unrest at Knockalisheen Camp that had reached such "dangerous proportions" that the possibility existed of the huts being burned down. "Expert agitators" in the camp were creating unrest because the Irish Red Cross could not answer their questions about paid employment and resettlement in other countries such as the United States and Canada. However, before addressing these serious allegations and the concerns articulated by the Hungarians in Knockalisheen, each department preferred to set out its position. The Department of Defense pointed out that that the furniture and fittings were the property of the army and were being looked after by an army officer, military police, and cooks. An army doctor was also present and would remain until relieved by the county medical officer of health or a local doctor. The Department of Defense might have to charge the IRC at some point in the future, but this question did not arise at the moment. The Department of Health and Social Welfare explained that the Hungarian refugees, as aliens, were in the same position as Irish citizens in relation to social services. The Department of Justice stated that the operation of the Aliens Act, 1935, had been waived to permit the entry of the refugees. The department therefore needed direction as to what system of control to operate in relation to the refugees. The Department of Industry and Commerce outlined employment regulations and the need for employment permits.

Fig. 3.2. Administration Knockalisheen camp, Mr. Murphy third from left, first row; Mrs. Barry first in second row. Source: *Irish Times*, October 14, 2006.

However, while the refugees could be employed as farm laborers or domestic servants, they could not gain access to industrial employment because of the numbers of unemployed.

It was decided that the Department of Justice should register all the refugees as aliens and also issue individual orders that would restrict their movements at the discretion of An Garda Síochána. Should a refugee refuse to obey a police order, then persuasion was to be used first, but with the option of arrest if all else failed, although it would be undesirable to arrest and charge a refugee under the Aliens Order. The feeling was that the refugees should be treated kindly and better than Irish citizens in this instance. Application forms and employment permits were to be given to Mrs. Barry for the Knockalisheen Camp.[28] The following day, Mrs. Barry wrote to the taoiseach that "yesterday's meeting was a great success and almost all the vexed questions which were upsetting the peaceful operation of the Camp were clarified to the satisfaction of all."[29] However, at this meeting the Hungarians had swiftly metamorphosed from heroic Christians fighting "Godless Communism" to aliens subject to controls, including the restriction of movement. The legitimacy of Hungarian refugees asking questions about their futures did not arise in the discussion with the result that their voices were silenced and their wishes ignored completely.

The second interdepartmental meeting, held on January 21, 1957, had four items on its agenda: malcontents again, refugees wishing to go to other countries again, arrangements for the medical care of the refugees at Knockalisheen, and employment.³⁰ Mrs. Barry had submitted an extensive report laying out details on the running of the camp and numbers of refugees, including a lengthy section on the pressing matter of malcontents. Apparently, this group's ringleader was the democratically elected Hungarian camp representative, Mr. László Pesthy, whose name appeared with ten other so-called agitators in the camp; they were all Catholics apart from two recalcitrant Calvinists.³¹ Mrs. Barry had visited the camp a month previously on December 20 to confer with Commandant O'Callaghan, Captain Brennan, army intelligence, Superintendent Lavan, Camp Controller Mr. Murphy, and the Reverend Dr. O'Neill, bishop of Limerick, who was present for part of the meeting. As a result of these discussions, "The UNANIMOUS suggestion from this meeting was that the malcontents should be removed from the camp. Through their activities these men had (a) Prevented willing Hungarians from cooking and helping in the camp. (b) Had broken into the coal stores and removed five tons of coal. (c) Had broken the windows of the stores. (d) Had threatened Red Cross personnel. (e) Had howled down and threatened a Hungarian resident in Ireland, Dr Scgoffory [sic, meaning Szövérffy], Folklore Commissioner, when he addressed the refugees." While there was concern about press reports damaging the employment prospects of all the Hungarians in the camp, the most pressing matter was Mr. Pesthy's character: allegedly, he had consorted with a woman of ill repute from Limerick.³²

A lady had arrived at the camp and was refused entry; she returned later with Mr. Pesthy and another refugee, and the trio forced their way past the gate and the sentry. The gardaí in Killaloe were notified, and an inspector arrived accompanied by a contingent of gardaí; with no warrant, they did not enter Mr. Pesthy's hut but remained on-site until the lady left. The following day, an angry Mr. Pesthy remonstrated with the camp controller to say that "they were supposed to be in a free country." Mr. Pesthy learned that Mr. Murphy "could keep people from the camp" and that "we must have law and order in the camp and that the refugees must obey the rules." Unimpressed by this explanation, Mr. Pesthy "replied that he would bring the lady to the camp any time he liked." The lady returned that evening but was turned away and informed that "she was trespassing and could be prosecuted.'" Two days later, she returned and asked for permission to retrieve the musical instruments she had left in Mr. Pesthy's hut: she had provided the Hungarians with the opportunity to play music. Even at that point, "a close watch was kept on her until she left," and "the refugees in the surrounding huts . . . [were] loud in protest against the lady's treatment."

However, as camp representative, Mr. Pesthy had other things on his mind than consorting with an apparent lady of doubt as he asked for a day pass and railway voucher so he could travel to Carlow and Dublin. On arrival in Dublin, he went immediately to the Independent Newspapers office, where he related concerns about the conditions at Knockalisheen. This visit was to no avail, as it resulted only in further silencing of Hungarian refugee voices: "The Independent got in touch with the Department of Justice but they promised not to publish the statement. He made threats also at the Independent that, if he was not received by high Government Officials he would ring the camp and there would be a big disturbance there. The Supt and other members of the Garda kept a close watch, but so far there has been no disturbance."[33] Mr. Pesthy was a persistent individual, and while it was noted that he did not travel to Carlow on the day he went to Dublin, he still managed to contact Mrs. Bielenberg in county Carlow; she translated a letter he had previously sent to the Irish Red Cross listing a number of complaints and requests.[34] He circulated this letter to the embassies in Dublin and the daily papers on January 7, 1957; the Irish Red Cross interpreted the letter as an attack on its administration. One of the requests in the letter was that all clothing in the stores "should be handed over to Hungarian hands for accountancy" because "rumor had it that not only Hungarians are benefitting by the Clothing Gifts."[35] There were certainly frustrations around clothing; the IRC stated that they were distributed as quickly as possible but the Hungarians were not waiting their turn and impeding the process. The Hungarians' perspective was that they should have control of clothing supplies. The rumor of pilfering did not appear in the papers.[36]

The Irish Red Cross executive received a report from Knockalisheen to say that "since the arrival of the Refugees we have been faced with unrest, no matter what is done for them there is always something else wrong." Mr. Murphy continued that "it is useless to continue a policy of appeasement. The present leader, one of the many chosen to represent them, is an unreliable man and a very bad influence over some of the refugees."[37] The executives decided unanimously to first ask for the Department of Justice to remove Mr. Pesthy and second to deal publicly with his letter of complaint in an official bulletin, subsequently posted throughout the camp on January 15, 1957. Unfortunately, the woes of the IRC did not abate, as there was a camp council election among the refugees; 193 over the age of eighteen voted, and eighty abstained. Four people put themselves forward, and Mr. Pesthy received 174 votes while the rival candidates received fewer than 10 votes each. Based on this evidence, Mr. Pesthy enjoyed significant support from the Hungarians in the camp in his endeavors to represent them. The IRC, however, had still not accepted the result of this free and fair democratic vote by the time of the second interdepartmental meeting.[38]

The second interdepartmental committee debated the IRC motion to remove Mr. Pesthy:

> This man has publicly defamed the Irish Red Cross by lies and insinuations to the world. He is an undesirable of the worst type of professional agitator who has terrorised some of his fellow refugees. Whether he is a genuine refugee or not is open to question. He arrived in Ireland among the first contingent of 153 unscreened Hungarians. We have only his own boasts which are very much at variance. On arrival he listed his occupation as a Galvaniser. In his early proclamations to the Press he has promoted himself to "Metal Engineer." Last week he described himself as a manager of one of the largest Engineering firms in Hungary, employing thousands. This man's removal from the Camp is both urgent and imperative if the Red Cross is to run the Camp in a humane and efficient manner.[39]

Mrs. Barry had read about refugees being sent back to Austria and wondered if the same could be applied in the case of the apparent agitator at Knockalisheen. However, Mr. Pesthy had refugee status: Article 32 of the Convention on Refugees, 1951, could not apply as removal was premised solely on grounds of national security and after due process. Only a formal directive under the Aliens Order 1946 could physically remove a refugee from Knockalisheen to another place and keep him there legally. Furthermore, the Department of Justice had been in touch with the superintendent "responsible for maintaining law and order in the camp and had received many reports from him, all of which indicated that there was no serious unrest at the camp." The Department of Justice had received a comprehensive report from Superintendent Lavan that summarized the situation at Knockalisheen as being "quite peaceable and orderly" and with "no lack of discipline present in the Camp." Superintendent Lavan was "not disposed to take [threats] seriously" and was "satisfied that there is not the slightest danger that any of the refugees would use or attempt to use force against any member of staff." The camp was enthusiastic about Mr. Pesthy's election and "showed no signs of being intimidated—quite the contrary." Superintendent Lavan, in agreement with Commandant O'Callaghan, was "satisfied that it is neither necessary nor desirable to have any particular individual removed from the camp in the interests of law and order." As Mr. Pesthy had applied for a job in England, the solution was to help him relocate. Mrs. Barry was not immediately satisfied and questioned the Department of Justice view, as Superintendent Lavan had not opposed the unanimous stance toward removing so-called malcontents at a prior meeting held in the camp. The Department of Justice pointed out that Superintendent Lavan's responsibility was to report to his own authorities.[40]

The depth of feeling emanating from the IRC related to reputational damage and the request for a government statement "re-affirming the Government's confidence in the Irish Red Cross and its recognition of the Society's efficient handling of a very difficult task."[41] However, the interdepartmental meeting took a more sober approach to the situation at Knockalisheen Camp and, in order for the IRC to avoid adverse publicity, advised that the organization accept the result of the election. In addition, the committee considered the IRC were overburdened with work at the camp and that an "experienced person should be sent to the Camp for a couple of weeks at least to organize a proper office system" and that "the clothing and supplies stores need an adequate staff." Some of those burdens were, however, already lighter as Mr. Murphy, the camp controller, had an assistant and the IRC intended to employ two more interpreters and another watchman.[42]

Since much of this second interdepartmental meeting was devoted to the management of the supposed situation at the camp, another pressing question received brief attention: the local employment exchange in Youghal did not seem to have cleared the employment of a few Hungarians at Seafield Fabrics. Such clearance was mandatory; employing aliens required a permit. However, the Seafield Fabrics manager declared that there was no one in Ireland "qualified for the highly specialized work offered to these refugees." The IRC proposed creating a special employment committee, and the interdepartmental committee approved this idea.

With regard to healthcare, the Hungarians had the same rights as Irish citizens so that an individual entitled to treatment would apply for a medical card from the local county council. The committee foresaw objections from Clare County Council because of the number of refugees at Knockalisheen. Finally, refugees wishing to go to other countries would have to wait, as the Canadians would be able to offer transport only in April. The United States, Australia, and Argentina would receive only Hungarians who had been sponsored. Thus, the aliens would be staying in Ireland until these migration impasses were resolved.[43]

Employment

Toward the end of December 1956, the Irish Red Cross advertised in the national press that skilled Hungarians were available for work.[44] In addition, the IRC carefully stated that prospective employers could apply for the necessary permits from the Department of Industry and Commerce by obtaining application forms directly from Knockalisheen. There were more than 150 individuals available for work at that time (see table 3.2). The list was a varied group and "because of its diversity (was) not likely to upset the labor market if employers were willing to give the refugees a chance." The local Red Cross would also help refugees find temporary accommodation if they did secure employment "until the refugee and his or her family could be rehabilitated in the local community."[45] A supportive editorial in the *Irish Examiner* pointed to the potential benefits the Hungarians brought to Ireland and to the fact that there was no conflict existing between the Hungarians, their potential employment, and the fact of Irish emigration: "Authority here proscribed ordinary employment, apparently on the ground that it would depress the labour market if the Hungarians took employment. It could be argued that with the heavy tide of emigration of Irish workers it would be anomalous to allow foreigners to take their place. The vast majority of our emigrants are unskilled workers, while most of the Hungarians are technicians of a class which Ireland requires." The Hungarian threat to the depressed state of the Irish labor market was precisely the premise on which the government based its argument for not accepting the full one thousand refugees as well as its almost immediate turn to contemplating their swift departure from Ireland.[46]

However, as the editorial points out, the refugees arrived with the kind of technical skills needed by a country slowly turning to the idea of modernization by expanding its industrial base. There were Hungarians who had the necessary technical skills to make serious contributions to industrial start-ups. For instance, in Tubbercurry, county Sligo, two brothers from Cashel, the Gallaghers, had created three industries including Industrial Foundries, which began operations in 1955. With 12 employees by November 1956, the company planned for a workforce of 150, so a skilled individual would have been a welcome addition.[47] In April 1957, Industrial

Table 3.2. Hungarian adults available for work

Situation wanted	Number	Situation wanted	Number
Plumber	1	Postman	1
Truck drivers	8	Textile merchant	1
Motor mechanics	8	Locksmiths	3
Weavers	9	Electrical engineer	1
Ironworkers	11	Dressmakers	2
Stokers	5	Optician	1
Laborers	2	Railway shunter	1
Welder	1	Waiter and land worker	1
Radio telegrapher	1	Battery factory worker	1
Precision instrument makers	2	Lens grinder	1
Tractor driver	1	Bookkeeper	1
Physician	1	Restaurant manager	1
Tool fitter	1	Railway draughtsman	1
Carpenters	3	Miners	5
Aeronautical mechanics	3	Fitters	4
Dockworkers	3	Brick factory worker	1
Central heating mechanic	1	Soldier	1
Teacher and nurse	1	Electrical mechanics	9
Draper	1	Farmworkers	2
Agricultural teacher	1	Galvanizer	1
Tailors	3	Joiners	2
Lawyers	2	Musicians	3
Ironworker and woodcarver	1	Glazier	1
Confectioners	3	Clerks	2
Horse trainer (trotting)	1	Storekeepers	2
House painter	1	Watchmakers	2
Bar manager	1	Radio technician	1
Artist and teacher	1	Factory workers	6
Machine fitters	2	Bank accountant	1
Metal polisher	1	Physicist	1
Journalists	2	Hairdresser/barbers	2
Paper factory worker	1	Architects	2
Auto mechanical instructor	1	Stonecutter	1
Engine drivers	3	Shoemaker	1
Civil engineer	1	Furniture factory worker	1
Stationmaster	1	Oil company laboratory assistant	1
Knitting factory workers	2	Cooper	1
Waiters	3	Butcher	1
Total number of persons seeking work			164

Source: Irish Red Cross list published in the *Irish Independent*, December 27, 1956, 12. Irish Newspaper Archive.

Foundries employed a skilled worker, Rezzo (Rezső) Filler, making molds to shape molten metal into castings used to make parts for industry. Soon he was promoted to the position of foreman at the foundry. A report on Mr. Filler, a young man, characterized him as having excellent habits and more than average intelligence, being a capable and efficient workman, and generally exhibiting a temperament that made work easy for himself and his coworkers. Unfortunately, he was not pleased with the rate of pay—approximately eight pounds per week—and did not appreciate "the fact that the Industry is only at present in its infancy" and that his earnings would improve once the company developed contracts and "the Industry begins to thrive." Mr. Filler threatened to leave for better opportunities in London, and it is not known if he stayed long enough to see the company flourish.[48]

The Entrepreneurial Spirit

By the end of 1957, after a year in Knockalisheen, over a hundred adults resided in the camp; half were women mainly categorized as housewives. At this point, the chief executive officer of Limerick Vocational Education Committee wrote to the technical education branch of the Department of Education with a view to organizing training for the refugees remaining at Knockalisheen. The camp refugee representative, Mr. Kukk, in conjunction with Camp Controller Mr. Murphy, confirmed that the refugees would attend any course that would secure employment. The question of English language skills or the language problem, as it was alluded to in the letter, arose, but by this time it appeared that "while they cannot express themselves in English they nevertheless understand most of what is said to them."[49] It is not evident that this idea went any further, but, regardless of the seeming language problem, there were enterprising Hungarians who had been attempting to make some money despite their situation.

However, not every activity was designed to create pocket money. In early December 1956, Béla Siráky, formerly a Budapest journalist, had begun the production of a camp newspaper that he hoped would have a daily circulation of about two hundred readers when the camp population was at its peak. Alternatively, moneymaking enterprises included creating and selling Hungarian handicrafts, an activity that began soon after the Hungarians arrived. The Irish Red Cross had appealed for donations of wool and knitting needles for the women in the camp and woodwork

Fig. 3.3. Family sharing the camp workload. Source: Sean Curtin Collection.

material for the men. At the beginning of December 1956, a small group of young men built their own loom using pieces of wood and metal piping and began the production of carefully designed colorful scarves at the end of the first week in December. Geraldine Fogarty organized an exhibition in the upmarket department store Brown Thomas lasting from March 12 until March 23, 1957, which showcased Hungarian arts and crafts: she considered that this approach could lead to employment for the Hungarian refugees. László Lovas, formerly assistant professor in the College of Art in Budapest, contributed watercolors, oils, and charcoal portraits. The exhibits were varied, with handmade painted furniture produced by Ferencz Vincze and János Letoha; Ferencz Takács, who had to make his own tools at first, created metalwork artifacts. The exhibition included felt appliqué work, needlework, and knitting where design and color were inspired by Hungarian folklore. The exhibit brought the Hungarians into the public eye from a positive perspective.[50]

Eventually, there were enough such small ventures to create an impact on the local Limerick economy, where the Hungarians spent their earnings. The *Limerick Chronicle* printed a letter raising concerns about a proposal to move the Hungarians from Knockalisheen to accommodation in Templemore: the potential loss of revenue would affect Limerick at a time when the city was facing the closure of local businesses.[51] Those who remained at Knockalisheen found odd jobs in the surrounding environs of the camp, even as far as Limerick, which was some three miles away, where they would sell toys or embroidery to local shops or through their own stall. A small shop outside the camp profited from the extra money brought in by this labor as the refugees would buy small items there. Mrs. O'Shea, who ran the shop, considered that she had the most dealings with the Hungarians in county Clare, and she went out of her way to learn some Hungarian; she considered her customers to be "impeccably honest." With their odd job pocket money, Knockalisheen Hungarians could walk into Limerick, where they socialized in two pubs—John Quins and Hassetts, where the sight of unaccompanied Hungarian women drinking caused a stir. The second evening this occurred, some of the local lads tried talking to the women, and they eventually reached the stage of introducing themselves. When the men heard the words *Buda* and *Pest*, they assumed these were the names of the two young women until a local wag, the pub intellectual, stepped in to explain that Budapest was the capital of Hungary. The term *drink on book* became part of the English vocabulary of those Hungarians who enjoyed pub life; it could be assumed that with all the comings and goings, some debts might have been left unpaid. However, one man who owed Maíre Quin for three pints called into John Quin's the day before he left Ireland to pay his debt. As Maíre Quin was not in the pub, he left the money in an envelope with a note of thanks.[52] Going to Limerick was not always essential for the consumption of alcohol: entrepreneurial ingenuity extended to the creation of a still to make *pálinka*, a Hungarian brandy brewed using a combination of potatoes and barley. A bread bin, copper piping, insulating tape, plaster of paris, a bucket, and empty milk bottles comprised the parts, and the ensuing quantities of alcohol supplied pálinka parties at the camp. Unfortunately, one reveler drank half a pint of pálinka which rendered him unconscious and in need of medical attention. Gardaí raided a hut in Knockalisheen, confiscated the still and spirits, but made no arrests. Their professional verdict on the still was that "whoever made the still was well up in the art. It was a very ingenious piece of work."[53]

Apart from such activities, people did find employment, through either connections outside the camp or perseverance. For instance, some Hungarians found part-time employment in the overseas department of the mail order shop at Shannon airport.[54] There were fortunate Hungarians

Fig. 3.4. Men sharing the workload. Source: Sean Curtin Collection.

such as János, an engineer, who began work with Arup Ove and Partners. He quickly settled into permanent employment, and a partner in the company commented that his designs were in accord with the best in Hungary and he was improving his English; his main difficulty was overcoming the challenge of no longer being able to make calculations using the metric system. A master confectioner, Karoly Kotek, found employment in a Cork restaurant, and a master baker went to work in Dublin.[55] Twenty-one-year-old Janos Keszi-Koch, a timpanist and percussion player in the Hungarian State Orchestra, obtained a temporary position with the Radió Éireann orchestra in the percussion section and said he was "most happy to be back in music."[56] One young woman eventually went into domestic service.[57] There was a steady stream of Hungarians taking matters into their own hands by going to England; likewise, English employers came to Ireland in search of skilled Hungarian workers. The Reverend William Mills, the Presbyterian chaplain at Knockalisheen, introduced Mr. George Tunna to the Hungarians. Mr. Tunna, manager of the engineering administration of the Ford Motor Works at Dagenham in Essex, was touring Ireland for recruitment purposes. He interviewed ten potential candidates for employment as Ford needed engineers, draftsmen, and other craftsmen. In contrast, at the end of the first week in August 1957, some ten days after Mr. Tunna's visit, six men aged between eighteen and twenty-one contacted the Hungarian embassy in London to see if they could return home. They were steelworkers and farmers who saw "no prospect of employment in this country."[58]

Near the end of September 1957, seventy-three adults, with twenty-two children accompanying their parents, left the camp; they too were departing for England. Fifty-five men and sixty-seven women remained in the camp with 126 children, making a total of 248 Hungarians.[59] As a number of these adults were part of family units, and as many of the women had already either self-identified as housewives or been categorized as such, the search for full-time employment would have involved only the adult men and some of the women, and people did find work. Through casual labor, the Hungarians were setting down roots in the localities around Knockalisheen, but these individual initiatives were temporary measures that would not equate with long-term resettlement. Furthermore, their resourcefulness, willingness to work, and general honesty were at odds with some views reported in the press about employment and the Hungarian refugees. Some related fears of competition in a limited labor market and others different expectations. The Irish Red Cross highlighted the problem of some Hungarians not keeping their jobs because "they find difficulty in relating the money to the living conditions here. They are mainly industrial workers who have been used to big wages and a much lower standard of living than we have here. They have a feeling that they are being robbed when they go to rent a house or otherwise spend their money." The trade unions, with a remit to protect Irish workers, could also contribute to these complications.[60]

A Constitutional Crisis

The hiring of a Hungarian refugee led to assertions by the motor garage branch of the Irish Transport and General Workers Union (ITGWU) that the minister for industry and commerce was failing in his duty to safeguard the constitutional rights of Irish nationals regarding employment. The origins of this accusation began in February 1957, when the Limerick

Motor Works dismissed an apprentice panel beater because of bad timekeeping and, at the same time, agreeing to a request from the administration at Knockalisheen, provided a Hungarian refugee with an internship in the garage body shop. The Hungarian, Sándor Bikkes, hoped to remain at the garage for two weeks in order to learn the English names of different mechanical parts, an advantage when seeking employment elsewhere. The union took up the case of the apprentice and was informed that a Hungarian had been employed in the body shop, sparking a union protest until the garage explained the nature of his presence there. At that point the union was satisfied, but several months later the Congress for Irish Unions sent a letter stating that the Limerick Motor Works had applied to the minister for industry and commerce for a work permit so as to employ an alien—namely, the same Hungarian refugee. Unfortunately for the company, they had requested that the Hungarian be employed as a panel beater at two shillings and sixpence per hour, which was one shilling three and a half pence per hour less than the going rate for that grade of work. Mr. O'Sullivan, assistant secretary of the Limerick branch of the ITGWU, informed the labor court in Limerick that two shillings and sixpence was "one and a half pence per hour less than the agreed rate of pay for unskilled labourers employed in garages." The Limerick Motor Works, therefore, was destabilizing the labor market not only by not adhering to agreed rates of pay but also by severely undercutting the rate of pay to an amount that was even less than that paid for unskilled labor.[61]

The union corresponded with Limerick Motor Works and on June 24, 1957, received a letter from them stating that the union had not checked the facts regarding the Hungarian. This statement implied that Mr. Bikkes had already received an alien's permit, and the following day the union was officially informed of this fact. Mr. O'Sullivan said, "It is indeed regrettable that a responsible Minister of State should have acted in this fashion and, in so doing, shown such a lack of appreciation of the principles involved, which we, in the Trades Union Movement, hold sacred, and which one would reasonably have expected would also have been held sacred by such a high public official." Mr. O'Sullivan continued that "the Minister had failed to safeguard the prevailing rate of pay and the natural, moral and constitutional rights of the youths of Limerick to the opportunity of being apprenticed to the panel beating trade if, in fact, the Hungarian was replacing the dismissed apprentice. If on the other hand, the Hungarian was a qualified panel beater the Minister in issuing the permit had failed to safeguard the prior natural, moral and constitutional rights of qualified nationals to securing employment in their native land." Mr. O'Sullivan did accept the fact that an apprentice had been taken on to replace the previously dismissed apprentice; he also spoke at length about the sympathy felt for the Hungarian people because of their suffering under the communist regime but that nevertheless, the situation raised critical concerns. The labor court chairman noted that the rate of pay was just over 33 percent less than that offered to a graded worker and queried whether this was a secondary issue to the union with regard to the employment of the Hungarian. However, Mr. O'Sullivan considered that both matters were involved.

At this point, Mr. Quinn, assistant secretary of the Irish Motor Traders Association, added to the discussion:

> There only remains one point which I want to explain, and it covers the case of the victim of Communistic tyranny, Mr. Sandor Bikkes. At the time of his original employment there was no intention whatever of providing him with semi-permanent work. When it was discovered that his standard of craftsmanship was of the highest order, it was decided, in the interests of the firm and its customers, not to be deprived of the services of this superior worker. That decision has been justified by results and the employers of Mr. Bikkes can see no logical reasons why they should be asked to displace Mr. Bikkes in favour of any less efficient sheet metal worker.[62]

The Labour Court ruling recommended that Mr. Bikkes should become a member of the union, that the union should accept his application, and that the court would not discuss the other matters raised by the submissions from both parties. Consequently, a degree of pragmatism also prevailed, particularly as there was a shortage of skilled craftsmen and technicians in Ireland.[63]

However, by the time of the apparent constitutional crises created by the hiring of Mr. Bikkes, there were far fewer Hungarians in Knockalisheen who were looking for work. The Labour Court's ruling in the Bikkes case occurred mid-month in November 1957. At the beginning of January 1958, there were 208 Hungarian refugees Knockalisheen: 53 men, 56 women, and 99 children. In effect, just over a quarter of the 208 refugees were potential employees—namely, the 53 men, assuming that the majority of the women still identified as housewives.[64]

Misbehavior

Very little crime occurred either inside or outside the camp given the length of time the Hungarians lived in the uncertain limbo of Knockalisheen. Among adults, there were instances of minor theft, scuffles, and brawls. In November 1957, Mr. B. became so drunk that he was found banging on the door of the medical hut at midnight, shouting for a doctor for his wife, who was ill. The medical hut was locked, so Mr. B. ran at the door, broke the lock, and fell headlong into the hut. Mr. B. then assaulted Camp Controller Mr. Murphy and tried to punch Garda Lowney, as well as biting him. Garda Lowney stated that Mr. B. arrived drunk and "was talking to himself in Hungarian or some strange language and was making a great deal of noise."[65] Reinforcements, called in from Killaloe, arrived at 2:00 a.m. to subdue the seriously inebriated reveler. Mr. B., who was carrying a cosh at the time, apologized in court and clarified the matter of the cosh by saying it was for self-defense as four Irishmen had threatened him in a bar in Limerick. This uncharacteristic and self-inflicted incident occasioned a fine of six pounds.[66] His actions were not as serious as the assault of a Hungarian man by compatriots at Knockalisheen in January 1958, which resulted in his hospitalization. Three men were kept in custody for seven days as they had issued threats. Superintendent Dunne referred to the use of a knuckleduster during the brawl and that some people had had teeth knocked out. Consequently, he could not let the "highly-strung" trio return to the camp. In court, with the aid of Mrs. Kovary, one of the interpreters, the three men in custody claimed self-defense and said they were not the perpetrators as they had intended only to talk.[67] A stabbing in August 1958 was the final of these incidents. A Hungarian, Terence, was charged with stabbing Karoly in the abdomen, with the wound requiring ten stitches. However, complications existed for the case as the accused was also potentially innocent. Mrs. O'Shaughnessy translated the court proceedings, and when Terence was asked if he had anything to say, he replied, "I do not wish to stay in prison and I'm not guilty." The solicitor defending Terence referred to his potential innocence and that he was a family man, with a wife and two children, who had already spent over a week in custody and was not likely to leave the country. Unfortunately, Inspector Harvey, stationed at Killaloe, opposed bail because of the serious nature of the crime.[68]

There were no further significant encounters between the Hungarian refugees and An Garda Síochána. However, there were disputes with the administration at Knockalisheen where some form of punishment resulted individually or collectively. The consumption of electricity across the camp became the focus of collective punishment. In April 1957, there was a rumor that the refugees had set up a shortwave radio transmitter, a fact denied by the Irish Red Cross, who did, however, say that the Hungarians had tapped into the electricity supply including the ESB meter boxes.[69] The Hungarians were overriding the time switches that had been installed in the huts—camp lights were automatically switched off at midnight—and consuming more electricity. At the end of July, Camp Controller Mr. Murphy considered daily consumption to be excessive once it doubled to 400 units, whereas previously consumption had been about 200 units. He instigated a seventeen-hour per day electricity cut so that from 4:00 a.m. to 9:00 p.m. daily, electricity was disconnected from refugee huts. Mr. Murphy stated that he would restore the supply if the Hungarians promised to cut down on their "excessive use of electricity and elected a new Committee as the refugee's democratically elected council of representatives was clearly not to the administration's liking."[70] The disruption to supply to the huts lasted just over a day and ended following the election of a new camp leader, Mr. Bihary, coincidentally an electrician.[71]

"Unauthorized home-made cooking and heating gadgets" as well as electrically driven lathes, used in the production of handicrafts for sale in Limerick, would have contributed to the surge in consumption. The IRC attended to safety concerns a few months later; in January 1958, Mr. Kukk, camp leader at this point, said the IRC had informed him the army was going to alter the wiring in the huts by removing any carried out by the refugees and allowing a single light plug in each hut. The IRC considered that "this would be in the best interests of the refugees" due to their use of unapproved equipment. Mr. Kukk iterated that the refugees had requested additional plugs in the huts for radios and had asked the IRC to make strenuous representations on their behalf. Being reduced to a single plug for a light would have the detrimental effect of depriving people of having separate cooking facilities in their huts so that they could not cook food for their babies. It would also affect those refugees who had been involved in handicrafts as they would lose the income from their work. Nevertheless, an IRC spokesman stated that the change related to fire prevention and that the refugees' requests "had been sent to the proper authorities." The Hungarians, therefore, had actions taken against their efforts to have a degree of autonomy over their lives, to feed their babies, do some of their own cooking, or endeavor to make some money.[72]

Punishment occurred for individuals who did not behave, such as Mrs. Palocz and her eleven-year-old daughter. Mrs. Palocz had been offered accommodation in Pearse Street in Dublin at a time when there were efforts to close the camp following the departure of most of the remaining Hungarians to Canada. She had rejected the accommodation because she would not be able to cook food there in Hungarian style. On returning to Knockalisheen, Mrs. Palocz was initially refused permission to enter the camp, and mother and daughter spent the night in a house in the Ballinanty area, though they were admitted to the camp the following day. Mrs. Palocz had tried to return to the shelter of Knockalisheen without permission; as punishment, neither she nor her young daughter received food rations. The camp had already closed officially but still housed a family of six and a separated child. Readmittance was on the condition that Mrs. Palocz and her daughter would return to Dublin, and the withdrawing of food was to force Mrs. Palocz and her daughter to return despite the fact that she wanted to obtain lodgings where she could provide her own food.[73] A spokesman for Knockalisheen Camp said, "Neither of those people has any right to be in the camp. We fixed them up in Dublin and they would not accept that accommodation. Now we have offered them a flat in Limerick but they have rejected that too. We have cut off their rations and have no intention of altering that decision."[74] Punishment, therefore, was a means of keeping the Hungarians individually and collectively in line. Collective punishment was incurred for the use of electricity, including no evening meal for 140 children and not being able to listen to news from Hungary. Punishment was proposed if people did not leave Knockalisheen so that the camp could be closed.[75]

The gardaí, however, proposed a more measured perspective, in relation to the question of discipline:

> I do not wish it to be thought that the Gardaí are interfering in any way with the functions of the Red Cross. They are not doing so. At the same time I think that it is only right that we should offer whatever advice we consider necessary or desirable. A point I would make in this connection is that the Red Cross authorities should be slow in applying punitory measures against individual

refugees who offend against discipline. The danger here is similar to the plight of an army unit advancing too far without securing its lines of communication and a safe avenue through which the troops can retreat in a dignified and orderly manner should the necessity arise. Where strong measures are taken and have later to be withdrawn the Authorities at the camp invariably lose ground. Any punishments in the way of stopping allowances, etc., should not, in my opinion, be enforced until all the pros and cons are carefully considered. In other words the Red Cross Authorities should not take a stand until it is fairly certain that it can be maintained.

Unfortunately, no one listened to this point of view.[76]

Conclusion: Deserving and Undeserving Refugees

This chapter, along with the first two chapters of this book, has presented perspectives on refugees and the interactions between refugees, the public, authorities, and organizations. At the end of the first part of this study, these themes require further elaboration of their contexts, particularly as refugee voices are mainly absent in the discussions involving their situation at Knockalisheen. Views of the refugees are rooted in a combination of factors including "the heat generated by the Cold War."[77] This heated international context combines with an entanglement of views of the needy, charity, the deserving poor, and acknowledging benevolence with gratitude. Instead of disentangling these perspectives from, for instance, the rights of refugees, organizations and people working with refugees confounded the concepts of need and charity with the concept of deserving and undeserving refugees.[78] Postwar efforts to rehabilitate DPs continued to resonate, as did the concept of apathy, which emerged in the DP camps approximately two years after their establishment. Scrutiny of the newly arrived Hungarian refugees revealed a lack of apathy and relief that they had "absolutely no desire to settle down to the listless and enervating life to which the displaced person is so often condemned."[79] This comparison ignored the relatively swift dispersal from Austria in contrast to the plight of DPs who languished in camps for years where "abnormal behaviour . . . could be regarded as a sensible adjustment to an abnormal situation."[80] However, there was consensus that the Hungarians required rehabilitating, a concept never exactly clarified despite years of postwar engagement with refugees. Rehabilitation, however, was associated with becoming fit to reenter society and was part of the mission of secular and religious organizations tasked with rescuing refugees who "were expected to be seen and not heard."[81] Joseph Szövérffy felt that Knockalisheen housed "an unfortunate composition" who would need rehabilitation as "Hungarians used to obey the authorities but the 12 years of Communist rule and the psychological repercussions of this wonderful rising, as well as the presence of this 'hooligan' group explains the difficulties." However, not everyone would have shared this view.[82]

One of the tangible, if temporary, outcomes of the 1956 revolution had been the heady organization of workers' councils where people could finally voice their concerns after years of silence. The steelworks in Csepel in Budapest was the site of such upheaval as well as witnessing some of the most brutal fighting in the last days of resistance. Mr. Pesthy, while nothing is known exactly of his circumstances except that he fled and his wife remained behind in Hungary, was a determined man who could well have been involved in similar activities. Workers councils had management committees, which would equate with Mr. Pesthy's own description of having been "a manager of one of the largest Engineering firms in Hungary, employing thousands."[83] As a democratically elected camp representative, he went to great lengths to make his voice heard on behalf of his compatriots. The press reported his words, which explain his actions: "The delay in finding work . . . the lack of information about our future and the attitude of certain officials towards us, are the main causes of the discontent. Because of this treatment, many refugees who originally wanted to stay in Ireland changed their minds." The Hungarians wished to be seen and heard and participate in the running of the camp rather than be grateful recipients of charity.[84]

The attitude of certain officials draws attention to the Irish Red Cross management of their remit—namely, "the reception, care and maintenance" of the Hungarians at Knockalisheen.[85] The IRC enjoyed an elevated presence in Irish society, where its executive officers mixed with dignitaries and politicians. The president of Ireland, Seán O'Ceallaigh; Taoiseach John Costello; Minister for Defense General Seán MacEoin; and Éamon de Valera, a TD in opposition at the time, attended an IRC convention of over five hundred people following the success of the national fundraising effort. The president of Ireland gave a speech in which he complimented the organization on the success of its appeal for Hungarian relief and their postwar work, which included sending relief supplies and working with refugee orphans.[86] Red Cross activities in Ireland had consisted mainly of addressing first aid and hygiene needs, water safety training, home nursing, elder care, and the care of tubercular children. The IRC water safety program was both innovative and progressive at the time, as it did not discriminate according to gender and performed a valuable public service with the laudable aim of preventing loss of life by drowning. Swimming had become a summer pastime in Ireland "but unfortunately, in many places enthusiasm had outstripped ability and the number of drowning and near-drowning accidents has reached alarming proportions." The Irish Red Cross had launched its water safety section in 1945, and it expanded quickly so that by 1947, water safety competitions began across the country with winning teams, "both male and female," attending the finals in Dublin.[87]

As a highly regarded organization, the IRC must have felt vexed by the critique in the *Church of Ireland Gazette*: "There is a tendency to regard this organization as sacrosanct and immune from criticism. But, while we are very ready to acknowledge the good work it is doing and has done in the past, we hold that the country has a right to expect competence in any organization to which it entrusts its good name and the expenditure of a considerable sum of money. It is no light thing to accept responsibility for the welfare of five hundred people. It is no task either for amateurs or bureaucrats."[88] First, the Irish Red Cross was caught between two extremes: administering the result of people's generosity toward heroic Christian warriors and the government's readiness to pass responsibility for the Hungarians at Knockalisheen into the lap of the IRC. The organization had already encountered its own version of difficulty with some of the *Victory*'s remaining passengers once they did not conform to behaviors inherent in the moral code of the times. The Hungarians, elevated to a position of heroic Christian warriors battling the evils of Communism, quickly fell from grace to a position of ungrateful malcontents who neither realized nor appreciated the efforts made on their behalf. Giving generously for the welfare of others had become a feature of Irish life, "slender though the means of the majority of its people may be." With an underdeveloped welfare state, charitable organizations such as the Saint Vincent de Paul society, in its annual appeal, called on people to donate generously "on behalf of the poor among us" as "Ireland knows too, that within its own boundaries there is need today for sympathy and aid, the sympathy and aid that can mean so much more to the deserving poor than State Welfare."[89] This generosity resulted in the collection of over £150,000 for Hungarian refugees, an unprecedented sum in the 1950s. The main issues were the Hungarians not behaving as expected for being the recipients of this charity and the Irish side's lack of curiosity as to where the Hungarians had come from, what they had experienced, or how they could contribute to the smooth running of the camp. Instead, pettiness and attempts at punishment came to public attention. Dissolving the position of camp leader because the organization did not like to work with the individual, only for him to be reelected, was the kind of overbearing and inconsiderate Irish Red Cross maneuver that the editorial of the *Irish Examiner* pronounced as being "inconceivable."[90]

With responsibility for the care of the Hungarians, the Irish Red Cross, with close links to the Department of Defense, interpreted the administration of Knockalisheen virtually as military control of a refugee camp.[91] The organization's secretary also held this view; being a military man, he felt that a retired army officer would have made a better commandant, as such a person would have had experience in maintaining discipline.[92] As there was already a visible military and police presence at Knockalisheen, further attempts at control seem to have been unwarranted; Superintendent Lavan had no misgivings about unmanageable levels of unrest at the camp. The IRC had no experience in the long-term resettlement of refugees, a fact that the secretary later admitted; the secretary also considered legitimate the criticism that they had not used people with experience in managing large numbers of refugees, instead of relying on voluntary workers. Likewise, sympathy at interdepartmental meetings was no substitute for some level of government involvement. The IRC was one of only three national Red Cross groups tasked by the government to become camp administrators, along with Austria, where there was already expertise among nongovernmental organizations, and Yugoslavia, where seventeen thousand Hungarian refugees had also fled. There were offers of help, but they too were misguided.

In a submission to Taoiseach John Costello, Joseph Szövérffy outlined a number of suggestions in relation to the 10 percent of the camp he felt were "hooligans and irresponsible elements" who were "terrorising the peaceful and grateful majority." He advocated halting any more arrivals, screening and rescreening in Vienna to improve the quality of persons arriving in Ireland, and expulsion from Ireland for individuals who "escaped" to Dublin to represent their compatriots. After addressing the group in Knockalisheen for five hours, he felt he had made progress by, for instance, organizing vocational groups, a Roman Catholic approach whose philosophy was not favored by government, in contrast to the three-man committee who had been democratically elected. The final suggestion proposed that he be permitted to continue reorganizing the camp "on Hungarian level," with the army in full control of the camp and having the authority to "enforce discipline by severe punishments."⁹³ Fortunately, these suggestions were not taken up. Szövérffy meant well: his worldview and academic experience could address the shortcomings of Communism if not the equally important shortcomings and failings of prewar Hungarian society and its moral collapse by the end of the Second World War.⁹⁴ There was no desire to return to it: the revolution had not been about looking backward.

Looking forward, and with the exception of those returning to Hungary, were the Hungarians leaving Knockalisheen. In April 1957, Sergeant Dolan documented that 120 people had left the camp for addresses in Ireland, with almost half of this group being children. A further 42 people had departed to other countries: two adults and one child to Canada, six adults to England, and seven adults and four children returned to Hungary. By far the largest exodus at this point was fourteen adults and three children to Argentina, and two adults and three children went to Switzerland. In all, 162 people left the camp. Mr. Pesthy too set sail, first to England, and then he "left for the Argentine and, oddly enough, all concerned are now agreed that he was an influence for good since his position and authority was recognized by the other refugees."⁹⁵

Notes

The epigraphs are from J. J. Lee, "Continuity and Change in Ireland, 1945–70," in *Ireland 1945–70*, edited by J. J. Lee, 166–78 (Dublin: Gill and Macmillan, 1979), and "Refugees Abscond to Britain from Knockalisheen," *Irish Times*, September 9, 1957, 4, ITDA.

1. Wyman, *DPs*, 108.
2. "Hungarian Refugees Arrive in Ireland," *Irish Independent*, November 26, 1956, 9; "Crowds Welcome the Victims of Russian Terror," *Irish Press*, November 26, 1956, 1; "Refugees Settle Down to Life in Clare Camp," *Irish Independent*, November 27, 1956, 7.
3. "Refugees Settle Down to Life in Clare Camp," *Irish Independent*, November 27, 1956, 7.
4. Department of External Affairs, note to British ambassador, December 7, 1956, DFA/419/33/11.
5. "Hungarian Refugees," report, Interdepartmental Conference, June 20, 1957, 1, 3, TSCH/3/S11007 D.
6. "Hungarian Refugees," report, Interdepartmental Conference, June 20, 1957, 1, TSCH/3/S11007 D.
7. Murphy to Mrs. Barry, January 17, 1957, TSCH/3/S11007 D.
8. Mrs. Barry, "Position of the Irish Red Cross Refugee Camp, Knockalisheen," report to Interdepartmental Committee, January 18, 1957, TSCH/3/S11007 D.
9. "Hungarian Refugees," memo, Department of Justice, January 19, 1957, TSCH/3/S11007 D.

Peter Berry was a longstanding, career civil servant who entered the Department of Justice in 1927. He became head of the department's newly-created intelligence section and remained influential in this role. He continued to maintain an interest in intelligence briefings, even though he changed departments, until his retirement in 1971. He is infamous for his opposition to the admittance of Jewish refugees before the Second World War and after.

10. Mrs. Barry, "Position of the Irish Red Cross Refugee Camp, Knockalisheen," report to Interdepartmental Committee, January 18, 1957, TSCH/3/S11007 D.

11. Mrs. Barry to General Sean McEoin, January 10, 1957, TSCH/3/S11007 D.

Leslie Bean de Barra, translated from Irish as Mrs. Tom Barry (used in this study as identified in archival and media files), had no hesitation in contacting government ministers as part of her modus operandi. Leslie de Barra, maiden name Price, participated in the 1916 Easter Rising as a member of Cumann na mBan. She married Tom Barry, commandant general in the Irish Republican Army during the Irish War of Independence. For a more detailed exploration of her time at the Irish Red Cross, see Lehane, *Irish Red Cross*. For her involvement in the 1916 Easter Rising, see her witness statement, Mrs. Tom Barry (née Price) document number 1754, in the Bureau of Military History at https://www.militaryarchives.ie/collections/online-collections/bureau-of-military-history-1913-1921/reels/bmh/BMH.WS1754.pdf. For further discussion of Leslie de Barra's role in the 1916 Easter Rising, see Taillon, *Women of 1916*, 55–56, 83–84, 114, 120–22. For an overview of women's involvement during this revolutionary period, see Connolly, *Women and the Irish Revolution*.

12. Mrs. Barry, "Position of the Irish Red Cross Refugee Camp, Knockalisheen," report to Interdepartmental Committee, January 18, 1957, TSCH/3/S11007 D.

13. Pálmai Bánki, "Crossing Borders," 134.

14. Ryan, "Hungarians in Limerick," 55.

15. Mrs. Barry, "Position of the Irish Red Cross Refugee Camp, Knockalisheen," report to Interdepartmental Committee. January 18, 1957, TSCH/3/S11007 D.

A 1957 Irish punt, or pound, was worth approximately €27.87 in 2020. Fifteen shillings approximates to €21 and ten shillings to €14. The sum of £60 would have been worth €1672 in 2020. In terms of buying power, a basket of goods and services that cost €1 in January 1957 would cost almost €23 in January 2020. Data derived from Irish Inflation Calculator 1922–2020 and the Central Statistics Office Consumer Price Index Inflation Calculator.

16. "Refugees Settle Down to Life in Clare Camp," *Irish Independent*, November 27, 1956, 7.

17. Note to Department of External Affairs, December 4, 1956, DFA/419/33/11.

18. Note to Department of External Affairs, December 5, 1956, DFA/419/33/11.

19. "Dail Tribute to Heroic People," *Irish Independent*, November 8, 1956, 10.

20. "Johanna and Josef Will Also Wed Tomorrow," *Evening Herald*, December 7, 1956, 1.

21. "Herald Readers Make a Dream Come True," *Evening Herald*, December 8, 1956, 3.

22. "Weddings of Refugees," *Evening Herald*, December 8, 1956, 1, 9.

23. "Weddings of Refugees," *Evening Herald*, December 8, 1956, 1.

24. "528 Refugees in Camp at Knockalisheen," *Irish Independent*, December 10, 1956, 9.

25. "Demands Listed by Camp Leader," *Irish Independent*, January 14, 1957, 8. See also John McMahon's efforts to reconnect with the family in later years and his recounting of events at http://s171621534.onlinehome.us/somodi.htm.

26. "Evening Herald Readers Make a Dream Come True," *Evening Herald*, December 8, 1956, 3.

27. "Refugees' Flat Refusal to Leave Camp," *Irish Examiner*, November 5, 1958, 9.

Mr. Hauser owned the first Mercedes in Ennis and was known for driving at high speeds. He died in a car crash in 1960. Joe Ó Muircheartaigh, "Rambling Down Memory Lane," *Clare People*, June 4, 2015 (unpaginated).

28. Interdepartmental meeting report, December 10, 1956, DFA/419/33/11.

29. Mrs. Barry to Taoiseach John Costello, December 11, 1956, DFA/419/33/11.

30. "Conference on Hungarian Refugees second meeting, 21 January, 1957," report, TSCH/3/S11007 D.

31. List of agitators with names of dependents and religion, TSCH/3/S11007 D.

32. Mrs. Barry, "Position of the Irish Red Cross Refugee Camp, Knockalisheen," report to Interdepartmental Committee, January 18, 1957, 2, TSCH/3/S11007 D.

33. Mr. Murphy to Major General Sweeney, January 4, 1957, TSCH/3/S11007 D.

34. Christabel Bielenberg had settled in county Carlow with her German lawyer husband. She had spent the Second World War in Germany and wrote two books, *The Past Is Myself* and *The Road Ahead*, which brought her fame. On December 13, 1956, the *Irish Times* published a letter from her about assisting Hungarian refugees. Whether Mr. Pesthy had heard of the letter or possibly knew about her from one of the translators is not known.

35. Mrs. Barry, "Position of the Irish Red Cross Refugee Camp, Knockalisheen," report to Interdepartmental Committee, January 18, 1957, 3, TSCH/3/S11007 D.

36. "Refugees Complain of Camp Conditions," *Irish Independent*, January 11, 1957, 6; "Refugees Biting the Hand?" *Pictorial*, January 18, 1957, 12, ITDA.

37. Mr. Murphy, report to IRC executive, Knockalisheen Camp, co. Clare, January 8, 1957, TSCH/3/S11007 D.

38. Mrs. Barry, "Position of the Irish Red Cross Refugee Camp, Knockalisheen," report to Interdepartmental Committee, January 18, 1957, 4, TSCH/3/S11007 D.

39. Mrs. Barry, report, "Position of the Irish Red Cross Refugee Camp, Knockalisheen," to Interdepartmental Committee, January 18, 1957, 4, TSCH/3/S11007 D.

40. "Conference on Hungarian Refugees Second Meeting, 21 January 1957," report, TSCH/3/S11007 D.

41. Mrs. Barry, "Position of the Irish Red Cross Refugee Camp, Knockalisheen," report to Interdepartmental Committee, January 18, 1957, 4, TSCH/3/S11007 D.

42. "Conference on Hungarian Refugees Second Meeting 21 January 1957," report, 2–3, TSCH/3/S11007 D.

43. "Conference on Hungarian Refugees Second Meeting 21 January 1957," report, 5. TSCH/3/S11007 D.

44. "Irish Red Cross Hungarian Refugees," *Irish Independent*, December 27, 1956, 12.

45. "Work Available for Refugees," *Irish Independent*, December 27, 1956, 2.

46. "Knockalisheen Strike," *Irish Examiner*, April 30, 1957, 6.

47. "Industrial Development of Tubbercurry," *Sligo Champion*, November 17, 1956, 3.

48. Report on Filler Rezzo in *Details of Refugees in Knockalisheen Camp* (following its closure in 1958). Undated. Private collection.

49. Limerick Vocational Education Committee to Department of Education, December 5, 1957, TSCH/3/S11007 D.

50. "Hungarian Refugees in Ireland," *Anglo-Celt*, December 1, 1956, 1; "Hungarians Find Jobs a Problem," *Irish Times*, December 11, 1956, 1, ITDA. "Refugees Display Arts and Crafts," *Irish Independent*, March 13, 1957, 6; Brown Thomas exhibition brochure, TSCH/3/S11007 D.

51. Ryan, "Hungarians in Limerick," 57.

52. Malone, "Hungarians in Limerick," unpaginated.

53. "Hungarian 'Poitín' Find," *Evening Herald*, February 23, 1957, 1.

54. Ryan, "Hungarians in Limerick," 57.

55. "Hungarian Happy in Dublin Post," *Irish Times*, February 16, 1957, 5, ITDA. "Exodus Leaves Refugee Camp Half Empty," *Irish Times*, September 21, 1957, 5, ITDA. "Refugee Remembers," *Irish Press*, November 26, 1957, 2.

56. "New Boy," An Irishman's Diary, *Irish Times*, February 23, 1957, 8, ITDA.

57. "Exodus Leaves Refugee Camp Half Empty," *Irish Times*, September 21, 1957, 5, ITDA.

58. "Knockalisheen," *Irish Press*, July 27, 1957, 2; "Hungarians Want to Return Home," *Limerick Leader*, August 7, 1957, 1.

59. Memorandum for the government, September 26, 1957, TSCH/3/S11007 D.

60. "Hungarians Are Free to Go Home," *Irish Times*, April 25, 1957, 7, ITDA.

61. "Employment of Refugee Charge against Minister at Labour Court," *Evening Herald*, October 11, 1957, 2; "Labour Court Ruling in Case of Refugee," *Irish Independent*, November 13, 1957, 3; "Job for Hungarian in Limerick Has Raised Constitutional Issues," *Limerick Leader*, October 12, 1957, 1.

62. "Job for Hungarian in Limerick Has Raised Constitutional Issues," *Limerick Leader*, October 12, 1957, 1.

63. "Labour Court Advises Union to Admit Hungarian," *Irish Times*, November 13, 1957, 8, ITDA. Daly, "Cultural and Economic Protection," 12.

64. "208 Refugees at Knockalisheen," *Irish Press*, January 4, 1958, 4.

65. "Refugee Assaulted Camp O/C," *Irish Press*, November 8, 1957, 4.

66. "Refugee Assaulted Camp Head and Garda," *Irish Independent*, November 8, 1957, 9.

67. "Hungarian Refugees on Assault Charge," *Evening Herald*, January 11, 1958, 3.

68. "Hungarian Refugee on Wounding Charge," *Nenagh Guardian*, August 2, 1958, 7.

69. Ryan, "Hungarians in Limerick," 56.

70. "Camp Light Dispute Settled," *Irish Press*, August 2, 1957, 3.

71. "Electricity Cut Ended at Knockalisheen," *Irish Independent*, August 2, 1957, 13.

72. "Refugee Camp Electricity Dispute," *Irish Independent*, January 9, 1958, 9.

73. "No Rations to Refugees Who Refused City Place," *Irish Press*, December 19, 1958, 3; Ryan, "Hungarians in Limerick," 59; "No Rations for Two Refugees," *Irish Times*, December 17, 1958, 3, ITDA.

74. "No Rations to Refugees Who Refused City Place," *Irish Press*, December 19, 1958, 3.

75. "No Rations to Refugees Who Refused City Place," *Irish Press*, December 19, 1958, 3; "Refugees Unwilling to Move," *Irish Press*, August 1, 1957, 1.

76. Superintendent Lavan, "Hungarian Refugees," report to C3, April 18, 1957, TSCH/3/S10749.

77. Brown, *Ireland*, 223.

78. These arguments, coupled with similarities in attitudes to recalcitrant Hungarians, including "real" freedom fighters as opposed to feckless and ungrateful Hungarian refugees are seen in Taylor, "Their Only Words," 127–42. They are echoes of earlier, more immediate

postwar perspectives on refugees and also with resolutely cheerful aid workers being met with ingratitude. See also Salvatici, "Help the People," 430–33.

79. "Pattern of Hungarian Rising Emerges from Exiles' Stories," *Irish Times*, November 27, 1956, 1, ITDA.

80. Bakis, "So-Called DP-Apathy," 85.

81. Gatrell, *Making of the Modern Refugee*, 20.

82. Joseph Szövérffy to Taoiseach, December 5, 1956, DFA/419/33/11.

83. Mrs. Barry, report, "Position of the Irish Red Cross Refugee Camp, Knockalisheen," to Interdepartmental Committee, January 18, 1957, 4, TSCH/3/S11007 D.

84. "Demands Listed by Camp Leader," *Irish Independent*, January 14, 1957, 8.

85. "Conference on Hungarian Refugees, 20 June meeting, 1957," report, 1, TSCH/3/S11007 D.

86. "Tribute to Red Cross at Dublin Convention," *Irish Press*, November 15, 1956, 5.

87. O'Brien, "Irish Red Cross," 8, 9, PRES/9 1367.

88. "Back to Hungary," *Church of Ireland Gazette*, May 3, 1957. Representative Church Body Library (RCBL), henceforth RCBL.

89. Editorial, *Connacht Tribune*, November 24, 1956, 20.

90. "Trouble at Knockalisheen," *Irish Examiner*, January 15, 1957, 8.

91. "Red Cross Chairman's Reference to Hungarian Refugees," *Irish Examiner* May 14, 1957, 9.

92. "More than Half of Hungarian Refugees in Ireland have Left Camp: Great Surge of Sympathy Has Dwindled," *Irish Times*, October 10, 1957, 5, ITDA.

93. Joseph Szövérffy to Taoiseach John Costello, December 5, 1956, DFA/419/33/11.

94. Joseph Szövérffy had expressed his interpretation of the situation in Hungary in his article "Hungary" in the journal *Studies*, published by the Irish Jesuits. In the article, Szövérffy reflects on "Hungarian Christian traditions," but this was not the only perspective or dimension of a complex political situation.

95. Sergeant Dolan, report to Department of Justice, April 24, 1957, TSCH/3/S11007 D; Superintendent Lavan, report, "Alleged Unrest at Hungarian Refugee Camp at Knockalisheen," to C3, TSCH/3/S11007 D.

4

THE HUNGER STRIKE

> It should be made very clear to the Hungarians that Ireland has done all in its power to assist them, notwithstanding the fact that a large number of our own citizens are unemployed.... Further, will the Minister inform the Hungarians that while they are living in this country they will have to behave themselves in a reasonable manner?
>
> —Mr. O'Malley, Dáil Éireann Debate

> Ever since they came to the Camp the refugees have been anxious to get to other countries—Canada, the United States, etc., where they expect to find suitable employment and establish homes for themselves and their families. They complain that the Authorities here—the Red Cross and the Government—are not presenting their case sufficiently.
>
> —Superintendent Lavan, "Hungarian Refugees"

Drawing Attention to Liminality

At the beginning of April 1957, camp representatives sent a letter to the taoiseach:

> We have a very great Request to you as President of Ireland. Give us the deputation of the Hungarian refugee Camp a permission to call and see you. We should like to thank you and the Irish nation for the magnanimity you did for us separated Hungarians from our country.
> We should like to continue a conversation about our position too, because the most part of the families don't see their own future ensured.
> We ask your Excellency to give the possibility to couple of minutes long conversation.
> On behalf of the Hungarian refugee camp.

The request was for conversation, not confrontation, to work through problems, real or perceived, so that the refugees would not feel forgotten in Knockalisheen. The reply, received a few days later, declined the request for a meeting and pointed out that the government had asked the Irish Red Cross to be responsible for the Hungarian refugees so that all concerns should be addressed to them, including government matters. As the hoped-for conversation did not occur, events began to move swiftly toward the end of the month.[1]

Near the end of April, Mr. Murphy, the camp controller, sent a note to Superintendent Lavan at the Killaloe station in county Clare to say that four members of the camp committee had come to see him.[2] They were concerned that there was general unrest at the camp and some trouble was going to occur, but no one knew what form it would take. Superintendent Lavan's opinion was that some form of demonstration, such as a march, might be staged in Limerick "in an attempt by the refugees to make their presence felt so as to force the Authorities to act." The move to action was triggered by a remark made at a talk in the camp that had led refugees to believe that Canadian representatives would be arriving during April. Superintendent Lavan suggested a meeting in Dublin because of his experience with

> general meetings at the camp where everybody seeks to join in questioning the speaker. Many of the refugees are very well informed and seem to be in close touch with the situation in other Countries. I think that the present Committee would constitute a reasonable and intelligent deputation. A statement of the efforts being made on their behalf might help to allay their fears.... I do not think that the threatened demonstration would take a violent form as I feel that there is a sufficient number of decent people in the Camp to prevent this, but there are some of the others too.[3]

Communication with families in Hungary had been established by the beginning of April 1957; some people had spoken by telephone to relatives left behind, and there had been a free exchange of letters and parcels in recent weeks. Relatives in Hungary had sent letters urging family members to return, although there were propaganda elements to such communication. Additionally, letters were arriving from Austria, the United States, and Canada, so the group of refugees in Knockalisheen were not cut off from the outside world and had their own lines of communication and information about conditions for Hungarian refugees elsewhere in the world.[4] They had a radio, which implied the possibility of listening to broadcasts made by the BBC, the Voice of America, Radio Free Europe, and other stations, including from Hungary. As Hungarians had listened to foreign broadcasts prior to the revolution, there is no reason to assume that this habit stopped, particularly as such broadcasts would have provided material for debate and discussion in Knockalisheen. However, with no senior figure responding to their concerns, the refugees began a hunger strike at the end of April 1957, which was conveyed to national and international audiences.[5]

The *Irish Times* reported that the refugees were to begin a hunger strike and passive resistance to draw attention to their future departures to Canada or the United States.[6] However, the paper was of the view that the hunger strike would damage the reputation of the refugees as well as "cause pain and embarrassment in this country" and concluded, "The circumstances of the refugees are the reverse of ordinary, for they have been the victims of fears and pressures almost inconceivable to most people in this country; and that is the heart of the matter. It would be a tragedy if Ireland were tempted to regret the impulse of generosity which introduced the Hungarians to their midst. At the same time, having brought them here, she cannot wash her hands of her responsibility."[7] While the government could ignore the *Irish Times*, it could not so easily overlook communication from the Irish ambassador in Washington stating that the *New York Times* was reporting on the hunger strike. The cable also reported that the Office of Refugees and Immigration Affairs in the US State Department had sought information on the number of Hungarian refugees in Ireland, the number wishing to proceed to the United States, and the number wishing to continue to Canada. The hunger strike, therefore, achieved its aim immediately by drawing attention to the apparently static situation at Knockalisheen as well as inadvertently embarrassing the government on the world stage.[8]

The Hungarians made full use of their situation. They sent a telegram to the taoiseach on May 1, the third day of the hunger strike, with the following question: "Hungarian Refugees who are continuing with hunger strike would like to know if the Irish Government willing to send to their Camp a representative for the investigation of grievances within the shortest possible time. Signed Hungarian Refugees Knockalisheen." The initial request for a conversation prior to the strike, which began on April 29, 1957, had escalated into a discussion of grievances and was again declined within this charged atmosphere. The hunger strike continued.[9]

Surveillance and Deception

Superintendent Lavan met with the Hungarian camp committee to ask for the hunger strike to be called off. The refugee representative committee said they would lose face and so could not agree to the request. The committee members said the paramount issue for them was moving from the camp to settle in other countries. Superintendent Lavan detailed an account of his visit during the first day of the strike:

> I visited Knockalisheen again at 7.30 on Monday the 29/4/57. On my arrival the four Committee members were patrolling the camp wearing arm bands with the Hungarian colours. None of the other refugees were about. Mr. Murphy had gone to Limerick to collect the mail and the interpreters. The Hungarian cooks had not turned up for work and did not do so during the day. Only four people, a man and wife and two children of other families turned up for breakfast and none at all for lunch or tea. About 20 refugees attended Mass celebrated by the Rev. Fr. Kiss, SJ, at 9 a.m. and they returned to their huts immediately after mass. One man left as usual for work in Limerick, but otherwise the Strike appeared to be complete, the refugees remaining in their huts all day. Late in the evening a lorry load of turf arrived in the Camp and the refugees turned out to collect their supplies. Members of the Committee went to the cook house during the day and collected some bottles of milk for the young children. There is reason to believe that most of the refugees had some food in their huts. I hesitated to believe that the children were allowed to go hungry.

He was also present the following day and saw children being fed by their parents, though they were not allowed out to play and stayed indoors for the duration of the strike. Mr. Murphy consulted him about a telegram from Dr. Szövérffy that was addressed to the refugee committee but that, after discussion within the Irish Red Cross, Mr. Murphy did not want to deliver. Superintendent Lavan pointed out that such action would be illegal. This attempt to illegally interfere with the postal service arose due to suspicion of Dr. Szövérffy and his motives. Apparently, his telegram said the matter of the strike had been taken up with the "prime minister," which implies that the telegram had been opened, translated, and made known to people other than its intended recipients. The reluctance to deliver the telegram arose in case Dr. Szövérffy was "seeking to add fuel to fire." Superintendent Lavan wrote in his report that it "would create a very bad impression and complete distrust if the Hungarians became aware that their letters and telegrams were being interfered with." Such a comment would be an understatement considering that the Hungarians had fled a state where the secret police had considerable powers of control through surveillance and an army of informers to spy on their neighbors and coworkers. The action of IRC officials—not only opening mail but also considering withholding mail from the intended recipients—demonstrates an extraordinary level of high-handedness and deceit that could have undermined all remaining trust between the Hungarians and any representative of Irish authority.

Superintendent Lavan added in this report, "At a press conference this evening the committee put forward the theory that the Irish Government were keeping them in this Country as a matter of prestige—that they do not want to admit that the country is so poor that suitable employment could not be found for them." He urged that a deputation be sent to meet with the refugees, who were serious in their intent, as was the situation.[10]

In a follow-up report the next day, Superintendent Lavan recorded the outcome of talks between Mr. Murphy, the camp controller, and the Hungarians where it was decided to exempt women and children from the hunger strike. However, the superintendent was most concerned about a rapidly deteriorating situation regarding the health of the strikers. The men involved had gathered in a hut that was usually used as a schoolroom, where they had the benefit of camaraderie and mutual support. Some of the men were refusing water as well as food, and they would require urgent medical attention. Irrespective of this escalation, Superintendent Lavan pleaded for some understanding of the Hungarians:

> I know that Irish public opinion is turning against the refugees owing to the apparent unreasonableness of their behaviour. It would be well, however, to consider their history and background. Communism has done its work to the extent that these people do not trust each other. Nobody can be certain that his neighbour—or even his wife—is not an active Communist. A great many of the Refugees do not agree with the action being taken, but they fear the taunt that they are not good Hungarians. It is only a person who has been in close touch with them who can appreciate, to some extent at least, their point of view. The majority are ordinary decent people. . . . I mention these things as I can understand that at a distance the actions of the Refugees must appear ungrateful and unreasonable.

Having typed up his report, Superintendent Lavan added a handwritten comment that an interpreter had heard talk of drastic action being taken if the government did not respond. He added that "one of the leaders presented himself at the administration hut this morning for the purpose of making his will." The intent of the hunger strikers was unambiguous, and Superintendent Lavan had a very clear understanding of the turn of events, including the refugees' determination. Echoing Superintendent Lavan's summary of the question of trust at the camp, Olga Murphy also commented on not being in a position to trust people at the camp as she did not know who they were. Apart from having one Hungarian friend, she had kept to herself, preferring to make friends outside the camp.[11]

A Series of Visits: Dublin Sends a Delegation

During the strike, the Hungarian camp committee met with reporters twice a day and reiterated that the Intergovernmental Committee on Migration (ICEM) had assured them in Austria that Knockalisheen was a transit camp, and, having remained in the camp for five months, they felt let down. The Hungarian camp committee was adamant that they had been led to believe their stay in Ireland would not be for long. The hunger strike, which they described as being *halálig*, or to the death, was a way of drawing attention to their situation, and "when they were queried on this melodramatic aim, they replied quietly but firmly, that they were prepared to go to this limit as they thought things could not get much worse for them." The Hungarian camp committee also rejected allegations that the hunger strike had been mooted by Communists among them in the camp. The committee considered that there were no Communists in the camp, and they themselves had never been members of the Communist Party. The matter of profound importance for them was that "they were tired of waiting and wasting time. They wanted to get to Canada or America, even though they must have a sponsor in Canada and a special law still had to be passed in America to allow refugees in. They said that they wanted the Irish people, and the Government, to whom they felt grateful for what had been done for them since the October emergency last year, to know their needs. The strike, they keep saying, had been agreed among the people of the camp as the quickest way to accomplish that aim." The Irish government initially deliberated the prospect of receiving a refugee deputation in the Department of External Affairs, although the IRC considered that it would be undignified while the hunger strike was in progress.[12]

The bishop of Limerick, however, conveyed the gravity of the situation and that it required urgent attention. In his opinion, there was no subversive influence at work in relation to the hunger strike, and he urged that a senior government official go to Knockalisheen as the refugees would be too weak to travel to Dublin. The taoiseach and the minister for external affairs decided that two senior departmental representatives, one each from the Department of External Affairs and the Department of Justice, should go to Knockalisheen to address the refugees. The bishop of Limerick, the Irish Red Cross, Superintendent Lavan, the army medical officer Captain McCann, the three interpreters, and Father Kis met the two senior civil servants. At this initial meeting, the Irish Red Cross was rather combative, complaining that not only had the bishop been kept waiting but "the state had been all too pusillanimous in its handling of the refugees and that stern action was what was required." At this stage, the bishop of Limerick thought that the refugees were beyond reasoning with. One of the department officials proposed addressing the Hungarians in German to do some plain speaking, as he understood a large number of the Hungarians understood the language. However, the people in closest contact with the Hungarians at Knockalisheen—namely, the IRC officials, the gardaí, and army representatives as well as the interpreters—said that in fact only a few of the refugees understood German and that this idea was ill-judged. Captain McCann was of the opinion that, as many of the men were too weak, the government representatives should not address all of them.

Eventually, the members of the hunger-strike committee were asked to join the meeting, where various officials spoke to them through an interpreter, some forcefully and at length, to remind them of their asylum, the conditions of their stay, and efforts to move them on to other countries. There was also the question of whom the strike was directed against, and was it "against the Irish Government and People who had befriended the refugees and who would inevitably suffer by reports in the pages of the world press?" Thus, a rather cross meeting ensued. However, the strike committee eventually replied via a prepared statement collected by Father Kis, in which they said they would accept the word of the government that no promise had been made that they would be free to go to the United States, Canada, or Australia despite what they thought had been said to them by an Irish visa official in Vienna. While ready to compromise, the hunger-strike committee's final view was deeply pessimistic: "We understood when leaving Austria that we would come to Ireland where we would find a home or be allowed to go to the USA or Canada etc.: we are here five months; we cannot get employment; we see no prospect of emigrating: we cannot return to Hungary: let us die, there is nothing to live for." Despite this gloomy and dramatic conclusion, talks continued, during which some of the refugees and the interpreters became quite emotional and distraught, but the result was to call off the hunger strike. The government representatives said they would make fresh approaches to the Americans, Canadians, and Australians regarding emigration to those countries and assured the hunger-strike committee that a government representative would return in a month to provide an update, keeping the channels of communication open.[13]

After two hours of talks, the hunger strike was called off at 9:30 p.m., and "there were scenes of rejoicing in the camp. Some of the hunger-strikers walked slowly to their womenfolk and embraced them. The women were in tears."[14] The Hungarian flag, which had hung symbolically over the schoolroom, remained in place until the end of the hunger strike, which had lasted four days, from Monday April 29 to Thursday May 2, 1957. Of the one hundred and fifty men who had gathered together in solidarity in the schoolhouse to undertake the hunger strike, seven collapsed; six were treated at the camp by Captain McCann, and the seventh was taken to Barrington's Hospital accompanied by Father Kis. The ninety-six women in the camp had been exempt from the strike, but, despite appeals, some fifty, including expectant mothers, had refused meals in solidarity with the men in the schoolhouse. One woman had collapsed during Mass and was taken to a hospital in Limerick but returned the same day. The camp itself gradually returned to life, with children, who had been kept indoors for the duration of the strike, able to go back to school as it reopened on Saturday, May 4. Mr. Murphy, having provided assistance to the men who had fallen ill, was cheered that same day. However, some bad feeling remained: one nonparticipant family began to take their meals after all the others had finished.[15]

The government issued a press release regarding the visit to Knockalisheen, in which senior officials expressed sympathy for the Hungarians' plight and pointed out that no admittance to other countries had been sought for the Hungarians, but efforts were being made to do so. Furthermore, over forty individuals had already secured entry to other countries, with the Irish Red Cross paying their passage, as it would for future cases. With regard to the Hungarians remaining in Knockalisheen, "an appeal was made to them to exercise patience, and they were assured of the goodwill and sympathy of the Government and of the Irish people."[16] There was no mention that five months earlier, the government had requested the Irish ambassador in London start making arrangements for employment in Britain for some of the residents of Knockalisheen.[17]

International Organizations and Representatives

The United Nations High Commissioner for Refugees (UNHCR) and the ICEM became aware of the hunger strike, and an official from UNHCR visited Ireland a few days after it ended. First, Mr. Wyrouboff had a meeting with the Department of External Affairs with the aim of providing assistance to Ireland. He indicated that there was some wiggle room in the impasse, as refugees in countries of first asylum were given preference for resettlement elsewhere—that is, in countries of second asylum. Ireland had attached no condition to the acceptance of the refugees and was, therefore, considered a country of first asylum. Italy had taken Hungarian refugees on the basis that it was a country of first asylum; some countries took Hungarian refugees on the basis of both approaches to asylum. Mr. Wyrouboff thus reiterated the contents of the leaflet provided to the Hungarians by ICEM while they were in Austria and from which they had argued their case for moving to another country. The Irish position was that Ireland's original intent had been to take children or suitable family groups who could be placed in Irish homes but instead had taken refugees indiscriminately. At the same time, Ireland had an unemployment and emigration problem to consider and the fact that the refugees had always thought they were going elsewhere.

Mr. Wyrouboff advised that all these points should be outlined to the UNHCR office, which, in turn, could communicate this news to ICEM and advise that Ireland be treated as a country of first asylum. ICEM had received more offers of permanent asylum than there were refugees to send, and ICEM's financial problem had been solved through donations from many governments, particularly the United States'. Mr. Wyrouboff thus considered the issue to be one of time needed for transport and screening and that ICEM could send a representative to interview each refugee in relation to resettlement. Although Ireland was not represented in ICEM, this would not present a problem. In turn, Irish officials informed Mr. Wyrouboff that the Irish Red Cross would be willing to pay the refugees' fares for resettlement. It was agreed that this course of action was to be in tandem with the Irish government also making its own efforts regarding resettlement of the Hungarian refugees.[18]

That same day, Mr. Wyrouboff visited Knockalisheen—something he must have specifically asked for, as the strategy in Dublin had been not to offer him a visit but rather to wait for him to ask for it.[19] At Knockalisheen,

Fig. 4.1. Meeting outside. Source: Sean Curtin Collection.

he met with a number of officials and the four members of the Hungarian camp committee. The meeting received press coverage, where Mr. Wyrouboff explained that five thousand Hungarian refugees had indeed gone to Canada from Britain but only because another five thousand still in Austria were to replace them and travel to Britain. As far as he was aware, the Irish government had not proposed a similar measure. He said, "We are most grateful to the Government of Ireland for having taken the refugees and for catering for them as well as they are doing at this camp. We will consider all possible ways of solving this problem and meeting the wishes of the refugees: but they will have to realise that it is not sufficient to express their wishes to have them fulfilled." In his view, three issues would hamper a speedy resolution to the situation of the Hungarian refugees in Ireland: finding a country to take them, funding, and transport. He referred to the ICEM document handed to refugees in Austria, indicating that they were going to a transit camp from which they could travel further afield such as to Canada or the United States. He considered the document open to interpretation in that no specific time frame had been laid down in which to move refugees on to their country of choice, although they would be transported as soon as it was possible.²⁰

The following month, in June 1957, Mr. Aarö, ICEM's chief of mission in Britain, came to Ireland.²¹ He visited the refugees at Knockalisheen, where he was met by camp officials and the Hungarian camp committee, with whom he held discussions about moving from Ireland. At the camp, Mr. Aarö said, "I can make no promises whatever, except that we will do our best. If the Irish government so desire, we will approach the Canadian and other Governments. When we have discussed the situation with the Department of External Affairs, we may be able to see if we can do anything further. We know the Irish Government has already made approaches to other Governments and all we could do would be to offer our good offices with the member Governments concerned." He did note that Ireland was not a member of ICEM, so the organization could not subsidize the passage of the Hungarians, but there were funds in place on the Irish side for transport. He also stated that, as hundreds of thousands of Hungarians were being resettled, the situation could not be resolved overnight. In other words, the Hungarians at Knockalisheen would still have to wait.²²

The Roman Catholic Church had become involved as well, and a month earlier, near the end of May, the Department of Justice had circulated a note to the Departments of the Taoiseach, External Affairs, and Defense stating that "the most Reverend Dr. John C. McQuaid Archbishop of Dublin phoned Mr. Berry, Assistant Secretary." The National Catholic Welfare Conference (NCWC), an American organization, aided the screening of Iron Curtain refugees on behalf of the American authorities.²³ This screening was being extended to other countries including Ireland. Their Paris representative, Mr. McCluskey, was sending Mlle Simone Delattre, chief emigration officer of the French mission of Catholic Relief Services, to Ireland, and as she was arriving in Dublin that very afternoon, "his Grace requested permission to send Mlle Delattre to the Department of Justice on arrival to meet the Minister, if possible, and officials to discuss the matter."²⁴ She intended to spend a week interviewing refugees at Knockalisheen, and following her visit she would report to the chief visa officer at the US embassy in Dublin.²⁵ A visitor of some significance, Mlle Delattre was received immediately in the Department of Justice. She explained that Mr. McCluskey was director of the French mission of the Catholic Relief Services, an agency of the NCWC, which mainly obtained private funding but had access to public money

Fig. 4.2. Child watching the meeting. Source: Sean Curtin Collection.

because of its connection to the US Escapee Program. Catholic groups such as the one Mlle Delattre represented worked directly with the World Council of Churches, their Protestant counterpart. As these groups worked closely together, she would be dealing not only with Catholics but people of all religions, and she would pass information to the appropriate body with regard to people of other faiths. This close cooperation between different faith groups came as a surprise to the officials at the meeting, who did not appear to be aware of the existence of the World Council of Churches. Mlle Delattre caused quite a stir in the department, where she was served tea, and officials felt "it would be appreciated if Mlle Delattre could lessen the group of refugees even by one or two." Officials agreed to provide a police car to be at her disposal, and she was also booked into a Limerick hotel once she had outlined her itinerary and plan.[26]

Mlle Delattre's visit to Knockalisheen yielded immediate results as she found people not only with relatives in the United States but who also had a possibility of sponsorship. Making discreet inquiries during her two-day visit, she discovered 40 cases consisting of 127 Catholics with sponsorship potential, 10 cases of 34 people who were Protestant, and 1 case of 4 people who were Jewish. Mlle Delattre was to follow up her investigation after having sent information to her agency in New York and to the US consulate in Ireland. In the meantime, the Irish government made representations to Australia, Canada, the United States, Argentina, Brazil, Colombia, and

Bolivia about relocating the Hungarian refugees while life continued at Knockalisheen Camp.

A Letter to America from Knockalisheen

The Hungarians in Knockalisheen were not idle. Shortly after the strike, the camp committee composed a letter destined for the US Congress and entrusted to one of the Hungarians relocating to Canada:

> It is the seventh month that we have been waiting for the news at the wireless with fresh hopes every night, that you have met a resolution in the case of refugees. According to broadcasts you were to attend our case after the Easter recess, but nothing happened. Here in Ireland there are only men with families who had promised by representatives of ICEM in Austria, that for a short transitory period until we can go farther to the USA or Canada much better conditions can be secured for our children than in Austria. Who however would wish can settle in Ireland, work and accommodation being secured for them. Our arrival here after our marvellous reception in Austria, was a great disillusionment. We, who never went abroad and were blindly trusting in the Western World, did not think that we would be deliberately mislead by someone. We wished to have our children waiting under better conditions here, and it is already the seventh month that—despite the undeniable good will and willingness to help of the Irish Government and Irish people—we are being kept in unheatable wooden huts, on unhealthy food, without the possibility of schooling. The Irish are a poor and unfortunate people with a population of 3½ millions there are 90,000 unemployed here at present. To find employment is accordingly impossible, as the Irish Trade Unions most understandably protest against our employment. Our possibility of going to other countries seems to become most hopeless. We are aware that the liberty war fought by us at home was fought for a Hungarian cause and it is no merit for us in the West. But your broadcasts, unselfish assistance during our hard days, promises of most extensive help for us in case we leave the country, were main cases that the Kadar "Government" could yet execute, imprison or deport to the Soviets approximately ten thousand of our comrades. We, after the defeat, have taken upon ourselves the hardships of exile solely on these promises. For this reason only and for the future of our children. If you ever knew the immense gratefulness and trust we felt when we arrived in the Free World! The enormous kindness of the Austrians and their great sacrifice made us believe what the Free Western world headed by the United States has understood and is appreciating our fight and will value us. We know that miracles last only for three days and two hundred thousand refugees are too much for you. We know that many of us have behaved unworthy and ungrateful, but let us ask you if you tore out 200,000 of the population of the US depriving them of their savings, earned by a life's work, and kept them locked up in camps in utmost hopelessness, would they behave differently? Would not have occurred

as many disturbances? There certainly would have. Why then do you blame the Hungarian refugees in general for the slightest mistakes perpetuated by individuals who perhaps were never liberty fighters?

We do not expressly wish you to transfer us to the US or Canada, but you have promised us life, not concentration camps, depriving us of work and the hope of life. We are grateful and we have to be so because you have done too much for us. We have to be grateful to you for recently admitting the closest blood relatives to your country. But we have to ask you. Your country is a great one, your people are charitable, and they live in wealth. The Austrians are a small nation and not wealthy. Yet, after tremendous sacrifices they are willing to accept 30,000 refugees to settle there. You have accepted approximately 30,000 and have given great material support. Most of the refugees are already working in jobs and living a human life. . . . We beg you to assist those who are unable to start a new life in the countries they are at present. Owing to utmost hopelessness already 18 fellow-refugees have returned to Hungary facing the horror of retaliation of the Communist government. And still more are thinking of the same horrible thing. Mr. Wyrouboff, emissary of the United Nations Refugee Committee, the Irish Government and local Red Cross had to admit that there are no possibilities for us in this country. From the point of ourselves and of our children the only possibility is for us to go abroad.

We could experience that not everything is true what they promise even in the West. This experience may be the result of some irresponsible officials who have brought us here. But most certainly we had to be disappointed. We ask you, please do not judge us for these bitter words. We ask you to consider our case this time not as administrative officials, but as good neighbours. We ask members of the Congress who have children to consider our case through the eyes of fathers who have children. We know that in the above, we did not recall the great sacrifice and assistance of the people of the United States, listing only our own bitter disappointment. We were doing this however as a sign of trust felt towards your country. Your country had the greatest sympathy towards ourselves after the liberty war of Kossuth and that is why we take the liberty of applying to you again. Please take up the case of Hungarian refugees and try to arrive at a just solution of same. We ask you further to impress governments of other countries and induce them to a further and last sacrifice.

Hoping that our letter will be read and considered we hand it to a fellow-refugee travelling to Canada to forward same to you in a speedy way.

On behalf of 370 Hungarian refugees
Members of the Hungarian Camp Management.[27]

The writers of this letter made good use of the Knockalisheen Camp radio and were knowledgeable about the international situation regarding the resettlement of the Hungarian refugees, in this case the long-standing debate between restrictionists and liberalizers of American immigration policy, which affected the ways Hungarians could be admitted to the United States. The letter also plead for recognition, for understanding, and, presumably, for a way forward that would take people out of a state of liminality in the halfway house of the camp. De Valera, then taoiseach, received a copy of this letter with the comment that it contained some very untrue statements. It is not known how a copy came into the hands of the camp administration.[28]

Communists, Workers, Ingrates?

The charge of the refugees being Communists surfaced again in October 1957, by which time the Hungarians had been in the camp for almost a year. Rumor alleged the presence of some two hundred Communists in the camp. At that point, Mr. Kukk, the camp's representative, wrote an open letter to the press to scotch such innuendo. The letter was not reported verbatim, but Mr. Kukk did say, "I am sure there were some amongst us, as we were strangers at home. But there could be only a few. If you took the trouble to think and calculate first, you would have found that your statement is impossible. We were about 520 when we arrived. This represents about 120 families, or 120 adult males. Even if you call all of us Communists, where do you take a surplus of 80? . . . It is a pity you rely on your feelings and not on facts."[29] The refugees, he continued, were not ungrateful and never would be, but they could not be blamed for seeking work. Their only sin would appear to be, he added, that they had not all been killed in the streets of Budapest. If that had happened, then no one could be blamed anymore. Mr. Kukk asked the critics of the refugees to try to understand the plight they were in. They had no fatherland, no home, and were separated by hundreds of miles from their loved ones, and "we ask those who would condemn them for seeking work and better conditions to co-operate with them, as there are only a few left." Mr. Kukk had begun by saying that Ireland was both a religious and a hospitable country and that the refugees had believed they could come and live in peace and happiness. However, "there was something wrong with hospitality when they could not find jobs," and "those who did get jobs were paid a wage lower than paid to the native workers."[30] Furthermore, "even if they were to work for nothing, only to learn the language, that would not do because of the presence of so many unemployed."[31]

A press report earlier in the year had covered the worsening unemployment situation in Ireland and considered that it was virtually impossible for the refugees to find employment, but there were also references to misunderstandings, both past and present. The article also referred to

Mr. Somodi, the electrical engineer from Budapest who moved to England eventually but still wrote a letter to the *Irish Times* to argue his case:

> I put my case to the Irish people. I fought against the Russians in Budapest. My father, mother and wife were killed in the street fighting. I had to take my little girl of 2½ and go to Austria. In Vienna, Irish government promised work for refugees. I thought Ireland would be good but to-day I see no work in Ireland. I am electrical engineer and I want to learn English. I work hard to learn English in six months. I am here in Ireland for over three months. My friends here . . . have a family friend in London who will give work to me but I cannot get a visa from the British Embassy to travel to London. What am I to do? I do not like to take charity but very much like to work.[32]

Not to be outdone, the Irish Red Cross issued a statement on employment, assimilation, and deserving and undeserving refugees, stating first that no Hungarian had taken an Irish worker's job. There had been troublemakers at the camp, and such activities had been reported in the press so that "through this publicity, the chance of employment and assimilation into Irish homes have decreased as also have their chances of emigrating." The IRC commented that "there are some willing to live as parasites on Irish hospitality and probably feel they need never work goes without saying, but these are being gradually weeded out and the refugee of better calibre will finally emerge." In the meantime, the situation at the camp continued to rumble on, including the return of some people to Hungary.[33]

The first to undertake such a course of action was a young couple, one of those recently married in Knockalisheen, as the mother of the young wife was seriously ill in Budapest.[34] Others decided to return to Hungary because they could not find work in Ireland. One group contained nine individuals including Mr. Pickarczyk. He was returning with his wife and two-year-old daughter "because this is a poor country, where we could find no work." He added, "But we thank the Irish for all they did for us. I speak from my heart. I spent five months in the camp at Knockalisheen. There was money, yes, but no work. So now we go home. I am glad to be going." Mrs. Pickarczyk did not seem to be as enthusiastic as her husband to return to Hungary, and these decisions were not taken without friction or consequences. These returns were also not without controversy, and the Irish Red Cross commented that the group was returning home against IRC advice and that "this group has organized its return on its own through the Hungarian Embassy in London." A spokesperson told the press that "we pay their fares as far as London and then they are taken over by the Hungarian

Government. They ignored our advice not to go, and believed that it was all propaganda." The Irish Red Cross also laid out the fact that they had raised the sum of £145,000 and that in April 1957 the camp's running costs were approximately £1,000 a week, including feeding the 370 men, women, and children still living there. At that rate of expenditure, there was enough money to maintain the Hungarians for two years. With little chance of finding employment for the majority, the Irish Red Cross was "always prepared to facilitate them by paying their fares to Canada or the Argentine."[35]

Mr. Pickarczyk's decision occasioned two letters to the *Irish Times*, including one from Sir George Mahon in Ballinasloe, who had offered "this man and his wife work, with a house, good pay and allowances." Sir George said that after accepting the job, Mr. Pickarczyk did not inform him of a change of mind; Sir George hoped "that not all refugees are so frustrated and demoralized, and that some, at least, carry home good memories of Ireland."[36] Geraldine Fogarty, who had come to know four Hungarian families well, wrote the following day to add that coincidentally she had spoken briefly to Mr. Pickarczyk about his intended return and

> some of his experiences both in Hungary and here, and of his reason for going back. I cannot believe that he appreciated that an opportunity for even a modest living here was available to him. My impression was necessarily a brief and imperfect one; yet the look in his eyes haunted me during the week-end, so that I telephoned to Knockalisheen Camp three times on Tuesday to urge that he be dissuaded from his return. The camp authorities, when I was able to contact them, were kind and sympathetic, but the man had already gone, and they said there was nothing they could do.

She felt that "in spite of language difficulties" the Hungarians were "cooperative, hard-working and most appreciative of anything done for them." Geraldine concluded by saying that an "energetic effort should be made now to deal finally, and without further delay, with the problem we created by our invitation to these unfortunate people."[37] However, further departures ensued. Mr. Akos, a motor mechanic, and his family were the first to leave for Canada after having been sponsored by relatives.[38] Seventeen left for Argentina following sponsorship, including Mr. Vilmos Bodinka, the eldest member at the age of forty-one, and the Babszky family. Mr. Babszky was listed as a glazier, and his six-year-old daughter was the youngest in the departing group. Their interpreter, Mr. Josef Wolf, said that they hoped to establish an electronics factory in Argentina as they had been unable to obtain permission in Ireland for the project.[39]

Conclusion: Critiques, Claims, Counterclaims, Disbelief

Immediately following the hunger strike, the *Church of Ireland Gazette* critiqued the situation: "It has been stated that the money subscribed through the Red Cross national collection will suffice to support them for some considerable time to come. It is to be hoped, however, that the time will not be considerable and that the refugee camp will not become a semi-permanent feature of the countryside as has happened elsewhere. Its inevitable frustrations and limitations are already becoming evident not only in the decision of some of the refugees to return to Hungary but in the day-to-day reports of unrest and discontent which come from the camp."[40] The critique must have struck a chord with the IRC, which immediately decided to attack such aspersions by engaging with the press and sending a letter to Taoiseach Éamon de Valera, as "it was highly desirable to see that the refugees recognise the laws of the country on the same basis as Irish citizens." The IRC also noted that the aid of the Department of Justice was critical if "the Nation's property is to be preserved, and most of all that the children of school going age attend regularly at the school we have opened in the camp."[41] While the tone of the letter was rather overbearing, the Irish Red Cross had an unenviable task that had no direction or endpoint: taking care of the refugees at Knockalisheen with no experience of working long-term with refugees in a camp. The Irish Red Cross was used to receiving praise, as it had during a series of meetings of the executive committee of the League of Red Cross Societies in Geneva in the month prior to the strike. Apart from Austria, Yugoslavia, and Ireland, most national branches of the Red Cross helped with supplies, acted in teams, or helped out in refugee camps, which were generally in the hands of the state. The IRC view was that "the Hungarian refugees in all countries have shown the same tendencies as those who came to Ireland"; they claimed that the countries to which they had been sent were simply temporary refuges so that they "decided to do nothing but wait until they could emigrate to the US or Canada." The verdict on this behavior was that "no one can actually settle who spread this report or whether it was ever issued."[42]

Unfortunately, this claim rests, once again, on the ICEM leaflet issued to Hungarian refugees in Austria. While the Irish Red Cross may not have received a copy, the government certainly had. It was among the batch of ICEM reports forwarded by Josephine McNeill, the minister plenipotentiary in Berne to the Department of External Affairs, and bears out the truth of the claim.⁴³ The refugees were also caught in the tangle between church and state, as the bishop of Limerick wrote to the taoiseach after the strike to comment on how it had "almost ended in disaster," that "neither bludgeon nor reason would have prevailed" and that the IRC had insufficient "support in the matter of discipline." The bishop referred to deception being part of the meeting with the strike committee, to "bluff—when all else failed. I would not think it good to give the refugees the impression that they have got the Govt on the run." In other words, there was persistent repetition of the same problems of miscommunication, attempts at so-called discipline, and obdurate, undeserving refugees.⁴⁴

The *Irish Times* sent an investigative reporter to Knockalisheen after receiving a plea from a young Hungarian man after the government refused to admit his fiancée. There followed a lengthy article:

> It is a pity that, before dealing with human beings, one cannot first practice on models. Live flesh and blood pays for your inexperience. Listening to the refugees, I felt my sympathy going out to the officials who could not fall back on my comfortable little formula: "I'm sorry, I do not know. I'm just a private individual."
>
> Here was the Department's letter refusing the fiancée a visa. There would be more hope if he could support her. A reasonable enough ruling in its way, but what was one to say when face to face with its penniless victim? He and other members of his hut had busied themselves making decorative workboxes. The materials were bought at retail prices, so that the final price was high. The boxes were most unlikely to sell well, and the energies of those who made them appeared to be misdirected.
>
> Here, most bitter of all, was the signature—indecipherable—on a medical document, of the official in Austria from whom they had understood that Knockalisheen would be a transit camp, a temporary resting place *en route* to the New World. There had also been, they said, a map showing the different Irish economic areas. Here be grasslands. Here be industries. Presumably, the unemployment exchanges went unrecorded.
>
> Hoping not to sound like a visit to the sick poor, we assured them that their sense of being forgotten was exaggerated, that they would not be left to rot indefinitely in a camp.
>
> They wanted us to tell our friends two things, firstly that the refugees appreciated all that had been done for them, secondly, that they were not a disorderly crew. They were simply beginning to feel desperate. The hunger strike had occurred for a number of reasons among which was engagement with a faceless bureaucracy; the certainty that Knockalisheen would be a transit camp; the swift circulation of rumours round the camp instead of actual news; a sense of being forgotten and that like most normal humans, they were not good at waiting for Godot.⁴⁵

From International to Local Perspectives

Staging a hunger strike was not unique to Ireland; Hungarian refugees took similar action in Newcastle-on-Tyne in England. However, this hunger strike, which began with the refusal of breakfast by eighty-two men in a hostel in South Gosforth, appears to have lasted around a day. The men began the strike because some of them were to be transferred to another hostel, and five men protested that they would be taken away from relatives or fiancées. The situation was resolved once their names were removed from the transfer list. When a bus sent to collect the men left empty, the matter appeared to be settled, and the situation did not deteriorate further.[46] Another short-lived hunger strike occurred at Margate in Kent; both groups had expressed a desire to relocate to Canada. As in Ireland, Hungarian refugees attempted to solve their grievances through a deputation, in this instance from the remote Belmont Camp near Forfar, Scotland to London, to the headquarters of the British Council for Aid to Refugees (BCAR), which had representatives from a number of organizations including the British Red Cross. With their case highlighted by the press at the beginning of January 1957, and including cold huts, unsuitable food, insufficient washing accommodation, no privacy for married couples, and no hairdresser, the response was positive, and BCAR and other authorities worked to ameliorate the situation. Like their counterparts in Knockalisheen, many of the Hungarians in the UK had intentions to settle elsewhere, and four hundred Hungarians were moved from Scotland at the end of January, first to Northern Ireland before their final transfer to Canada.[47]

The situation could have been much worse: in Austria, the United States had announced the end of the Hungarian refugee program and a return to its usual immigration laws. *Die Presse* reported that "the doctors of the Vienna psychical clinic have their hands full: in the last few days of the previous week as many as 47 suicide attempts in refugee camps were registered. The number of nervous breakdowns and acute cases of 'camp blues' among Hungarian refugees are increasing every week and the psychological pressure is becoming stronger every day. Impatience grows at the same time as restlessness." The news "struck the refugee camp inmates in Austria like a hammer blow. Nine out of ten refugees want to emigrate to America. The Hungarian refugees are in despair." Not only was there despair, but the article addressed the question of restlessness among a number of the Hungarians in Austria who had received offers of employment.

Approximately half of six thousand Hungarian refugees with jobs did not stay in the employment because "they are restless. They wish to go abroad and are not particularly interested to settle down to work in Austria." *Die Presse* stated that the camps were "not a long-term solution of the refugee problem. Everything must be done to give a future prospect to the refugees. Otherwise the mental institutions will be as overcrowded as the camps."[48] Restlessness was also evident in Knockalisheen. Employers offered jobs only to discover that a potential employee took a different course, such as returning to Hungary. An IRC official described Hungarians as being "browned off" and commented that twenty had returned to the camp despite having been employed. Some had left "very good employment," but all of them were "browned off" because they were unable to go to Canada and were waiting.[49]

In the Dáil, the minister for external affairs received questions concerning the strike and if he was aware of the level of anxiety at Knockalisheen; whether any of the Hungarians had asked the department for permission to leave Ireland for Canada or other countries; and if arrangements were in the works for admission to these countries. The Hungarians did not require such permission and were, according to the minister, "quite free to leave at any time. We have simply given them asylum here for the period that circumstances compel them to remain with us." This version of events presents the Hungarians as temporary sojourners rather than having been offered permanent resettlement in Ireland. While this position could be the case, as Mr. Wyrouboff had explained regarding the content of the ICEM leaflet provided to Hungarian refugees following their arrival in Austria, this was not mentioned in the Irish offer to UNHCR. However, the discussion in the Dáil turned to unemployment, the hospitality extended to the Hungarian refugees, and their behavior while "we have a lot of people who have not got rashers and eggs for their breakfast but these people have got them." Taoiseach Éamon de Valera intervened in the debate to say that the government was trying to resolve the situation, that it would take time and patience. He reminded the chamber that "we have not passed through the trials which they have" as a response to the nationalist preference for "looking after our own."[50]

Members of the public, however, had already critiqued government inaction months before. Heather Pennefather and Christabel Bielenberg had voiced astute disquiet in letters to the press in the second week of December 1956. Heather wondered if the Hungarian refugees were to "remain at Knockalisheen carving wood and making lace." She wondered if Professor Szövérffy had in fact "restored morale," as reported by the Irish Red Cross or, as rumor had it, the opposite. She acknowledged the situation of domestic rising unemployment but also that decisions would have to be made quickly "before more despairing young Hungarians leave Knockalisheen for Dublin or anywhere else in order to get away from what they may think is the Irish version of the free world—an internment camp with some privileges." She also suggested that, following the example of other countries, the voluntary sector could pool their resources and come to the aid of the Irish Red Cross rather than allowing it to try to manage alone: "What of the Knights of Malta, the St John Ambulance Corps, the Irish Save the Children Fund, the Society of St Vincent de Paul? Beyond collecting clothes and money, have they no suggestions to make which would help the Red Cross Society in its task?"[51] Christabel Bielenberg considered that many others had reached the same conclusions and that "a number of social workers in Co. Carlow have decided to pool their resources . . . to form a Co. Carlow Resettlement Committee for refugees, designed to work with and help the Irish Red Cross Society in the task of absorbing a number of refugees into our county community." Unfortunately, there had been no decisive action on the part of the two governments involved apart from assigning "care" to the Irish Red Cross. The frictions and misunderstandings, suspicions and disbelief of refugees had culminated in a hunger strike less than six months after the arrival of these Hungarians at Knockalisheen.

Notes

The epigraphs are from Dáil Éireann Debate, vol. 161, no. 6 (May 2, 1957, Private Notice Question—Hungarian refugees, statement of Mr. O'Malley), available at https://www.oireachtas.ie/en/debates/debate/dail/1957-05-02/25/, and Superintendent Lavan, "Hungarian Refugees," report to C3, April 18, 1957, TSCH/3/S11007 D.

    1. Camp Committee to Taoiseach, April 8, 1957; Assistant Secretary, Department of the Taoiseach to Camp Committee, April 11, 1957, TSCH/3/S11007 D.

    2. Mr. Murphy, note to Superintendent Lavan, April 26, 1957, TSCH/3/S11007 D.

    3. Superintendent Lavan, report, "Alleged Unrest at Hungarian Refugee Camp at Knockalisheen," to C3, April 27, 1957, TSCH/3/S11007 D.

    4. "Jobs Being Found for Refugees," *Irish Times*, January 31, 1957, 4, ITDA.

    5. Stations like Radio Free Europe and others were part of the Cold War propaganda wars, and "Communist regimes spent considerable time, energy, and resources fighting

foreign broadcasts through jamming"; Risso, "Radio Wars," 145. Radio also "played a highly significant part in the Hungarian uprising"; Webb, "Cold War Radio," 237. For an overview of the Voice of America and the Cold War, see Heil, "Voice of America," 25–48; and for radio jamming in Hungary, see Rév, "Just Noise," 239–58.

    Surveys of Hungarian refugees found that 83% to 97% had listened to foreign broadcasts and 80% relied on such broadcasts for reliable news, Webb, "Cold War Radio," 223.

6. "Refugees to go on Hunger Strike," *Irish Times*, April 29, 1957, 1, ITDA.
7. Editorial, *Irish Times*, April 30, 1957, 5, ITDA.
8. Ambassador in Washington, cable, May 2, 1957, TSCH/3/S11007 D.
9. Camp Committee, telegram to Taoiseach, May 1, 1957, TSCH/3/S11007 D.
10. Superintendent Lavan, report to C3, April 30, 1957, TSCH/3/S11007 D.
11. Superintendent Lavan report to C3, May 1, 1957, TSCH/3/S11007 D.
12. "Children of Refugees in Clare Camp Given Food," *Irish Times*, May 2, 1957, 1, ITDA.

    As ICEM had issued a document stating that Hungarians did not have to decide immediately on their futures, a document in the possession of the Department of External Affairs (see chapter 2), it is strange that this question remained so contentious and that the refugees were not believed throughout their stay.

13. Summary document, Department of the Taoiseach, TSCH/3/S11007 D.
14. "Refugees End Strike," *Irish Press*, May 3, 1957, 1.
15. "Hunger Strikers Get Medical Aid," *Irish Press*, May 2, 1957, 1; "Hungarians Call Off Hunger Strike after Talks," *Irish Times*, May 3, 1957, 1, ITDA. "Cheering Refugees 'Mob' Red Cross Man," *Irish Press*, May 4, 1957, 1; "Ten Hunger Strike Refugees Are Seriously Ill," *Irish Examiner*, May 2, 1957, 7.
16. Press release, May 2, 1957, TSCH/3/S11007 D.
17. Cabinet meeting minutes, December 4, 1956, TSCH/3/S11007 C.
18. Report on Mr. Wyrouboff's visit to Knockalisheen, May 11, 1957, TSCH/3/S11007 D.
19. Correspondence relating to strategy during Mr. Wyrouboff's visit, TSCH/3/S11007 D.
20. "UN Spokesman at Knockalisheen, Hungarians Told of Emigration Difficulty," *Irish Independent*, May 9, 1957, 12.
21. "Migration Head at Knockalisheen," *Irish Press*, June 26, 1957, 1.
22. "Conference at Clare Camp, Hungarian Refugees' Problems Discussed," *Irish Independent*, June 26, 1957, 7.
23. The NCWC was a permanent bishops' council formed in the United States to respond to government, domestic, and foreign policies that affected Catholic interests. The War Relief Services, WRS, was an agency of the NCWC that worked with local organizations during and after the Second World War to bring relief to war-torn countries in Europe and Asia. In 1945, the WRS organized with other associations to create the National Catholic Resettlement Council to help resettle displaced persons in the United States. The WRS changed its name to Catholic Relief Services, CRS, in 1955.
24. Department of Justice, note, May 23, 1957, TSCH/3/S11007 D.
25. "Emigration Officer to Interview Hungarians," *Irish Times*, May 25, 1957, 5, ITDA.
26. Memo of meeting with Mlle Delattre, TSCH/3/S11007 D.
27. Camp Committee to US Congress, May 13, 1957, TSCH/3/S10749.

    Lajos Kossuth (1802–94), a great hero of the nation, was defeated in the 1848–49 War of Independence against the Habsburgs. His defeat was guaranteed once Tsar Nicholas

1 sent his army to aid his cousin Emperor Francis Joseph. Kossuth went into exile and died in Trieste.

28. At this stage, the taoiseach was no longer Fine Gael's John Costello but Fiánna Fail's Éamon de Valera, who had won an absolute majority at the age of seventy-four in the general election held in March 1957; Lee, *Ireland 1912–1985*, 327.

29. "Hungarian Camp Leader's Open Letter," *Limerick Leader*, October 19, 1957, 1.

30. "Reply to Critics of Refugees," *Irish Examiner*, October 19, 1957, 9.

31. "Hungarian Camp Leader's Open Letter," *Limerick Leader*, October 19, 1957, 1.

32. "Few jobs Are Offered to Refugees," *Irish Times*, February 14, 1957, 5, ITDA. According to the visa section of the British embassy, no Hungarian refugee had been refused a visa as far as was known.

33. "Statement on Refugees," *Irish Independent*, March 12, 1957, 6.

34. "Refugees Return to Hungary," *Irish Independent*, April 4, 1957, 11.

35. "Party of Refugees Going Home," *Irish Times*, April 24, 1957, 1, ITDA.

36. Sir George Mahon, letter to the editor, *Irish Times*, April 25, 1957, 5, ITDA.

37. Geraldine Fogarty, letter to the editor, *Irish Times*, April 26, 1957, 5, ITDA.

38. "Hungarian Family on Way to Canada," *Limerick Leader*, April 20, 1957, 9.

39. "Off to a New Start in Life," *Irish Press*, April 24, 1957, 2.

40. "Back to Hungary," *Church of Ireland Gazette*, May 3, 1957, 1, RCBL.

41. Irish Red Cross to Taoiseach, May 13, 1957, TSCH/3/S11007 D.

42. "Refugees' Tendencies the Same in All Countries," *Irish Independent*, May 14, 1957, 12.

43. Text of the leaflet given to the Hungarian refugees in Austria. Intergovernmental Committee for European Migration, *Hungarian Refugee Program report 8*, annex 2, December 21, 1956, DFA/419/33/11.

44. Bishop O'Neill to the Taoiseach, May 3, 1957, TSCH/3/S11007 D.

45. "Refugees, a Visit to Knockalisheen," *Irish Times*, May 10, 1957, 8, ITDA.

46. London Letter: 59 Fleet Street, "On Hunger Strike," *Irish Times*, January 31, 1957, 7, ITDA.

47. Taylor, "Their Only Words," 138–39.

48. "Growing Depression among Hungarian Refugees," *Die Presse*, April 7, 1957, 1–2. Sent by Josephine McNeill, minister plenipotentiary, Irish legation, Berne, April 9, 1957, to Department of External Affairs, DFA/419/33/10/1.

49. "Refugees in Clare Fear for Relatives," *Evening Herald*, April 24, 1957, 1.

50. Dáil Éireann Debate, vol. 161, no. 6 (May 2, 1957, Private Notice Question—Hungarian refugees, statements by Minister for External Affairs Mr. W. Murphy and Taoiseach Éamon de Valera).

51. Heather Pennefather, letter to the editor, *Irish Times*, December 11, 1956, 5, ITDA.

PART II

Part 2. Child's artwork: Sailing to Australia and goodbye to Sister Immaculata. Source: Sister Immaculata Collection in Mercy Congregational Archives, Dublin (MCA).

5

THE LIVES OF CHILDREN

> Today is World Red Cross Day. To honour the memory of the founder of the Red Cross, Henry Dunant, members of the Irish Junior Red Cross will present gifts to the Hungarian children at Knockalisheen camp. Many of the gifts have been made by the juniors themselves—frocks, cardigans, gloves, cot covers, etc.—and they will distribute a wide variety of toys, sweets and fruit.
>
> —*Irish Times*, "World Red Cross Day"

> States Parties shall assure to the child who is capable of forming his or her own views the right to express those views freely in all matters affecting the child, the views of the child being given due weight in accordance with the age and maturity of the child. For this purpose, the child shall in particular be provided the opportunity to be heard in any judicial and administrative proceedings affecting the child, either directly, or through a representative or an appropriate body, in a manner consistent with the procedural rules of national law.
>
> —United Nations, *UN Convention on the Rights of the Child, Article 12*

Children of the Revolution

There is some difficulty in arriving at precise figures for children crossing and recrossing the border without a family member or other adult to look after them. In 1957, Hungarian official figures identified 21,196 children age fifteen and under as having gone abroad illegally.[1] To complicate matters, a total of 18,200 people returned to Hungary, including separated children.[2] The Kádár government had provided a short amnesty so that 11,500 people had returned by the summer of 1957; in addition, some 5,000 to 8,000 people were out of the country temporarily, crossing and recrossing land borders without the knowledge of the authorities. In May 1957, the Hungarian

Ministry of the Interior calculated that 3,665 children remained in Austria from fourteen to eighteen years of age, but, with constant movement out of the camps, they did not all remain or receive their education in Austria.[3] The press reported engaging stories of teenager participants of the revolution; one fifteen-year-old boy in Eisenstadt recounted his exploits with Soviet tanks with some bravado:

> My parents died when I was only one year old and I was brought up in a state orphanage. I don't think I have any relatives. When things got warm in Budapest my pals and I felt we ought to do our bit. So we collected a lot of bottles, filled them with petrol and corked them with rags. When a Soviet tank came by one of us would jump on the front and slap a wet rag over the slit with the driver. Another boy would cling on to the turret and stick another wet rag over the periscope. When the crew opened the lid we dropped a burning "Molotov cocktail" in their laps. A friend and I settled ten tanks that way.

Many children, especially those who had participated in the revolution and had nothing to return to or simply feared returning, remained in the refugee camps.[4]

From November 1956, the Hungarian government demanded the return of all separated children in Austria and Yugoslavia.[5] UNHCR referred some of these children because "in the early days of the Hungarian refugee problem . . . a number of minors were included in mass transportation movements and have thus become spread over many countries. The Office of the High Commissioner has intervened with the Governments concerned in order to emphasize the importance of deciding on the future of these children in accordance with the principles of family unity and the best interest of the individual child."[6] The UN had no presence in either Hungary or the Soviet Union and worked closely with the International Committee of the Red Cross (ICRC). Initially, the ICRC had representation in Vienna and Budapest to coordinate the control of relief supplies into Hungary, with cooperation extended later to the repatriation of civilians and minors. The ICRC began efforts to reunite families that same month, November 1956, by starting radio broadcasts over its own wavelength and the Swiss shortwave service, announcing the names of refugees searching for information about their relatives.[7] The ICRC also began a register of Hungarian refugees in early 1957 to initiate a tracing service to reunite families. The request from the Hungarian government, however, began a process of politicization of family reunion, which made it difficult for the ICRC to act in its traditionally neutral mode.[8] The two organizations discussed the situation of minors at an urgent meeting held in Geneva on December 13, 1956, and agreed that children under fourteen years of age would have to be repatriated if both parents remained in Hungary, with applicants having to submit a written request to the ICRC. There were foreseeable problems—for instance, if parents could not be traced, if only one parent was alive, or if the child was an orphan—and in such instances the best interest of the child was considered paramount. Another significant problem could arise in instances where both parents requested the return of a child to Hungary but the child was unwilling to return. In all cases, "the legal authority of the country concerned . . . was judged to be competent in this matter."[9] Countries providing shelter to minors had already turned to the ICRC as they did not feel the Kádár government's reasoning—that all such children had been claimed by their parents and, consequently, belonged with their families in Hungary— provided sufficient basis for repatriation. The United Kingdom refused to repatriate a single child until the ICRC could guarantee that the parents had not been intimidated and forced to make inquiries about their children.[10]

Austria and Yugoslavia also had different views on the process of repatriation with the Austrian government providing lists of unaccompanied children to ICRC but with no desire to engage with repatriation until knowing what awaited a child on return. In contrast, the Yugoslav Red Cross dealt directly with the Hungarian Red Cross by passing on a list containing the details of thirty-four children to return to Hungary but only as long as parents desired the return of their child. In fact, the Austrian government refused to engage in a bilateral agreement with the Hungarian government's demand on November 29, 1956, for the return of all minors, preferring to establish a legal basis for any movement of minors out of Austria. Cases concerning unaccompanied minors involved the Advisory Council on Asylum in Austria, whose role was to advise the Ministry of the Interior on decisions. The Ministry of the Interior, the Ministry of Justice, and the Ministry of Foreign Affairs had representatives on the council, as did UNHCR, although in an observer capacity. UNHCR accepted the Austrian process as being in accord with Article 12 of the Convention Relating to the Status of Refugees 1951, which stated that the personal status of a refugee was governed by the law of the country of residence. This interpretation of Article 12 meant that guardianship resided with the authorities in Austria, as they were competent to authorize the movements of an unaccompanied minor. Overall, the Austrian example demonstrates the extent to which a government had to take responsibility for the unaccompanied Hungarian refugee children and that individual departments had to collaborate to arrive at a decision in the best interests of the child: whether to return to Hungary, to stay in Austria, or to be permitted to leave Austria for resettlement elsewhere.[11]

Conversely, individual and country representations began to flow to the International Committee Red Cross to help with the process of family reunion in cases where children had been left behind in Hungary. At the beginning of 1957, the Hungarian government appeared to agree in principle to allowing children to leave Hungary.[12] However, the Hungarian government remained a reluctant actor in the two-way process of return to or departure from Hungary so that hardly any progress occurred. The Nineteenth International Red Cross conference held in New Delhi in November 1957 debated the controversy over the reunion of Hungarian families, and the conference came out in support of the ICRC's position through the adoption of its Resolution XX. This resolution called on all national societies and governments to "facilitate by every means the reunion of persons, both adults and children, with their families in accordance with the wishes of . . . the recognized head of the family no matter where domiciled."[13] This resolution, however, would not have solved some of the bitter disputes over children whose parents were separated or divorced and where the concept of head of the family would be inadequate in defining a more complex set of family relationships. ICRC drew up a proposal for minors: reunion with family up to the age of six, possible consultation with minors age six to fourteen regarding their wishes, and, finally, clear consultation with all minors age fourteen to eighteen regarding their wishes. The Hungarian government rejected the proposal outright as it dismissed the principle of reciprocity, so the case of children being reunited with family or remaining in their host country remained unresolved. Furthermore, ICRC had no permanent mandate to remain in Hungary after June 1957, which made such operations difficult to establish. Due to this impasse, some countries such as the United Kingdom made their own arrangements in child repatriation cases, in this instance by using the British consulate in Budapest as an intermediary with parents in Hungary.[14]

Unaccompanied Children in Ireland

In Ireland, the many offers of homes for Hungarian orphans that preceded the arrival of the 1956 refugees were no doubt seen as a sign of welcome, even if the offers were not needed due to the emphasis on selecting families in Austria.[15] A small number of unaccompanied children had reached Ireland as part of the initial wave of arrivals, but the majority arrived with at least one family member. In April 1957, Superintendent Lavan counted 220 children under sixteen at Knockalisheen, comprising almost half the camp.[16] By June 1957, two children had been born in the camp. Numbers fluctuated considerably due to the significant level of coming and going from the camp with, for instance, 95 children reported in the *Irish Press* in the first week of December 1957, which rose to 99 by the following month.[17] Ten children had also arrived with no family: 8 unaccompanied boys and 2 girls from twelve to fifteen years of age (see table 2.2 in chapter 2). As many of the children were of school-going age, their education would, or should, have been a major concern. However, early attempts to integrate children into local national schools had not produced positive results, and the camp bulletin, issued mid-January 1957 to answer refugee concerns, stated that "there is no objection to the attendance of Hungarian children at the local National schools. In fact this is encouraged."[18] The same month, the Irish Red Cross raised the question of whether the Department of Education should attempt to further the situation and secure places for the children in Limerick. The department, however, declined to act and pushed the matter back into the hands of the IRC.[19] Anna Letoha, a trained teacher in Hungary, brought her teaching skills to Knockalisheen and, with the aid of the IRC, helped set up a camp school with morning classes for the children; the schoolroom hut also provided space for classes in the afternoon for adults. She taught anything she could, from arithmetic to choral singing; the children even sang for a radio show broadcast nationally. Unfortunately for the school, Anna remained at the camp with her husband for a mere six weeks until, aided by Dr. Szövérffy's contacts, they relocated to Dublin for full-time employment. An interpreter then took on the teaching role for adults and children. Initially, adults did not attend these classes wholeheartedly, despite admonitions about English being essential for prospective countries of resettlement. Children also attended classes sporadically, but by June 1957, their attendance had improved significantly.[20]

One newspaper reported in March 1957 that education was a cause for some concern, but following the appointment of an additional interpreter there were "three full-time competent interpreters and classes in English, a regular schedule, and . . . [as] they were opening a national school in the camp, they were hoping the whole situation would become more

Fig. 5.1. Children sitting outside church after mass. Source: *Irish Press*, October 26, 1957, 7. Irish Newspaper Archive.

satisfactory.[21] Local national schools claimed they could not take primary-school-age Hungarian children due to capacity; on being asked to take the older boys, the Christian Brothers also cited capacity as their reason for refusal, even when the IRC offered to bus the children to the school.[22] The situation remained unsatisfactory, and at a special meeting held at Knockalisheen in August 1957, the camp representative, Mr. Bihary, stated that all the children were taught by one teacher who also served as the camp interpreter. The refugees requested a bus for 140 children so they could attend school in Limerick instead. At a further meeting on August 22, which lasted four hours, the IRC announced the cooperation of Limerick schools. All girls would attend the Convent of Mercy national school in Ballynanty at the beginning of the new school year in September 1957, and older boys would go to the Christian Brothers school on Sexton Street in Limerick.[23] A school bus, operated by the IRC, would take the now 120 children involved to and from the camp, and teaching would involve "special instruction . . . and languages." It had taken almost a year to introduce education and integrate the children into local schools.[24]

Sister Immaculata: Teacher, Confidante, and Hungarophile

In September 1957, education for fifty-one Hungarian children, comprising girls up to the age of eighteen and preschool boys, finally became a reality in a vacant classroom in Ballynanty School. Sister Immaculata had the task of teaching English to the children, and, looking back on this stage of her life she said:

> Can you imagine my feelings on the 4th September 1957 when I stood in front of 51 Hungarian children, aged 3½ to 18 years? I hadn't a word of Hungarian and they apparently hadn't a word of English. Let me explain, they had been learning English in the camp from their Hungarian teacher but it was a totally different experience for them to hear English spoken in a non-Hungarian accent and in a Cork brogue. Sign language came into play and got us out of all our problems. The children were bright, intelligent and very anxious to learn. I loved those children and can still see them in front of me in the classroom. I did a lot of English with them, also music, art, drama and of course Religion. Fr. Kiss S. J. was very supportive. He escaped from Hungary to Vienna tied on under a train! He provided me with the necessary books—all in Hungarian of course. The children soon loved Ireland and even asked me to teach them our National Anthem in Irish. They had no trouble with the pronunciation. They got great praise when they took part in the Schools' Musical Festival.[25]

The children were taught in Ballynanty until their departure in 1958 and formed a warm relationship with Sister Immaculata that, for some, endured for many years. Sister Immaculata said that she "gave my best" to the children as she wanted to provide an experience of life that they might have "lost" under Communism, such as a spiritual dimension. In her class, she empathized with the children's situation and tried to ameliorate their circumstances, particularly some of the older ones. She was saddened by the fact that older children in her care had been exposed to one of the particularly violent aspects of the revolution—in Budapest, they had witnessed the gruesome lynching of an individual suspected of being a secret police informer. Being sensitive and resourceful, Sister Immaculata secured art materials through the IRC, providing some short-term therapeutic relief for the children as they painted pictures about events in their lives, such as going on a journey to a new country overseas and bidding goodbye to Ireland. Unfortunately, such materials were considered to be "too expensive" at some point, and their provision was discontinued.

As a nun, Sister Immaculata was a woman of her time in 1950s Ireland, but she was also ahead of her time as she made the effort to learn Hungarian, a singular feat as it is not an Indo-European language. In her classroom,

Fig. 5.2. Hungarian songs for the Ballynanty school choir. Source: Sister Immaculata Collection MCA.

she created a culture where English, Hungarian, and Irish became the spoken norm. As part of this enlightened, inclusive approach to the language spoken at home and the languages of school, Sister Immaculata helped organize a bilingual English-Hungarian prayer book, *Az Én Imakönyvem* [*My Prayer Book*], which was printed abroad at no cost: Irish printing presses could not print all the diacritics used in Hungarian. She was particularly glad that no money was involved as it meant she did not have to ask for any yet again. As she was musical, she created a choir that she entered into a *feis*, a traditional cultural festival; while there was no hierarchy of results, each troupe received a critique, and the choir received "a good one." Sister Immaculata created a book of Hungarian songs, complete with musical notation, so that singing was part of the multilingual activities in her classroom. She taught the children Irish, specifically to sing the national anthem; the Christmas play, however, was in English.

As a teacher, Sister Immaculata also observed her pupils to see what they considered to be normal behavior on their own terms rather than simply imposing the norms of Irish national (primary) school culture on them. For instance, when she described her class, which was a mixed group of older and younger pupils, she saw that older pupils attended to the needs of younger ones without asking permission, as would have been the case then in an Irish national school. She watched one of the older girls go and help her younger brother blow his nose without seeking permission to get up from her seat; she let this behavior unfold as she felt that the children had a different way of doing things. From her observation of cultural differences—that is, culture as the practice of everyday life—Sister Immaculata was struck by the differences between the Hungarian children and their Irish peers. Poorer children fit into the group and were not looked down upon, which she believed would not have been the case in Ireland at the time. The older girls joined in games with the younger children, which again she felt would not have happened in Ireland. In effect, hierarchies of age and class were absent from the life experiences of these children, and poverty was not a crime.

She commented that at first the Hungarians appeared to be difficult, as nothing was right and nobody could do anything right for them. However, she became aware of a different landscape in Knockalisheen Camp in its early days once the lights went out: people woke up at night screaming and not knowing where they were. At that point, she would not have been able to do anything with the children as their parents were so unsettled. Children were also troubled, and she mentioned one boy who was sent back to Hungary because of a disturbing incident with the children's pet kittens, which were disappearing. Nobody knew what was happening to them until it was discovered that the boy was hanging them up by their tails and killing them. To Sister Immaculata's knowledge, it was clear that some aspects of the so-called problematic nature of some of the Hungarians were due to the processes of psychological disturbance, hopefully accompanied by recovery in the liminal space of the refugee camp.[26]

The children wrote Sister Immaculata letters from Knockalisheen illustrating their anxieties, which instinctively they may not have confided to their parents: they could see their parents already had their own worries and uncertainties amid the comings and goings in the camp. One young girl wrote about her father going to England and her fears for her grandmother back in Hungary: "I got a letter from home, they are very well but my granny is sick again. I get every night very lonesome about them and I cannot stop crying, but no one can hear and see me in the dark. I am praying very much about it and you and for myself that I love to be a mercy nun just like you. I like Ireland, it is a beautiful and holy land." The distress this young girl felt was endured alone but also confided to Sister Immaculata as

Fig. 5.3. Children with their pets. Source: Sean Curtin Collection.

a trusted adult the child could turn to. While such a letter demonstrates the closeness between Sister Immaculata and the Hungarian children she came into contact with, it also provides a different perspective on the apparently problematic Hungarian refugees.[27]

The experience of being a Hungarian child growing up in Ireland, in effect developing a bicultural self, is illustrated in a letter to Sister Immaculata addressed to "Dear Sister!" and headed by a crest drawn by its young writer. The crest contained a cross flanked on either side by a Hungarian and an Irish flag bearing the labels of "Hungarian" and "Irish." This child had left Knockalisheen but visited to maintain friendships: "I send it this croset [crest] for you. Thet is a gift for you. How are you? I am well. It is not to bad. Dear sister maybe I will go to the camp on Saturday but not too sure. We have here very bad weather. And now Sister, I am Thank You for yoo, what are you made it for me, when I was in the school, you are theach me the english and the sounds, you teach me the songs and you teach me the Christmas play. Thank you very much for everything!!!"[28] Whether writing from the camp or elsewhere in Ireland or following their departure from

Ireland, children corresponded with Sister Immaculata, who remained a point of contact for news of others:

> Dear Sister, I got your letter on the last week. Thank you very much for the nice small pictures. . . . We are very well Thank God. I hope we will meet again I sud like to see you very much. I cud not forget that you were very nice and very good to me to my little sister and to my little brother. Every children says in the camp Sr M. Immaculata was very good and she was very nice. The Hungarian people like you very much because you workd very hard whith the Hungarian children. Eva and Zoltán says that they will write to you.
>
> O did not go to mass on Sunday. I don't think that she will be good.
>
> The D and Sz family is arrived in Australia. They are all very well. Is Erzsébet write to you? Because she is not write to.
>
> God bless You, with love from Your Hungarian friend.

Children and parents valued Sister Immaculata's concern for her pupils and remained in contact with her even as their lives unfolded elsewhere.[29]

Crime and Punishment: The Darker Side of Irish Culture

Unfortunately, the complexity of relations between children and Irish culture in the 1950s surfaced in the case of two boys at the camp in Knockalisheen. Superintendent Lavan had remarked that the Hungarians kept a close eye on their children, who were well-behaved, and parents were solicitous of their welfare.[30] However, unaccompanied minors, as they were called at the time, did not have the advantage of the close presence of adults to provide checks on impulsive actions that could lead to unwelcome consequences.[31] An incident occurred in the camp that had a very serious outcome for two boys as they experienced the full brunt of not only the law but also the social and cultural ramifications surrounding attitudes toward children and juvenile wrongdoing in Ireland in the 1950s. In a hearing of the children's court in Ennis in October 1957, two boys from the camp were charged with larceny. While Mr. Murphy, the camp controller, was present at the hearing, as the theft concerned the property of the Irish Red Cross, no one else is listed as being present, such as a translator or another Hungarian adult. Consequently, there was no one to explain any of the proceedings to the boys or support them during the experience of a court hearing in a foreign country whose laws were neither known nor explained. The theft involved the following, as taken from the court record: "Larceny of clothes, child's case. Gyula K, aged 15 years and 3 months, Knockalisheen Refugee

Camp. The defendant did on 30.9.57 at Knockalisheen Refugee Camp steal, take and carry away two blankets, one sheet and two towels, total value £4.15.0p property of Irish Red Cross Society. Minor offence trebled, summarily accused consents to summary trial and pleads guilty. Mihaly B, 15 years 5 months. Plea of not guilty. Custody Order commit to Daingean Reformatory School for two years."[32] These two boys, who may or may not have spoken some English, were thus sentenced to two years in a case that could have been one of mistaken intentions and outcomes, particularly when there had been early grumblings among the Hungarians over failures of organization, waste at the camp, and preferring to have their own control of the clothing store.[33]

Admittance to an industrial school implied that a child came from one of the lower socioeconomic groups comprising low-income and large families and single-parent families, or that the child was an orphan or mentally ill. In contrast, children sent to the reformatories had usually been convicted of a crime and were eligible to be sent to such a residential institution from the ages of twelve to eighteen. Saint Conleth's in Daingean, a village in county Offaly, was run by a religious order, the Oblates of Mary Immaculate, and received a capitation grant for each child in its care. The Department of Education was responsible for such schools as it provided finance and was mandated to see that rules and regulations were adhered to and that finances were used properly, and to make sure that reasonable standards were maintained.[34] The Department of Education carried out inspections of the schools, including one of relevance to conditions in Daingean close to the time the two Hungarian boys were sent there. A Department of Education inspector and Dr. McCabe, the medical officer, carried out an inspection in 1955. Publications relating to conditions at the reformatory have discussed, referred to, or quoted from this report. Regardless, permission was not given by the Department of Education to copy this record for research purposes.[35]

What follows is an imagined narrative where the academic author assumes the role of a 1950s Department of Education Inspector:

> *At the beginning of August 1955 on a beautiful summer's day, filled with blue skies and sunshine, I set off for Daingean, and here is the report of my (imagined) visit in early August 1955. We saw Saint Conleth's through the main gate and were pleasantly surprised by the sight of flower beds, mature trees, and a well-kept lawn. The façade of the building is rather pleasing, although it was used as a cavalry barracks when the British occupied our pleasant land. We had*

made the arrangements beforehand to come to the reformatory, but the resident manager was not able to meet us as he had to attend to matters elsewhere. Father ---- was my replacement companion during the inspection. From this point, I inspected the premises thoroughly, including the farm, to see where and how the boys lived and labored. I should add that at present there are 130 boys at Saint Conleth's and thirty cows on the farm.

In the reformatory building I saw the dormitories, the play halls, and metalwork and woodwork rooms that provided a practical education, as well as the kitchen and dining area. The dormitory was a nice bright room, and there were about eighty to one hundred beds for the 130 boys, all made and all in rows. There is a large chapel, decorated wholesomely with the Stations of the Cross, with ample room for worship. Things, however, start to go downhill from this point. The play hall had a stage, which had potential, but was cold and untidy and had a concrete floor. The playground outside was in need of serious attention as the ground had no smooth surface. Unfortunately, I was told that the Oblates did not have the necessary funds for the work and any improvements would require further financial input from the state.

As for education, there does not appear to be any sign of formal education, and the woodwork and metalwork rooms appear disused despite having plenty of resources. The brothers I saw seemed to act as custodians, and I did not get the impression that they had anything to offer the boys. While I did not speak to them, I am sure they are all good, kind-hearted men and are considerate to the boys. I am not able to say if any of their influence rubs off on the boys, though I say again that they did seem to act more as wardens than educators. The boys do, I'm told, like the principal, who calls his charges "seekers." However, I continue to have the feeling that the boys are not being reformed at all and that the tradition of the Oblate Fathers and their general attitude is not really one that works for a reformatory. A brother or priest is in charge of each group of boys laboring at Saint Conleth's, and I saw one such group go to the bog to cut turf. The other groups were working diligently on the farm: getting hay into the barn, doing the milking, and looking after the chickens. The Grand Canal is just next to the reformatory, and all the laboring boys are allowed to go outside its high, thick walls and swim and wash in the canal. Unfortunately, they put back on the same horrible, dirty clothes they had been wearing before marching back inside in military fashion to eat their evening meal in the dining hall.

Regrettably, my equanimity was disturbed by the sight of the kitchen and the dining hall, and I have to use the word Dickensian here to describe both rooms, with the full living force of the nineteenth century in that word. Dickens described the social conditions of his time so well, and, unhappily, such conditions are applicable to what I see here. In the kitchen there are three boilers, with one used for making stews, the usual dinner for the boys. Another is for tea. While the management had been urged to buy an electric chip-making machine and this has been done, the machine stands idle as no one in the kitchen has used it. The dining hall is shabby, dark, and depressing and has a bare floor. There is a covering of sorts on the tables, though the original pattern on the oilcloth is hardly discernible. A small group of boys, usually six to eight in number, sits at each table, and they were eating their evening meal when I arrived. There was bread and margarine and tea, with each boy drinking from a tin cup. A loaf of bread was shared between four boys, and I did notice that the boys were having difficulty cutting the inside of the bread even though it was freshly baked. They preferred to spread their bit of margarine on the crust, which they ate. The boys could also help themselves to porridge, which was not served with either milk or sugar, and it looked particularly unpleasant when I peered into its aluminum container. Hardly any of the boys were eating it.

Thankfully, after these dispiriting scenes, I brightened up when I saw the farm, which was a model of order, tidiness, and cleanliness though it did rather show up the conditions the boys were kept in. Mercifully, the herd of dairy cows were well, even excellently looked after. There is good land here and a splendid 290-acre farm that is leased by the Oblate Fathers, who pay an annual rent of £350 for the property. Overall, the farm is managed very well, and "I am of the opinion that very handsome profits are made on the farm, but I can see no evidence of any of the profits being ploughed back for the benefit of the boys or for the improvement of the buildings." The father provincial and the principal insisted that they needed plenty of boys, who should stay for the full term of two years if they were to be successful in reforming them. "I could not help forming the impression that if the institution and the farm attached to it were part of the one business it should be a matter of very little difficulty for the authorities of the school to make very considerable improvements in the interests of the boys without appealing to the department for an additional grant."[36]

Unfortunately, Daingean Reformatory was no ordinary school, as it was one of the institutions forming part of the Commission to Inquire into Child Abuse, which was set up in 1999 to investigate physical, emotional, and sexual abuse and neglect in industrial and reformatory schools from approximately 1940 to 1999. Regardless of the here-imagined inspector's findings, no action was taken to ameliorate the conditions at Daingean, and the Oblates, undisturbed in their ways, continued to run Saint Conleth's as before for a further sixteen years. Consequently, conditions encountered by the two Hungarian boys cannot be interpreted as being outside the scandal of the way such establishments were run, including the battery of psychological, sexual, and other physical abuses that occurred in Saint Conleth's.

The Senator and the Schoolboy

Senator Owen Sheehy Skeffington was no stranger to the dark side of the Irish educational system, having a keen interest in educational reform and campaigning against corporal punishment in Irish schools, a practice that Hungarian children were well aware of.[37] Senator Sheehy Skeffington had become aware of the abuses in the system from his contact with Peter

Tyrrell, who had spent time in Saint Joseph's Industrial School in Letterfrack, county Galway.[38] A Hungarian refugee boy sent to Saint Joseph's in Letterfrack in November 1958 came to his attention, and Senator Sheehy Skeffington acted immediately. He contacted Mr. Murphy, the camp controller, who replied that he was not in a position to advise on the matter and requested the senator write to a superior in the Irish Red Cross.[39] Senator Sheehy Skeffington wrote to the minister for justice to inquire about the boy's name, "the nature of the original offence for which he was committed to a school," and whether the boy had any relatives in Ireland.[40] The response from the office of the minister for justice was that "it is a matter for the Department of Education," and the letter was forwarded to that department.[41] The information from the Department of Education stated that the boy was "committed to St Joseph School, Letterfrack under the terms of section 58 (1) (b) Children's Act, 1908—having a parent who does not exercise proper guardianship."[42] Half the children placed in industrial schools entered under the charge of destitution, though the charge did not actually have to be proven. Poverty or neglect was enough.[43] However, this boy's parents, in one sense absent by being in Hungary, had already applied for his repatriation through the International Committee Red Cross, and he was to be released from the school once he was in a position to travel. The summary of his case from the session of the Children's Court in Ennis in November 1958 states that the boy had a "guardian who does not exercise proper guardianship" and as a result had no one to care for him, though this was a moot point if his parents were inquiring about him.[44] Furthermore, the boy had been sent to a previous industrial school where he had created such havoc that he had been sent back to Knockalisheen. Within a short space of time, Letterfrack became his second industrial school; the court decided to send the boy for a period of two years, until the beginning of June 1960. Mr. Murphy said at the hearing that it would be "unfair" to leave the boy on his own, presumably destitute, as the refugee camp was closing and that "efforts would be made" to return him to his parents in Hungary.[45] The Irish Red Cross and Clare County Council agreed to share the costs for his maintenance at the industrial school, with the IRC paying twenty-two shillings and six pence weekly. The council representative made it clear that Clare County Council was the only council in the country to bear such additional costs due to the presence of the Hungarian refugees at Knockalisheen. The boy, Lajos H., was taken to his new accommodation on November 17, 1958.[46]

Senator Sheehy Skeffington became aware of much of this information once he received a detailed letter from the Irish Red Cross in January 1959:

> This boy, together with another refugee boy, was sent to Mount Melleray College in October 1957 to undergo secondary school education. At the end of 1957–58 academic year we were told by the President of the College that [the boy] had proved to be incorrigible and that under no condition would he re-admit him to the college; following damage to property and to animals caused by the use of a catapult and bows and arrows he was sent to Glyn industrial school on 22-10-58 with the object of having him trained in a useful craft but due to his conduct there he was returned to Camp the next day. On 14 November 1958, he was committed to Letterfrack Industrial School, Co Galway at Ennis Court, on the application of the Camp Controller, on the grounds that the camp was not a proper place for an unaccompanied boy and that the boy required supervision and education. He has no relatives in Ireland, and a request has been received from his mother through the Hungarian Red Cross and the International Red Cross for his repatriation. Steps are now in train to give effect to this request.[47]

Using his knowledge of the case, Senator Sheehy Skeffington wrote back to the Department of Education regarding the nature of the boy's offense, though he did confuse the number of industrial schools that had admitted Lajos H.: "I am disappointed that you have not answered one of my three questions, which was as to the nature of this boy's first offence. He is now in his third Irish industrial school, according to the press reports. Was he sent to the first of them also for 'having a parent who does not exercise proper guardianship?'" There was no reply to this query, which was pertinent to the case as parents searching for their child after a revolution can hardly be deemed negligent.[48]

Lajos H., however, did not remain friendless at Letterfrack, as Senator Sheehy Skeffington wrote him a letter:

> Dear Lajos H, you will not know me, but I have been trying to find out since last November both your name and the nature of the "offence" for which you have been sent to 3 of our industrial schools. I have just been given your name, by the Minister for Education, to whom I wrote on December 23, and the information that there is a move on to allow you to be repatriated to Hungary. I became interested in your case when I saw that two other schools found that they could not hold you. I don't know what kind of a fellow you may be, but it is obvious that you have some spirit! Now my reason for writing is that I think it possible that you might find it useful to have someone in Ireland to write to, or to help you in some way. I am an independent member of the Irish Senate, and a Lecturer in French at Trinity College, in the University of Dublin. I get the impression, perhaps wrongly, that you have not been treated in every circum-

stance as you ought to have been, and if I can in any way help you please write and tell me so. I don't know how free you are to write in the ordinary way, but I cannot imagine that the Brothers would prevent you from dropping me a line.

I am particularly anxious to be assured that you get this letter so that even if you see no way in which I can be useful to you, please write to me anyway. I am enclosing a stamped addressed envelope.

I may say that I know something about our Irish Industrial Schools, and about Letterfrack in particular; and when I say "know," I mean know. So you can count on my sympathy and help if you can see a use for it.

Yours sincerely
Owen Sheehy Skeffington

Unfortunately, there is no response to this letter, so it is not clear whether Lajos H. received it or even whether he could write anything back in English. There is no further trace of the boy.[49]

Senator Sheehy Skeffington knew that his letter had some power of protection as Letterfrack Industrial School was in a remote part of Connemara where, given its isolation, physical and sexual abuse took place away from scrutiny. Additionally, while the school catered to destitute children, children without proper guardianship, and children who had committed crimes, this policy had changed in 1954, when Letterfrack became a detention center for juvenile delinquents, as the Christian Brothers had restructured their industrial schools due to a fall in income resulting from fewer children being placed in institutions. Due to this change, fewer boys arrived in Letterfrack, and the school continued to take destitute boys, but overall the school was not financially viable, a state of affairs that impacted the level of care deeply. In 1958, there were ninety-eight boys at the school at the receiving end of a harsh regime, corporal punishment, and punishment emanating from brothers' frustrations. Punishment was inevitable for the children in Letterfrack. For some there were the added horrors of child sex abuse, seen as a "chronic problem" in the school, where, generally, one or more abusers were present.[50]

Unaccompanied Children: International Cooperation

The "irregular relationships" of incomplete families that the sole Irish official had referred to in Austria in November 1956 had resulted from family decisions made in haste during the heat of revolution. These decisions created heartache on both sides of the Iron Curtain divide; at times these family fractures provided additional fuel to the feuding left over from broken marital relations and, as the Hungarian government politicized the process of family reunion, served as useful material for Hungarian propaganda relating to the contested fates of unaccompanied children.[51] Through the actions of the Red Cross and UNHCR, acceptance of the two-way system of requests—namely, return to or departure from Hungary—finally appeared to be resolved with the Hungarian government. Deputy High Commissioner for Refugees James Read sent an aide-mémoire to the Irish legation in Berne in February 1958 seeking information on four children: three boys, Tibor, Lajos R., and Mihaly B, serving his sentence in Saint Conleth's reformatory in Daingean; and a girl, Erzebet. The aide-mémoire referred to High Commissioner Gustav Lindt seeking information on how the Irish government proposed to make its decisions regarding Hungarian minors: "The High Commissioner would also greatly appreciate it if your Government would inform him of the legal procedure it has followed, or intends to follow, in taking decisions on the future of these children, whether it be for their local settlement, for their repatriation or for their resettlement in other countries." The Irish Legation in Berne forwarded the query to the Department of External Affairs, initiating a series of communications lasting several months, mainly between that department and the Irish Red Cross, whose administration, until this point, had been the de facto decision-maker regarding the welfare of Hungarian children.[52]

The Department of External Affairs sent a letter to Major General Sweeney, the secretary of the Irish Red Cross, on March 6, 1958, with the request for information from UNHCR. The reply came the following day with brief details of the four minors:

> Mihaly B—This boy was sentenced to two years detention in Daingean Reformatory. He wishes to return to Hungary and we have no objection. I understand that the Department of Justice would waive the sentence should he be recommended for repatriation.
>
> Tibor—This boy has returned to Hungary. We were not consulted about his travel arrangement.
>
> Lajos R—This boy is unfit for secondary education according to the Superior of the Cistercian College, Roscrea. On 24.2.58 the Camp Controller received a letter from him stating he is in possession of a ticket from Dover to Hungary. We have no objection to his repatriation.
>
> Erzebet—This girl and her father were resident in Knockalisheen Camp. Co. Clare, until this week, when they were found to be absent and it is surmised that they have gone to England.

As one child had already returned to Hungary and Erzebet was accompanied by her father, two children remained of concern: Mihaly B. in Saint Conleth's, who at that point had served over five months of his two-year sentence, and Lajos R. The inquiry from the UN Deputy High Commissioner James Read regarding the four children, did, however, draw the Department of External Affairs and the Irish Red Cross together to some extent once they both engaged in the repatriation of separated children or reunion with children left behind in Hungary. Their perspectives, however, differed.[53]

Mrs. Barry had attended the Nineteenth International Red Cross Conference in New Delhi in November 1957 and had presented the Irish Red Cross view on the reunion of Hungarian families: it was a matter for governments, as they had admitted the refugees. Regardless of the Irish view, the agreement on the two-way process of return to and departure from Hungary emerged. The following February, the executive director of the International Committee Red Cross, Mr. Gallopin, sent a rather optimistic letter to the Irish Red Cross stating that the Hungarian Red Cross, in agreement with the Hungarian government, was in a position to reunite families where family members had remained in Hungary. As part of the process, the request would have to be accompanied by proof that the family were settled in a country of asylum and could support the family unit. He felt that care should be taken in the cases selected: "Requests of this sort forwarded to the Hungarian Red Cross Society should be restricted to a few carefully chosen cases, such as those, in particular, where children or wives of refugees are concerned, which by their very nature might afford some hope of success." Mr. Gallopin advised the Irish Red Cross to contact their Hungarian counterparts directly, while keeping the ICRC in Geneva informed, as requests must exist regarding children left behind.[54] Regardless of the ICRC view, the Irish Red Cross reiterated its position that reunification was a matter for government and forwarded the letter to the Department of Defense almost a week later. Furthermore, Mr. Gallopin would be apprised once consent was given for a few test cases, as so far there had been no such requests from Hungarian parents in Ireland.[55] In fact the Irish government had already allowed refugees to return once they had signed and submitted a statement of intent to the Irish Red Cross, and all such returns had occurred because of family left behind. Mrs. Barry and the Department of External Affairs were in agreement to "hold our hands on returning these children" as "no one can tell of the pressure put on parents in Hungary to write those letters to the Hungarian Red

Cross asking for the return of their children."⁵⁶ Major General Sweeney, the Irish Red Cross secretary, was able to draw on these positions on receiving a follow-up letter from the first secretary, Department of External Affairs, in mid-April 1958, which looked for further information on the four children.

As with the Irish Red Cross, there was reluctance at the Department of External Affairs to act swiftly due to political concerns, but there were other diplomatic concerns in the department:

> We have been thinking over your letter of March 7th on the question of the unaccompanied minor Hungarian refugees and it appears to us here that we should be reluctant to let these children return to Hungary without making some enquiry as to what reception they may get. If your Society saw no objection we would ask the High Commissioner in confidence what his experience had been with other repatriated cases and also what arrangements other countries were making as to the guardianship of these minors. This last point has also arisen, you will remember, in connection with minors refused entry to Canada. As regards furnishing information to the High Commissioner on the cases listed in his enquiry, it seems to us that in view of the fact that these are unaccompanied young people we should perhaps give a more complete picture of their situation. For example perhaps the charge on which Mihaly was detained in Daingean might be mentioned, and a more detailed account of the reasons why Lajoz [sic, Lajos R.] is not considered fit for secondary education. It would, we think, be undesirable to give the impression that we were disinteresting ourselves in these people's future. . . . Against this background we would hesitate to give the impression that we were anxious to relinquish the responsibility for these minors which we freely assumed.

The Department of External Affairs contacted the Canadian embassy in Dublin and the Irish legation in Berne to ascertain the policies of other countries as part of the process to craft a reply to Deputy High Commissioner James Read, whose inquiry had set events in motion.⁵⁷

Mr. Devlin, the Canadian attaché, replied to the Department of External Affairs in March 1958 stating that under Canadian immigration regulations persons under eighteen years of age were considered minors and would therefore require parental or legal guardian permission to migrate to Canada and, furthermore, would have to have a relative in Canada to sponsor the application. Because of the latter stipulation, an application would have to originate in Canada for the admission of a minor, and in the case of Hungarian refugee minors no visa would be granted unless settlement arrangements had been approved in Canada.

The Department of External Affairs then requested that the Irish legation in Berne make unofficial inquiries to UNHCR about whether families and minors returning to Hungary suffered repercussions as well as asking about legal guardianship measures in other countries. The letter referred to the delicacy of the matter and Irish Red Cross unwillingness:

> Our attitude to the return of unaccompanied Hungarian minor refugees to their parents in Hungary is that while basically we would favour reuniting families where possible, we would wish to be reasonably sure that neither the children nor their families would be victimised in any way on their return to Hungary. . . . I will add that we are not entirely satisfied with the attitude shown by the Irish Red Cross in this matter. There has been a tendency, due no doubt to the inadequacy of the existing organization to meet emergencies of this kind, for the Society to disassociate itself as far as possible from any direct responsibility for these children. The replies furnished by the Red Cross to the Deputy High Commissioner's enquiries on the four individual cases submitted by the Hungarian government exemplify this tendency. In view of the fact that the persons in question are unaccompanied minors, we feel that the brevity of the information given would tend to give the impression that we were disinteresting ourselves in the future of these young people for whom after all we had freely assumed responsibility. We have accordingly asked the Red Cross to let us have a fuller report of each case.
>
> In view of the fact that the attitude of our own Red Cross leaves something to be desired in respect of the care and supervision of minor refugees, you may consider that it would be better to approach the Deputy High Commissioner unofficially, either by correspondence or, if you consider that the occasion warranted the journey to Geneva, by calling on him in person. It would be most undesirable if the impression were created that the future of these young people were a matter of indifference to us.

However, *indifference* was perhaps an apt description of the government's own attitude in initially distancing itself from the care of children and referring the care of minors back to the Red Cross, as had occurred initially with the education of the children in Knockalisheen.[58]

Minister Plenipotentiary Josephine McNeill, at the Irish legation in Berne, held a discussion with Mr. Kelly, who was dealing with repatriation at the Office of the High Commissioner for Refugees in Geneva. He stated that there were no guarantees in place to ensure that minors or families would not suffer if an unaccompanied minor returned to Hungary. Up until the previous year, UNHCR had been sure that children who had returned were interned in a camp or kept in a prison of some kind: after children had been repatriated, letters continued to arrive in Austria from their parents inquiring about their whereabouts, so it was evident that these children had not been reunited with family but were probably being held captive. As no such reports had emerged for a year, it was assumed that whatever the practice had been, it had ceased. In Mr. Kelly's opinion, a sixteen-year-old would be considered capable of looking after himself and could not be prevented from returning. He suggested "it might be dangerous for any refugee to return to Hungary without having heard from his family and being reasonably sure that they were not in any political danger, since such a person on his return would find himself involved in the same difficulties as his relatives. Where, however, a refugee was in touch with his relatives, and had no reason to believe that they were politically involved, there did not seem to be any great risk attached to his repatriation." Overall, there were risks to repatriation and family reunification, but the nature of the risk depended on each individual case.[59]

Individual Cases: Requests for Returns and Departures

Individual cases illustrate the differences between each instance of family reunification, whether from repatriation to Hungary or reunification in Ireland. The requests for information about the whereabouts of children or requests to return children were not always straightforward, as with the case of Erzebet, one of the four children on the UNHCR list sent to the Department of External Affairs. Erzebet's mother had sought the return of her child on the grounds of her husband being mentally ill. She had visited the British legation in Budapest in February 1958, inquiring about her daughter, who, she said, had been removed without her consent. She had no desire to see her husband again. At the legation, she produced a court order confirming her right of custody. From her contact with the International Red Cross, who, in turn, had relayed the request to the Irish Red Cross, she had learned that the Irish Red Cross were not in a position to do anything, as the child was accompanied by her father and he wished to keep her in Ireland. At the British legation in Budapest, Erzebet's mother was told not to be optimistic but that the legation would inquire to ascertain any change in the situation. Approximately a month later, Dublin had confirmed that the father and daughter had moved to England and were residing in Bedford.

At approximately the same time in February 1958, in a separate case, the mother of a young boy who had left Hungary with his father made inquiries to the Hungarian Red Cross, which were then forwarded to the Irish

Red Cross. In this instance, the mother had divorced and remarried and had custody of the child. According to the mother, the child had a good relationship with his stepfather, but left Hungary to join his father after learning in December 1956 that his father had left. The letter received by the Irish Red Cross suggested that the father had lost custody of his child due to his behavior:

> The child was greatly deceived about his father and wishes to return to his mother. Although he is still young, his decision is unshaken and his letters show that he has himself taken the steps regarding his repatriation. But the father wishes to prevent him and has appealed to every place so that the son should not obtain permission to leave Ireland. From what the boy says your Society should equally know about this. The father and the mother are in correspondence and the father grudges giving the child to the mother, who cannot understand the attitude of the father, particularly, if he is not pleased with his son, and according to the mother the husband's morals—he is already living with his fifth wife (woman)—are by no means a good influence for the child. The latter says he cannot get on with his father, they do not understand each other, and the son is much attached to his mother. He writes very nicely: "a mother has more right to her child than the father." The mother has declared that she would ask nothing better than that her son should return to her.[60]

Mr. Murphy, the Knockalisheen Camp controller, sent a short rebuttal to the charge that the father ill-treated his son: "There is no truth in the allegation that the Society sent this boy to College because the father ill-treated him. The boy was a little wayward when he came to the camp and his father had to be strict with him. The father is very happy that the boy is in College and states that under no circumstances whatever will he allow him to return to Hungary." There are different explanations that prevent a simplistic interpretation of the stance taken in the letter from Hungary: some families there were coerced into writing letters searching for family members, and the sad remnants of a marriage may have been refashioned to present a strong case; alternatively, these two cases involving Erzebet and the young boy represent desperate parents willing to go to any lengths to reclaim their children. Regardless of motive, these cases do, however, reveal the tragedy of families fragmented at the time of the revolution and, from the political perspective of 1958, remaining so indefinitely.[61]

Hoping to reunite with a child left behind in Hungary, Mr. Lipot had written to the Irish Red Cross in June 1957:

> Please do not regard this letter of a Hungarian father an impertinence. My son had unfortunately to remain behind last October because he was too ill to

travel in the depth of winter. I thought that there would be no difficulty in his way and that he could join us when he got well. . . . You are probably aware, I have been working in _____. . . . I could therefore fully support my son and he would not be a liability to the country. I am willing to pay the fare to Ireland. I know that you are very busy with affairs similar to mine, but I would appreciate it very much if you could put my case before the government, and indeed no human gratitude could repay you if you succeed in re-uniting a family.

The Irish Red Cross contacted the International Red Cross Committee about the case, but the case could not proceed further as the family had departed unofficially for England.[62]

The third boy on James Read's original list of four children, Lajos R., had been sent to the Cistercian College in Roscrea and, on his mother's instructions, had written to the Hungarian Legation in London from his school, asking "you to help me to go back home. My parents are living in Hungary and I wish to go back to them. Please, if you are able to help me, get for me the transit-visa from Dublin to London."[63]

Lajos R. received his return papers from the Hungarian Legation in London, and his parents also sent his ticket there. In his last letter home, dated February 10, 1958, he had written that he would return shortly. However, his parents informed the Hungarian Red Cross that he had never set off on this return journey. The Hungarian Red Cross contacted their Irish counterpart: "We beg you to be good enough to undertake that the boy may realise his early return by securing the ticket from where he is now living to London and on to Dover, from where he already has his ticket as far as his home which has been deposited at the Hungarian legation. We hope that you will not refuse the help which we are requesting of you and that you will help the young boy to undertake his return journey to his own country."[64] The verdict on Lajos R.'s performance during his stay in Cistercian College was that he was uneducable despite the fact that he was literate in his mother tongue, so already capable of reading and writing, as evidenced by his correspondence. It is not clear whether, as a young teenager, there was an expectation for him to learn English at an unprecedented pace and proceed in the Irish education system or whether there were social and cultural aspects of his behavior that, in some way, did not fit the ethos of the private Roman Catholic boys' school. Lajos R. was still at Roscrea on September 5, 1958, according to an article in the *Irish Press* that also stated that he was one of two boys who had been rejected for resettlement in Canada as he was an unaccompanied minor. By December he was in Knockalisheen, where "powerful influences were at present working to have the boy rehabilitated. That would be done in a day or two."[65] As the camp closed that month, he was moved to Limerick. He remained in Ireland.[66]

Conclusion: Mixed Responses and Outcomes

Unwillingly, the government and the Irish Red Cross became involved with the repatriation of children, with each considering the other to hold the greater responsibility. In the Departments of Justice and Defense, neither minister had any "observations to offer in this matter."[67] The Department of External Affairs did take a humane stance on the question of repatriating minors, particularly as most of the refugees would depart in 1958: "Until we have a fuller account of all the circumstances we should not assent to these boys returning. We will shortly have most of our refugees off our hands thanks to Canadian generosity. I feel we might at least assume a more human responsibility for those few who will remain and who will be all either invalids or minors."[68] The difficulty, however, as the Department of External Affairs noted, was balancing the wishes of parents and children against a potential negative outcome for a child who returned:

> This Department has felt considerable anxiety over the ultimate fate of these young people if repatriated. There is no guarantee that they and their families will not suffer as a result of their return. On the other hand it is undoubtedly true that their parents have a prior claim in this matter and, therefore, if the Red Cross is reasonably satisfied that the applications from the parents for the return of their children are bona fide and that the young persons themselves have been adequately informed of the circumstances at issue and know their own minds, this Department will raise no objection to their repatriation.

Despite being of the view that return to Hungary was a matter for government, the Irish Red Cross still became involved with repatriation; it would have been difficult to remain aloof as the process had become a matter for the ICRC and national Red Cross Societies.[69]

The Irish Red Cross indicated that it had been considering the question of the return of children and the "Society would be obliged for a ruling from the Government."[70] This is not to say that there was no concern for children; the IRC paid school fees for unaccompanied boys so that they attended good secondary schools where they could complete their education. As secondary education became free only in 1967 in Ireland, this support for the refugee boys was a combination of generosity and privilege.

Fig. 5.4. The first baptism. Source: Sean Curtin Collection.

At the beginning of January 1958, six boys, not all unaccompanied, were attending Mount Melleray College in Waterford and the College of Mount Saint Joseph Abbey in Roscrea, boarding schools run by the Cistercians, and Multyfarnham Agricultural College, run by the Franciscans, with the IRC paying their fees. The two boarding schools for boys, infused with the religious ethos of the Cistercian, or Trappist, Order, would have provided a strict regime in contrast to the chaos of revolution, of flight and the unsettling liminality of refugee camps. Such an ethos, though, may not have suited every child. In contrast, the intuitively intercultural approach taken by Sister Immaculata resonated over time and across continents with the children formerly in her care.[71]

Similarly, given the context of 1950s Ireland, the Irish Red Cross did not ignore the religious welfare of the children in Knockalisheen, which

Fig. 5.5. Departure. Source: Sean Curtin Collection.

culminated in first communions, a significant rite of passage for Irish children, and confirmation. As religious instruction formed a core component of the Irish national primary school curriculum, the Christian Brothers, Sexton Street, Limerick, helped to prepare boys for confirmation at the camp, and the nuns of Mercy Convent, Ballynanty, Limerick, instructed the girls. A total of thirty-five children were confirmed, and thirteen children made their first Holy Communion in March 1958; the Irish Red Cross had bought blue and white dresses for the girls and suits for the boys so that the Sacrament was celebrated in full Irish style. The bishop of Limerick performed the ceremony and addressed the parents beforehand with a reference to "Godless Communism": "I am happy to have the honour of confirming your children. We would prefer to see them receiving the Sacrament in their own country, but at least they are fortunate to receive it in a country where religion can be practised freely." A newspaper article commented on parents weeping joyfully at the ceremony, which had begun with the children walking in procession through the camp carrying religious banners while singing hymns and reciting the rosary. This event was a major ceremony at the camp, in keeping with the communion and confirmation ceremonies taking place throughout the country; the public staging of the ceremony underlined its social significance of belonging yet set it apart at the camp and in its status in the Ireland of the 1950s.[72]

Finally, the Irish Red Cross also took responsibility for the saddest of outcomes for a child, as thirteen-year-old Tibor Polczer died after staying as a patient in Our Lady's Hospital for Sick Children in Crumlin from April to July 1957. Following a requiem mass celebrated by Father Kis at the hospital, Tibor was buried in Deansgrange Cemetery on July 13, 1957. Mr. Murphy traveled with members of the Hungarian camp committee to Dublin to shoulder the coffin to the cemetery. Funeral costs were paid so that Tibor received a proper burial, also a rite of enduring significance in Irish culture. His status as a young Hungarian refugee remains memorialized in the Register of Interments.[73]

Notes

The epigraphs are from "World Red Cross Day," *Irish Times*, May 8, 1957, 7, ITDA, and Article 12, UN Convention on the Rights of the Child. Adopted and opened for signature, ratification, and accession by General Assembly resolution 44/25 of November 20, 1989; entry into force September 2, 1990.

1. Hoblicsek and Illés, *1956-os kivándorlás*, appendix, "Az illégálisan külföldre távozott személyek főbb adatai," 17.
2. Goodwin-Gill, "Politics of Refugee Protection," 8–23. See also the historical overview by Long, *Where You Once Belonged*, 7.
3. Lénárt, "Emigration from Hungary," 371, 380.
4. "Boys Destroyed Ten Tanks," *Irish Independent*, November 10, 1956, 12.
5. Vonèche Cardia, *Hungarian October*, 50.
6. UNHCR, Reports to General Assembly, January 1, 1959.
7. Perret, "ICRC Operations," unpaginated.
8. Vonèche Cardia, *Hungarian October*, 51.
9. UNHCR, *State of the World's Refugees*, 34.
10. Vonèche Cardia, *Hungarian October*, 50.
11. Pask, "Unaccompanied Refugee and Displaced Children," 204–6.
12. Vonèche Cardia, *Hungarian October*, 51.
13. Perret, "ICRC Operations," unpaginated.
14. Vonèche Cardia, *Hungarian October*, 55, 56.
15. The motive behind offering homes to children was not always solely humanitarian but more complex; it could include a welcome for another pair of hands to help with the labor of a family farm, as in the case of Operation Shamrock. Motivations and outcomes were complicated in the experiences of children, as Brandis, *Children from Operation Shamrock*,

indicates. Emotive attitudes toward refugee children are discussed in Taylor, "Don't Just Look for a New Pet."

16. Superintendent Lavan to Department of Justice, April 24, 1957, TSCH/3/S11007 D.

17. "Conference on Hungarian Refugees, appendix, June 1957," TSCH/3/S11007 E. "Boy Refugee to Rejoin Father," *Irish Press*, December 7, 1957, 1; "208 Refugees at Knocklalisheen," *Irish Press*, January 4, 1958, 4.

18. Irish Red Cross, camp bulletin, January 16, 1957, TSCH/3/S/11107 D.

19. "Conference on Hungarian Refugees January 1957," report; reconfirmed in the June 1957 report, TSCH/3/S11007 D.

20. Conversation with Anna Letoha, July 25, 2017.

21. "Statement on Refugees—Employment Chances Have Decreased—Mrs Barry," *Irish Independent*, March 12, 1957, 6.

22. "Conference on Hungarian Refugees, June 1957," report, 2, TSCH/3/S11007 D.

23. "Hungarian Refugees Want School Bus," *Irish Independent*, August 14, 1957, 3; "School Plans for Refugee Children," *Irish Examiner*, August 23, 1957, 3.

24. "Refugee Children to Attend Schools," *Irish Independent*, August 23, 1957, 3.

25. Sr. Immaculata's contribution at the Commemorative Celebrations in Knocklalisheen, 2006, Sister Immaculata Collection.

26. Interview with Sister Immaculata, May 16, 2014.

27. Letter, Sister Immaculata Collection.

28. Letter, Sister Immaculata Collection.

29. Mária, to Sister Immaculata, (?) 27, 1958, Sister Immaculata Collection.

30. Superintendent Lavan, report to C3, May 1, 1957, TSCH/3/S/11107 D.

31. Unaccompanied children, or, as they are called now, "separated children," are "children under eighteen years of age who are outside their country of origin and separated from both parents or their previous legal/customary primary caregiver. Some children are totally alone while others ... may be living with extended family members. All such children are separated children and entitled to international protection under a broad range of international and regional instruments"; UNHCR, "Separated Children in Europe," 2. Not all children were unaccompanied, as they could become separated in emergencies.

32. Justice's Minute Book, The District Court, DC/2002/115/18.

33. "Refugees Biting the Hand?" *Pictorial*, January 18, 1957, 12.

34. Ryan, *Commission*, vol. 4, 208, 1.

35. Following a Freedom of Information Request that went unanswered and was followed up by an appeal, one part of my request was denied; I was allowed to see this report but not copy it. Consequently, I am re-creating this imaginary version. Additional references to this report are in Raftery and O'Sullivan, *Suffer the Little Children*; Arnold, *Irish Gulag*; and Ryan, *Commission*.

36. Ryan, *Commission*, vol. 4, 185. The Ryan Commission was able to view the 1955 inspector's report and quote verbatim three times from it in vol. 4, page 185. Consequently, I have taken two extracts from those quotes and incorporated them into my imaginary text.

37. Pálmai Bánki, "Crossing Borders," 159.

38. Peter Tyrrell posted a series of manuscripts to Owen Sheehy Skeffington from November 1958, which eventually became the publication *Founded on Fear*. He had written to Owen Sheehy Skeffington earlier in the year and related what had happened to him. Owen Sheehy Skeffington wrote to Peter Tyrrell on August 18, 1958, about Letterfrack so that he was

152 | *Suitable Strangers*

aware of the institution and its goings-on. This knowledge may have contributed to Senator Sheehy Skeffington's interest in the case of Lajos H. Tragically, Peter Tyrrell burned himself to death on Hampstead Heath in April 1967.

39. Mr. Murphy to Owen Sheehy Skeffington, November 24, 1958, MS40, 512/2 1959, National Library of Ireland, henceforth NLI.

40. Owen Sheehy Skeffington to the Minister for Justice, December 2, 1958, MS40, 512/2 1959, NLI.

41. Office of the Minister for Justice to Owen Sheehy Skeffington, December 23, 1958, MS40, 512/2 1959, NLI.

42. Mr. Dukes, Department of Education, to Owen Sheehy Skeffington, January 23, 1959, MS40, 512/2 1959, NLI.

43. Ferriter, *Occasions of Sin*, 327.

44. Justice's Minute Book, the District Court, DC/2002/115/19.

45. "£120,000 Spent on Refugees," *Evening Herald*, November 18, 1958, 2.

46. "Red Cross Seeks Accommodation for 40 Refugees," *Irish Examiner*, November 17, 1958, 4.

47. Major-General Sweeney to Senator Sheehy Skeffington, January 12, 1959, MS40, 512/2 1959, NLI.

48. Owen Sheehy Skeffington to Mr. Dukes, January 25, 1959, MS40, 512/2 1959, NLI.

49. Undated letter from Owen Sheehy Skeffington to Lajos H., MS40, 512/2 1959, NLI.

50. Mr. Justice Ryan, *Commission Child Abuse*, vol. 1, 289 and vol. 4, 291, 315, 321, 356.

51. This is not the only instance of the use of children for propaganda or ideological purposes. See Bradford, *Revolution Children*, for instance, for protest in Cuba in 1960 in the early days of the Revolution in Catholic schools supported by the Catholic Church, 107–9, and from the United States, 127–29.

52. James Read, aide-mémoire to Irish legation, Berne, February 25, 1958, DFA/6/419/33/15.

53. Irish Red Cross to Department of External Affairs, March 7, 1958, DFA/6/419/33/15.

54. Mr. Gallopin to Irish Red Cross, February 5, 1958, DFA/6/419/33/15.

55. This was incorrect, as there had been a request the previous year from Lajos Lipot to reunite his family with their baby son, who had been left behind in Hungary.

56. Mrs. Barry to Major General Sweeney, DFA/6/419/33/15.

57. Department of External Affairs to Major General Sweeney, April 14, 1958. DFA/6/419/33/15.

   Máire MacEntee, Máire Mhac an tSaoi, worked in the Department of External Affairs, later Department of Foreign Affairs. She was also an Irish-language poet and scholar and was elected to Aosdána, the body honoring outstanding Irish artists, in 1996. She renounced this privilege a year later in protest at the elevation of Francis Stuart to a position of honor as he had broadcast for the Nazis in the Second World War. She married Conor Cruise O'Brien in 1962, when she resigned from the Department of Foreign Affairs. The couple adopted two children.

58. Department of External Affairs to Irish legation, Berne, May (month only), DFA/6/419/33/15.

59. Josephine McNeill to the Department of External Affairs, May 9, 1958, DFA/6/419/33/15.

60. Hungarian Red Cross to Irish Red Cross, February 28, 1958, DFA/6/419/33/15.

61. Mr. Murphy to Major General Sweeney, March 11, 1958, DFA/6/419/33/15.

62. Laszlo Lipot to Irish Red Cross, June 18, 1957, DFA/6/419/33/15.

63. Undated and translated copy of letter sent by Lajos R., DFA/6/419/33/15.
64. Translated letter from the Hungarian Red Cross, March 6, 1958, DFA/6/419/33/15.
65. "Future of Refugees Uncertain," *Irish Independent*, September 5, 1958, 12; "No Rations to Refugees Who Refused City Place," *Irish Press*, December 19, 1958, 3.
66. "Returned from Dublin to Knockalisheen," *Irish Independent*, December 15, 1958, 7. Lajos R. declined to be interviewed, so further insight into his circumstances and the influences on his decisions are not available apart from the fact that he did choose to remain in Ireland.
67. Department of Justice, May 31, 1958, and Department of Defence, June 12, 1958, to Department of External Affairs, DFA/6/419/33/15.
68. Maíre MacEntee, internal communication, July 1, 1958, DFA/6/419/33/15.
69. Department of External Affairs to Department of Defence, August 7, 1958, DFA/6/419/33/15.
70. Major General Sweeney to Department of Defence, June 16, 1958, DFA/6/419/33/15.
71. "208 Refugees at Knockalisheen," *Irish Press*, January 4, 1958, 4.
72. "Refugee Children Confirmed," *Irish Press*, March 24, 1958, 3. First Holy Communion remains an important rite of passage for children in Ireland; it has lost virtually all of its religious or spiritual impact and has significance for the amount of money a child may receive and for the element of dressing up for the occasion.
73. "First Hungarian Refugee to Die in Ireland," *Limerick Leader*, July 13, 1957, 1; Registry of Interments, 31–33, Dublin City Library and Archive.

Admission information courtesy of Our Lady's Children's Hospital, Crumlin.

6

DOMESTIC PROBLEMS, INTERNATIONAL SOLUTIONS, DEPARTURES

In the past many people were content to remain assisting on their home farms for virtually nothing more than their subsistence—some hoping to inherit the farm, others in expectation of dowries. This way of life was accepted as inevitable, and emigration from farms was confined to those who were obliged to go through sheer necessity. Nowadays fewer people are satisfied with a subsistence standard of living and they find an easy alternative in emigration.
—*Commission on Emigration and Other Population Problems 1948–1954*

All the refugees were under the impression that they were only coming to Ireland in transit for the U.S.A. or Canada. The Irish Red Cross has been in touch with the situation in Britain, Belgium and France where the same impression was held by the refugees and the same problems encountered.
—"Statement on Refugees 'Would Be Going to US' Belief," *Irish Press*

Problems

By the end of June 1957, a series of problems emerged from interdepartmental committee meetings concerning punitive measures, language, employment, and well-being, with a summary report recommending government attention. The matter of wandering aliens such as Huibe Huiré (see chap. 3) had resulted in Hungarians requiring a permit to leave Knockalisheen and the "law governing the residence of aliens . . . being enforced in respect of these Hungarians." The restriction order requiring garda permission to be absent from Knockalisheen for more than twenty-four hours was still in force several months after their arrival. Unsurprisingly, language difficulties also remained even though children initially attended school in the camp, and adult attendance was sporadic. As a result there were "formidable barriers to clear understanding between the refugees and the Camp authorities who are almost entirely dependent on two or three interpreters to convey and receive messages and that the lack of something to do results in the refugees standing about in groups in the Camp throughout the day gossiping and conjecturing as to their prospects of employment or emigration." Enforced idleness, gossip, and rumors were dangers to avoid in the long-term, but there were already symptoms of malaise evident in the camp.[1]

Efforts to intensify employment fell to the Irish Red Cross, either to finance any Department of Industry and Commerce–approved scheme that offered employment to a minimum of six Hungarian refugees with the proviso that such a scheme be marketed, or to sponsor any home craft scheme set up in the camp in tandem with a local voluntary marketing committee. The IRC had already taken the initiative by publishing a list of the trades and skills of workers in the camp followed by penalizing anyone who left their employment without a valid reason, especially as employers had taken the trouble to visit the camp. Pocket money was withdrawn for a period of five to six weeks to discourage such behavior. Apart from the lack of commitment to employment, the camp administration worried about the approach of a second winter. Superintendent Lavan and Captain McCann, the medical officer, were concerned about the camp's isolation, the recurrence of illness over the winter period, and the potential for hunger strikes and suicides. Captain McCann felt that "for psychological reasons, the isolated location of the camp, is unsuitable, particularly in winter time."[2] Language competency, commitment to employment, isolation, and feeling the combined effects of power and powerlessness in the face of punitive measures were inextricably linked. Commitment to employment in Ireland implied the fading of dreams of Canada, the United States, or Australia; as the time spent in Knockalisheen lengthened, the dream was the only hope.

During the first winter in Knockalisheen, a large number of children developed bronchitis.[3] With Knockalisheen deemed "a relic of the war emergency with little future in front of it," McCann Barracks in Templemore offered a solution to move to better quarters.[4] Having learned a lesson from the hunger strike, government and Irish Red Cross officials attended a meeting with the whole camp on August 21, 1957. The contingent included the IRC, government officials from the Department of Defense, and Commandant O'Sullivan; they addressed the gathering of refugees by saying that the camp medical officer was concerned for the health of both adults and children if they were to stay in Knockalisheen for another winter.[5] Furthermore, they asserted, the Hungarian camp leader had already visited Templemore at the end of July, taken photographs of McCann Barracks, and shown them on his return to support the assertion that everyone would be much more comfortable there during the winter. Mr. Bihary, the camp refugee representative, used the meeting to ask about the installation of cooking facilities in the huts rather than everyone using a communal kitchen, but the proposal was rejected on the grounds of being a fire risk. There was no need for people to cook their evening meal on their own stoves as "the communal kitchen is always there."[6]

The Hungarians, however, had no appetite to move from being close to Limerick to a small town and had already written a letter, signed by eighty-five families, detailing their objections:

> We the undersigned being Hungarian refugees at present resident in Knockalisheen camp desire to express our thanks to the Irish Government for the help you have given to us during our stay in Ireland. We appreciate very much the kindness behind the proposals that £10,000 should be spent on our behalf renovating the military barracks at Templemore.
>
> We should like to inform you before this work begins that it is the desire of the undersigned to remain in Knockalisheen camp. During our stay here we have made many friends among the Limerick people. Many of them have lent us radios, bicycles and other accessories which would all have to be returned should we move to Templemore. In addition quite a number of Refugees have been able to acquire temporary jobs in or around Limerick . . . [which] itself is quite a big place and there is always some form of entertainment to which we can go. The actual accommodation here in the camp has been improved by the huts being partitioned and stone paths being laid. Many of us have installed makeshift electrical appliances which also help to make conditions here more bearable.
>
> The psychological effect of moving to a more remote district would also be detrimental. Those of our number who have visited Templemore have told us that it is off the main road and is very small in size as compared with Limerick.

The letter elicited some surprise, as there had been many complaints about Knockalisheen.[7]

An *Irish Examiner* editorial examined the pros and cons of the situation and found that "there is something to be said for both sides, even if on balance the merits seem to be on the side of the refugees." It was also reasonable to wonder why the government had not chosen Templemore initially. Templemore council, meanwhile, was looking forward to a cash injection into the town of some thousand pounds a week. But, despite official assertions to the contrary, the group of Hungarian representatives taken to Templemore to inspect McCann Barracks had remained unimpressed by them, by Templemore, and by its amenities. Neither Knockalisheen nor McCann Barracks offered a permanent solution, but the Hungarians had developed tentative roots in Limerick and its environs and

> even found measures of employment. They have no desire to live on other people's charity or benevolence but are avid to fend for themselves. It is natural that they dislike the idea of being forced to change from a district they have learnt to know to one in which they have no contacts and where, in a sense, they would have to begin life over again. The authorities on this side would do worse than meet them halfway by executing such improvements at Knockalisheen as would render their life there easier for the coming winter. It should be remembered that they are highly intelligent people who know what they want and what is best for them.

The move to McCann Barracks was abandoned.[8]

The Hungarians remained in Knockalisheen and celebrated the first anniversary of the uprising with a requiem mass in the camp presided over by the bishop of Limerick. A choir sang, patriotic poems were recited, and Limerick bandleader Mr. Clancy sounded the *Last Post*. An *Evening Herald* editorial commented, "Whatever controversies may have arisen on the question of the Hungarian refugees since they came amongst us, there can be little doubt that on this anniversary of their gallant revolution the thoughts and prayers and sympathies of the Irish people are with them." A second winter came to the camp, followed by a glimpse of spring and hope in 1958.[9]

Screening for Canada

In January 1958, the Hungarians numbered about 190, and the Irish Red Cross continued to run the camp from the funds collected against "Godless Communism." Running costs had decreased from £2000–£2500 to approximately £1000 a week as people left the camp for other countries. People preparing to leave "draw from those who remain envious glances, for leaving appears to be the main ambition of most of those at the camp. A family is to go shortly to Australia; another to Argentina—it was held up by the birth of a baby. The rest hope that when Canada 'reopens' to immigrants in the spring there will be better opportunities for them to go there." This was a period of restlessness, hope, and preparation for resettlement, not only in Canada but in the United States and Australia as well.[10]

Even the children knew that at some point they would leave Ireland and relocate elsewhere. One of Sister Immaculata's pupils, Mária, wrote as her eighteen-month stay in Ireland drew to an end and as she received a group picture taken at the school in Ballynanty:

> Dear sister, I am very sorry that I did not wright to you in the last week but I was very busy. We are very wel. The pictures what the man was taking in the school is readi they are very nic and very good.
>
> I did not go to Éva's house in the last week but I will go in this week to her house. I hope Éva's father will let Éva come out to the Camp. I think Éva is very lonely their.
>
> We are going to mass every Sunday and we are praying for you. I say my rosary every day and pray for you to. The B family will not go to Australia on the 17 July they are weathing for us because our visa is not ready. Mabey we will not get the visa but mabey we will get. We sud like to go to Australia but we are not sure cud we go or we cud not. Please pray for us and mabey God will help us.
>
> Dear Sister I am very sad after you because I like you very much I no now I was bold some times in the school but I am very sorry. Please furgat my bad manurs. I will never forget you because you were very good to me and to my little sister. Mabey we will meet again in September but I hope we will go to Australia.

Anxiety, prayer, hope, loneliness, more hope, more anxiety: the seesawing of these emotions in the letter no doubt mirrored the emotions of the adults who were also waiting.[11]

As the child's letter indicated, three families, eleven people, had been cleared to leave for Australia, and the families expected to travel in May 1958. To facilitate these departures, Miss Regan, secretary of the Irish mission of the Catholic Relief Services, the agency of the NCWC that aided Catholic emigrants seeking to go to Australia or Canada, was already at the camp. A Canadian emigration team followed at the end of March 1958 to spend two days interviewing the Hungarians to ascertain their health and probe their characters.[12] The Canadian government had initially broached the question of resettling Hungarian refugees with a certain degree of caution. A rather optimistic economic forecast had dissipated this caution in 1957 as it expected a shortfall in available labor. The Canadian Minister for Integration Mr. Pickersgill would have been "anxiously looking for immigrants fit to work." The Irish government had had great hopes for the speedy departure of the Hungarians before their second winter in Ireland, but this optimism was misplaced as there followed reports of a Canadian recession. However, Canada did admit Hungarians from Austria and a group residing in the United Kingdom, all of which left the Hungarians in Knockalisheen stranded at the back of the queue until spring 1958.[13]

In Knockalisheen, the Hungarians received a form addressed to the male head of the family, typed as usual without diacritics, which aimed to create a list of all those wishing to move to Canada. The form began, "*Kedves uram, Egy nevsort keszitenek azorrol a menekkultekrol akik Kanadaban akarnak letelepedni. Ha on kivan menni, irja le a nevet, es a felesegenek es gyermekeinek a nevet.*" (Dear Sir, A list is being created of those refugees who wish to settle in Canada. If you wish to go, write your name, your spouse's name, and those of your children.) The questionnaire asked for the *foglalkozas*, the trade or profession of the applicant and, most importantly, *orszag ahova szeretne menni*, the preferred country of final destination. The form contained the proviso that "*nem valoszinu hogy tovabbi lehetoseg lesz meg Kanadaba menni. Ezt a kerdoivet azonnal vissza kell kuldeni, Dublinbe,* Westland Row, 25." (There may not be another opportunity to go to Canada. This questionnaire should be returned immediately to 25 Westland Row, Dublin.)[14]

The Canadian commission in Knockalisheen rejected 51 of the 205 Hungarian refugees who wanted to go to Canada, including six boys who, as separated minors under the age of seventeen, were automatically ineligible for entry. Even young Mihaly had received this form in the reformatory at Daingean, with the typed entry for his final country of destination showing "Hungary"; he would have been ineligible to travel to Canada without a Canadian family member sponsoring him. Some of the rejected group of fifty-one were ill, and there were further investigations in store for seventeen Hungarians. The Canadian team also considered one Hungarian, Josef Csoka, a champion weightlifter, to be too short; he became a sacristan and found refuge in the Roman Catholic Church in Ireland. Mr. Kukk, the elected camp leader at the time, who later traveled to Canada, said that others who had not passed the entry tests were Communists, even though some known Communists had been accepted. The lucky Hungarians who had passed all the tests continued to have a sense of unease and worry because of the downturn in Canada. Even so, they were still prepared to try their luck as "after all, we have spent 16 months trying to find work in Ireland." At this point, there was no further thought of returning to Hungary.[15]

Goodbye to Knockalisheen

In late August 1958, preparations began in earnest for the departure to Canada of the first group of refugees, more than seventy Hungarians, and culminated in a farewell concert at Knockalisheen. The concert mingled aspects of Irish and Hungarian cultures, and representatives of the church—Franciscan priests, Christian brothers, Mercy nuns, Presbyterian Minister Reverend Mills, Commandant McCarthy of the Twelfth Battalion representing the army, and Assistant Red Cross Area Director Mr. Lynn were in attendance. A performance by the Hungarian children's choir became the highlight of the concert as they sang in Irish, English, Latin, and Hungarian. The children also performed a Lourdes play created by their teachers, the Mercy nuns of Ballinanty convent. Further entertainment came from the Penny School of Ballet and Dancing and from other Limerick and Ennis artistes.[16] Mr. Murphy, the camp controller, made a speech and said that "when the refugees came to this country they were running away from tyranny and coercion and the Irish people received them with open arms because they fully understood their feelings. The Hungarians, he said, would take with them memories of the Irish way of life. From his experience of the past two years he had learned that the life of a refugee was not an easy one." In response, Mr. Kukk, the final Hungarian camp leader, expressed gratitude to all: "He wished to express the refugees' thanks to the Irish nation, and say how grateful they were to all who had given money to the Red Cross to help maintain the refugees in Ireland. He asked the Irish people not to forget them, and said the refugees would never forget the goodness of the Irish people."[17] Two days later, on August 29, 1958, final preparations were in full swing for the group's evening departure from Shannon.[18]

The refugees celebrated mass in the morning with their friends and then checked out of the camp by returning all their regulation issue utensils, furniture, and bedding to the army quartermaster stores at the camp. Mr. Stewart, a member of ICEM, was on hand to check papers. Many of those departing spent much of the day finishing handicrafts such as souvenir boxes, crochet work, and paintings that they presented to the staff in Knockalisheen as thanks for the kindnesses shown to them. At the same time, the children said goodbye to their pets, as puppies and kittens could not travel with them to Canada but would remain behind with new owners. In the evening, the group boarded several army trucks which took them to Shannon. Seventy more Hungarians left for Canada on September 1, 1958,

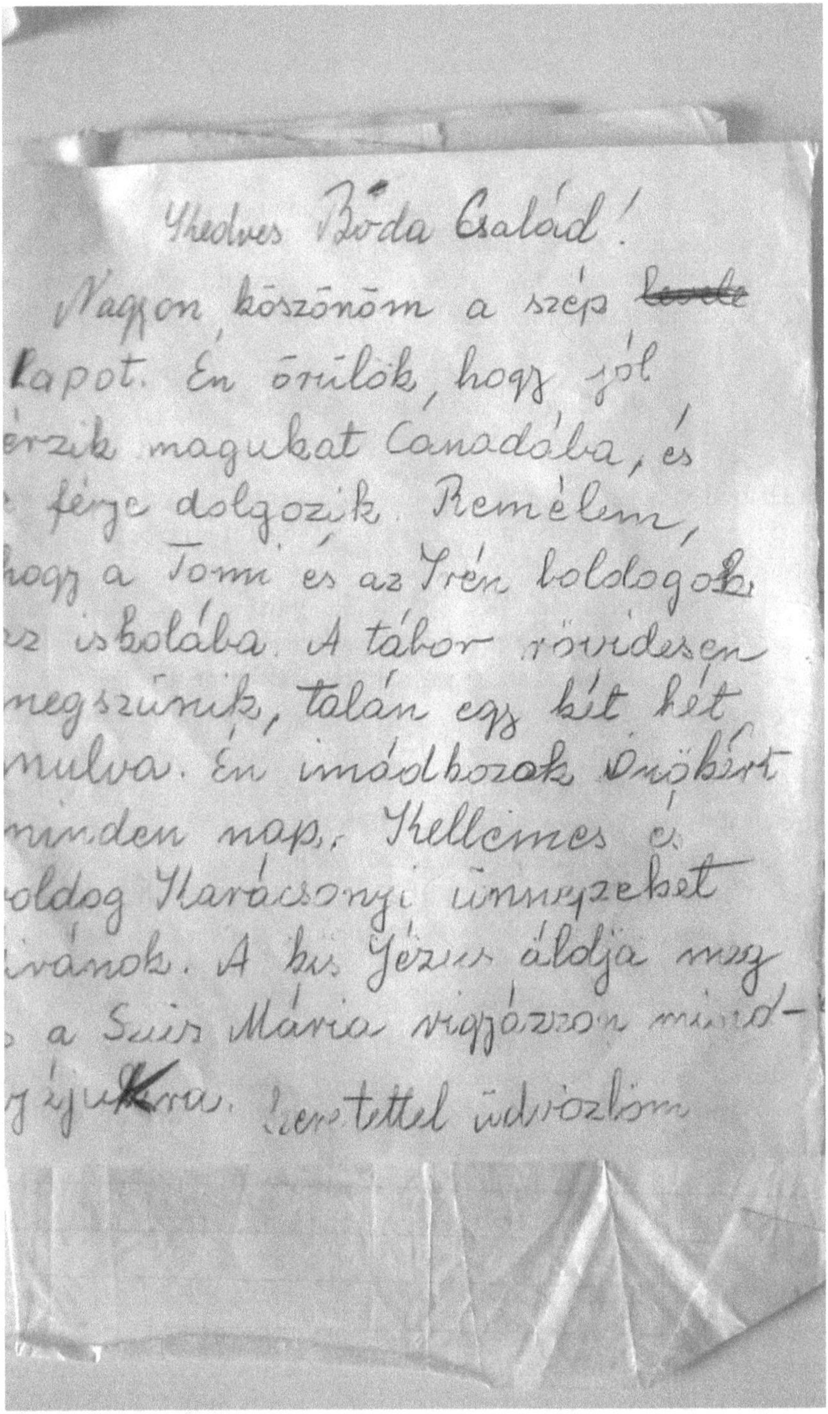

Kedves Böda Család!

Nagyon köszönöm a szép ~~levele~~ lapot. Én örülök, hogy jól érzik magukat Canadába, és a férje dolgozik. Remélem, hogy a Tomi és az Irén boldogok az iskolába. A tábor rövidesen megszűnik, talán egy két hét mulva. Én imádkozok Önökért minden nap. Kellemes és boldog Karácsonyi ünnepeket kívánok. A kis Jézus áldja meg és a Szűz Mária vigyázzon mind-nyájukra. Szeretettel üdvözlöm

Fig. 6.1. Letter to a Hungarian family. Source: Sister Immaculata Collection MCA.

in the second Canadian government airlift so that over 140 departed from Ireland to settle in Canada. Not everyone leaving was unemployed. The departing group included Paul Safari, a Hungarian who had worked as a waiter at the Shannon airport for almost two years. A designer who had secured a job designing raincoats in Dublin and was earning twenty-five pounds a week also left for Canada with his wife and two children. There would be further departures from Shannon airport and from Cobh, where Hungarians sailed to their new futures in Australia and the United States.[19]

Winding Up the Camp and Rehousing the Remaining Hungarians

There had been optimistic talk of closing Knockalisheen by the end of June 1958 as the camp was emptying steadily with departures for Argentina and Australia and the expectation of most of the refugees being admitted to Canada.[20] After the exodus, finding suitable housing for the ten remaining families became the most pressing concern for the IRC following its decision to return Knockalisheen camp to the Department of Defense. The alternative was to let these families become dependent on the state because the costs relating to the running of the camp had virtually drained the appeal fund, as a reminder to the public indicated: "Those who wish the remainder of the refugees to be kept at Knockalisheen would do well to note some items taken from the audited accounts for the six months ending on March 31, 1958, when there were a little over 200 refugees still to be catered for in the camp. Provisions, £6,337; clothing and footwear, £1,853; fuel and light, £4,017; school bus £540; salaries and wages, £2413—a complete charge of £18,348."[21] As an interim measure, the IRC would continue to pay allowances to families, allocating two pounds ten shillings to parents, ten shillings for each child, sixty pounds for rent and furniture, and twenty-five shillings for pocket money. The heads of households traveled to Dublin to inspect the corporation houses in East Finglas offered to six families on a weekly tenancy basis. The initial reaction was unfavorable, as they were unfurnished; everyone turned down the offer and returned to Knockalisheen. Once again a battle ensued with the IRC, who stated that the Hungarians had to accept the accommodation offered. However, a fuller story emerged the following day when Mr. Lorincz said that everyone had turned down the houses in Finglas not just because of the few items of army furniture but also because the IRC secretary had refused to see them in Dublin. Following discussions that lasted all morning, the Hungarian secured a written promise that the Red Cross would provide £60 worth of furniture for the families going to live in Dublin. Following the agreement, a notice written in Hungarian and English, both in red letters, appeared at the camp stating it would be evacuated on November 15, when it would be handed back to the army. The Irish Red Cross in Dublin also threatened the Hungarians with punishment by stating that those refusing to leave the camp would receive neither food nor finance. The result was that four families settled in Finglas, with one family accompanied by a small flock of hens.[22]

Knockalisheen did not close on November 15, 1958. Over forty Hungarians remained at the camp as accommodation proved difficult to find.[23] The IRC found two flats, and nineteen-year-old Olga, who was to marry a Cork man in January 1959, occupied one of them. This was the first Irish-Hungarian wedding to take place since the arrival of the Hungarians in 1956.[24] IRC members began to canvass house to house in their endeavor to find homes for the Hungarians, but the Department of Defense granted a further extension to the IRC for the use of the camp.[25] The IRC turned to Limerick's city council to house seven families, but on Monday, November 24, when there was a debate at the council meeting, the request became contentious as "there were far worse cases in Limerick then in the Hungarian camp," and with twelve hundred housing applications, it was difficult to see how Limerick could aid the Hungarians. The mayor was sympathetic, "but there was such a crying need to house people in Limerick that the council could not see its way to accede to this request from the Red Cross." There were also murmurings about the level of benefits the Hungarians received; some of them in the camp were drawing bigger state allowances than Irish people in similar circumstances, and thousands of pounds had already been given "by the people of Ireland and Limerick to the Red Cross Fund" for their maintenance. There were times to "look to our own," and the council did so.[26]

The IRC began to search further afield and located a Georgian house, 150 years old and a former rectory, that could house four families.[27] Unfortunately, plans to rent and house the Hungarians in Castleconnell fell through because of objections by villagers and the local branch of the Irish Red Cross. The parish priest, also chair of the local branch of the IRC, explained:

> It is the last place in the country to choose to send refugees, because of the poverty that exists here. There are over 200 labourers cottages in the parish and from every second house people have emigrated to England in search of work. The arrival in the village of refugees might even mean trouble. For they would

be maintained in what would appear to be a luxurious standard of living compared with that of our people. It would be better if some form of industry was started here where local people are not even permitted to take as much as an eel from the River Shannon.[28]

Following reports in the national press about local protests in Castleconnell, an indignant resident wrote to the *Limerick Leader* to complain about their sullying of Castleconnell's name: "Rarely in recent times has a more dastardly attack been made on innocent people as has been made by the Dublin Press on the people of Castleconnell within the past week. They have been accused of not wanting Hungarian refugees, holding public meetings of protest, and secret meetings behind closed doors. Facts about the whole matter may now be disclosed and Castleconnell's honor, so vilely smirched, can be vindicated." The Castleconnell branch of the Irish Red Cross held a meeting at which it was suggested to the higher authorities that, because of rampant unemployment in the locality, it would be morally good neither for the refugees nor the people of the district if large numbers of Hungarians were sent in to accentuate present difficulties. They also pointed out that schools in the locality were overcrowded. These facts had to be brought to the notice of the Red Cross authorities in Dublin, and the local branch would be failing in its duty if it acted otherwise. At no time did the local Red Cross, or the people of Castleconnell, refuse to accept the refugees, and therefore sympathies must go out to Castleconnell for so gross a misrepresentation of facts.[29] Meanwhile, thirty-four Hungarians remained at the camp, with numbers dwindling. Two families left in December 1958 to travel from Cobh by ship to the United States under the auspices of the World Council of Churches. Mr. Kozak, traveling with his wife and three children, had been a temporary waiter at Shannon airport and was journeying to California to take up a post in the metallurgical division of the University of California under Professor Cornelius Tobias.[30] Mr. Kun and his family were traveling to New Jersey to join relatives.[31]

Subsequently, three families went to Ballyfermot in Dublin, and one family did go to live in the old rectory in Castleconnell; the camp closed officially a few days later on December 15, 1958. Nine refugees remained, comprising a family of six, the separated child Lajos R., and Mrs. Palocz and her eleven-year-old daughter. Mrs. Palocz locked herself in a wooden hut that had no heating, and the IRC cut off electricity on Wednesday, December 18, and they also had no food from that day. Lajos R. left the camp on the evening of December 22 to live with a family in Limerick—a move in contrast to Lajos H., the other separated child remaining in the camp, who was sent to an industrial school (see chap. 4). The Baracskai family of six departed on Thursday, January 8, 1959, after which the camp remained empty apart from Mr. Murphy; his assistant, Miss Clancy; and army personnel. They were due to leave once the accounts had been finalized.[32]

Following the departure of the Hungarians, Knockalisheen was a ghost camp during the few weeks the IRC spent winding up its affairs and carrying out its own audits of the camp accounts. They had spent over £130,000 during those two years, which meant that the Hungarian collection of over £150,000 had not been exhausted. Throughout the 1960s and up until 1972, the remaining money continued to be spent on the remaining Hungarians for paying school and university fees and providing interest-free loans to people wishing to start a business or those experiencing financial difficulties.[33] The army, aided by the Irish Red Cross, carried out an audit to finalize the cost of repairs and alterations for the two-year Hungarian occupation of the camp. There was also an auction at the camp at the beginning of February 1959 during which one thousand blankets, five hundred mattresses, one thousand pairs of sheets, pillowcases, four hundred chairs, medical supplies, boots, clothing, hardware, and kitchen equipment were on offer to the public. The auction was well attended, with buyers coming from as far away as Cork and Donegal to view and buy the eight hundred lots of eight thousand items left at the camp. Knockalisheen closed officially on Monday, February 2, 1959, when the Irish Red Cross, in a short, wordless ceremony, handed the keys back to the army, represented by Lieutenant Colonel Joseph Dundon of the Twelfth Battalion, Sarsfield Barracks Limerick. Mr. Murphy; his assistant, Miss Clancy; and Mrs. O'Shaughnessy, the interpreter, left the camp following the ceremony, and Mr. Murphy said he would make a statement concerning his future with the Red Cross at the Red Cross meeting in Ennis the following evening.[34]

O Canada! Our Home and Native Land

As mentioned, Canada had been cautious in its response to the refugee crises unfolding in Austria but changed direction due to the pressure of public sympathy for the Hungarians. Minister for Immigration Mr. Pickersgill stated on November 16, 1956, that Hungarian refugees who had a "reasonable prospect" of being able to earn a living in Canada would be admitted but only if they satisfied medical requirements for migration to Canada.

Parliamentary opposition and the conservative press protested this position as being "selfish." The initial plan for Canadian officials to screen Hungarians in Austria for admittance was unviable as selection would have impeded the flow of people out of the camps, whereas the Austrian government had wanted to move people as quickly as possible. At an emergency session of the federal parliament on November 26, the minister explained:

> It does no great harm to anyone to be sent to Switzerland, Sweden, Germany or some other adjacent country from which he could go back home without too much trouble and where he can remain while he makes up his mind. They told us that what they wanted was to have the United States, Canada and Australia deal promptly with those people who had indicated that they were interested in going to one of those countries. They told us that they would send such people to us, and that is the way the thing has been proceeding so far.

Thus, Mr. Pickersgill explained the resettlement process outlined in the ICEM document presented to Hungarians in Austria. His enthusiasm for admitting Hungarians followed his visit to Austria in December 1956, when he saw firsthand the demographic of the refugees—young, healthy, and skilled—who were welcome in Canada.[35]

Federal, state, and local resources contributed to the effort to resettle Hungarians in tandem with the voluntary sector, such as the Canadian Council of Churches, as well as aid from Canadian Hungarian organizations.[36] Canada had waived the usual immigration formalities and even used commercial planes to facilitate the flow of refugees from Austria; by the end of 1957, it had accepted an estimated 37,000 Hungarians for resettlement. NATO was aware that this number included 958 students.[37] Almost the entire staff and students of the faculty of forestry of Sopron University relocated to the University of British Columbia and with another contingent, the technical group, to the University of Toronto.[38] Consequently, the Hungarian refugees represented an immediate and also future source of skilled labor. This is not to say that resettlement proceeded smoothly, as Mr. Pickersgill admitted during a parliamentary debate on the matter:

> I believe that up to the present we in Canada have been able to provide adequate reception for everyone who has arrived, perhaps not quite as nice as we sometimes would have liked it, but it has been pretty satisfactory, thanks, not nearly so much to the government as to the great generosity of the Canadian people, for which I am sure everyone in the house is grateful; and I have no doubt that if more facilities are needed in one way or another they will be provided either by the federal government or by provincial and local authorities,

and I hope in large part by voluntary agencies. Up to the present the facilities have been adequate to meet the flow but this present week is going to see the biggest flow yet of Hungarian refugees across the country.

News filtered back to Knockalisheen as people wrote of their experiences in their new country to their compatriots.[39]

Early communication in September 1958, some two weeks after the two contingents had left Knockalisheen, did not depict the new destination as a country where everything was easily obtainable: only one had so far found work in Canada. Another, faced with the immediate magnitude of making a new life from nothing, commented positively on his experience in Ireland: "It is only now I realise what a wonderful place Ireland is. I can't tell you much now, but the Irish camp is the best in the world." Alongside this regret, it came as a shock to find that Hungarian refugees received no pocket money in Canada and had to accept family separation, even if temporary, and, in Woodstock, New Brunswick, board with English residents. Added to these indignities was the news that employment was not easy to obtain and that the Hungarians would probably have to wait until the spring of 1959 before finding work. Such information had a positive effect on those remaining in Knockalisheen, and an official commented, "They realize they're not too badly off here, they have their pocket money as well."[40] Just over a month later, in the middle of November, Mr. Murphy was able to say, "As a matter of fact, I had a letter the other day from Bela Kis-toth. He still regrets that he had to leave Ireland, where he had such a wonderful time and met such nice people."[41]

Once the camp emptied, correspondence still continued, with Sister Immaculata serving as the link between Hungarians in Canada and the ones still residing in Knockalisheen. Mr. Kukk, the former camp leader, wrote to her soon after his arrival to say, "We are living alone in our Immigration building. I am no working. I am very sorry we came in Canada. Eva no goes to school here. We are unhappy here." The Hungarians did not immediately forget their sojourn in Ireland, and individuals and families corresponded with Sister Immaculata for many years, exchanging greeting cards and presents and, in longer letters, writing about the significant aspects of their lives. These glimpses into the early lives of families and their children in Canada present the difficulties and the successes of (re)settling into their new homes: the immediate stress of finding work, finding a home, and placing children in schools; and for the children, after the anxiety of making sense of their stay in Ireland, came another adjustment to a new culture, as well as maintaining ties with old friends and making new ones.[42]

Mária, a former pupil at the school in Ballynanty, wrote to Sister Immaculata about the immediate circumstances of the Hungarians after their arrival in Canada:

> I'm very sorry that I did not write to you a long time ago but we were in St John in the camp and I have nothing write to you from there. Now we are in Ottawa I am writing this letter from our house. We arrived in Canada on Szep 2 at 3 o'clock. The joarney was very long but it was nice we were in the air plane the 16 ours that is a long time. I were in Saint Jonh in school there were sisters there were very nice to me. That was a catholic school. I was in the VIII grade. It was very hard for me but it well be esayer later on. I will go to school here on monday. I will go to the grade VIII. My sister Anna will go to the grade IV. My father has a job not in a factory it is on the road he is making the roads. he has a good money for that. We have a nice home. We have two rooms a kitchen a bath room toilet and we have one more room but I dont know what is that room name. Here is a hungarian catolic priest he is very nice he do everythings for as what he could do. He got very much clothes and we got table chairs beds blankets pillos seets plaits cups and alot home mor thing. The catholic church is very good to us. Here is near me Sipaki Gyoni and some more Hungarian family who is from Ireland. I will write to you their address. Boda family is in Edmunston. They are very well Irene and Thomas is in a convent sister is teach them their is EIRIS sister. I will write to you their address. Dako is in Saint John they are well to the parents are working. Bodas Sipakis and Gyonis father working too they have lovely home too. Lipoczi Besenyödi is in Toronto I don't know any more about Lipoczi Besenyödi. I heard that Mr. Sarvary has not work but they have money because he was working for one year in Ireland. I forgot P Kukk they are in Ottowa too they are very near to us. I will get their address. I think Murányi Németh is in Mongton I don't know any more of Murányi and Németh Zoltán is in Fradincton. I don't know where is Károly Mária Ötvős Mária.
>
> Dear sister don't think that I did forget you because I write my first letter only now I always pray for you. . . . I will never forget Ireland I will never forget the Knockalisheen camp. I always thinking about the camp and the school you did teach much nice thing too us. You were very nice to us. Your friend who will never never never forget you and who always pray for you.

The information about individuals and families that Mária supplied meant that Sister Immaculata could, in turn, relay such news through her own correspondence as she received letters from England, Australia, and the United States as well as Canada. She served as a conduit for people to keep in touch, particularly children who would probably have not been able to stay in contact with friends who moved to different countries.[43]

While letters may have become less frequent over time, some people followed events in Ireland and continued their correspondence with Sister Immaculata. In 1966, Mr. Kukk wrote at Christmas, and he still retained fond memories of Ireland: "Thank you very much for your letter, and the beautiful stamps. We are very well. The children are doing very well in school. Yes they are groing quickly. Or are we getting older? I never forget the Saint Patrick's Day I spent with Mr. Murphy. And I never found anyone like the Irish."[44] Likewise, a letter from Ottawa in 1971 referred to good memories of Ireland: "We hear about the trouble in the North. We always listen to the news anxiously. We pray there will be peace and that communism will not find a place in Eire, we are afraid for Eire because we know what it would be like. We remember Ireland fondly." The sojourn in Ireland was a deep and long-lasting memory for some.[45]

Once people left the camp, Sister Immaculata wrote to them, including in Hungarian, and likewise received correspondence where some English was followed by Hungarian:

> Bocsánat a rosz angol irásomért. Külön köszönjük a Magyar sorokat és szentképet . . . hála Isten minden jól vagyunk és ugyaneszt kivánjuk Önnek is. Kérjuk hogy továbban is gondoljon ránk, mi is mindig szeretettel gondolunk Önre és az Ir népre akik olj sok segitséget adtak, nekünk és menekült honfitársaiknak. A jó Isten áldja meg! [Apologies for my bad English writing. We thank you for the lines of Hungarian and the holy picture. . . . Thank God we are all well and we wish you the same. Please continue to think of us, we will always think of you with love and the Irish people who gave so much help to us and our refugee comrades. May the good Lord bless you! From O family.]

While people made the effort to write in English, they could also rely on Sister Immaculata's understanding, given that she had made the effort to study and learn some Hungarian. Some of the correspondence between Sister Immaculata and families who had settled in Canada lasted into the first decade of the twenty-first century.[46]

Language: From Hungarian to English to French

Arrival in Canada meant further changes to people's sense of self as adults and children had to make the effort to integrate into different spaces such as school or work. This was not always easy, as suggested by Gabriella, one of Sister Immaculata's pupils, who wrote from Montreal: "Here where I go to school I do not have as much friends as I used to have in Ireland. Even my teacher cannot be compared with you. You always helped me when I asked.

I would like to thank you for teaching me to speak English all I can. I didn't learn anything else here except how to spell them a little better. My mother and father and brothers mention you, especially when it comes to our homework." She proceeded to write about still speaking and writing a little Hungarian, but this "little Hungarian" was in competition with an English- or French-language education system and would, over time, remain little.[47]

Edit, who worked in a hospital, wrote:

> There in the hospital is everybody is French, and now I must learn the french, it is very dificold for me because now I learn the french and the English. I remember when we were doing the Christmas play I was very happy and now how we come here and I can't do nothing just vork and to learn the frence and the English. I'm very busy with that, because it is very difficult for me, but now I can speak a little bet I will wright you one or two frence. Je suis fatigué. Va a la maison. Bonjour. Maman je vais dormer and Merci beaucoup and I can speak more.

Additionally, she encountered the combined religious and linguistic fault lines of Canadian society: "I worked in a hospital I came away from their because there was a sister who was very angry with me allways, because I can't speak france and after when she saw how I learned the france she said why are you protestant why are you not catolic and I said will be not catolic again I will be protestant forever and sister did not like it how I say that but I was very angry." Edit might have submitted to the pressure to conform and be Catholic in Ireland, but she discarded this aspect of herself in Canada and was quite prepared to let Sister Immaculata, at a safe remove, know these frustrations.[48]

Sailing to Australia

The Hungarian refugees who went to Australia were, in general, fortunate, as the Australian government did not impose restrictions and they arrived in a period when jobs were plentiful. Many Hungarians were soon in the position of being able to practice their trade or profession or even take up two jobs in order to make ends meet. They also benefited from the help and expertise of Hungarians who had arrived postwar, and many made significant contributions to Australian public life.

At the beginning of her voyage to Australia with her family, fourteen-year-old Erzsébet wrote to Sister Immaculata from the "Hungaryan Hostel" in London:

> The food here very, very good. Here are 45 Hungaryan people who will come to Australia on the same ship with us. We can't go to my sister for visit because

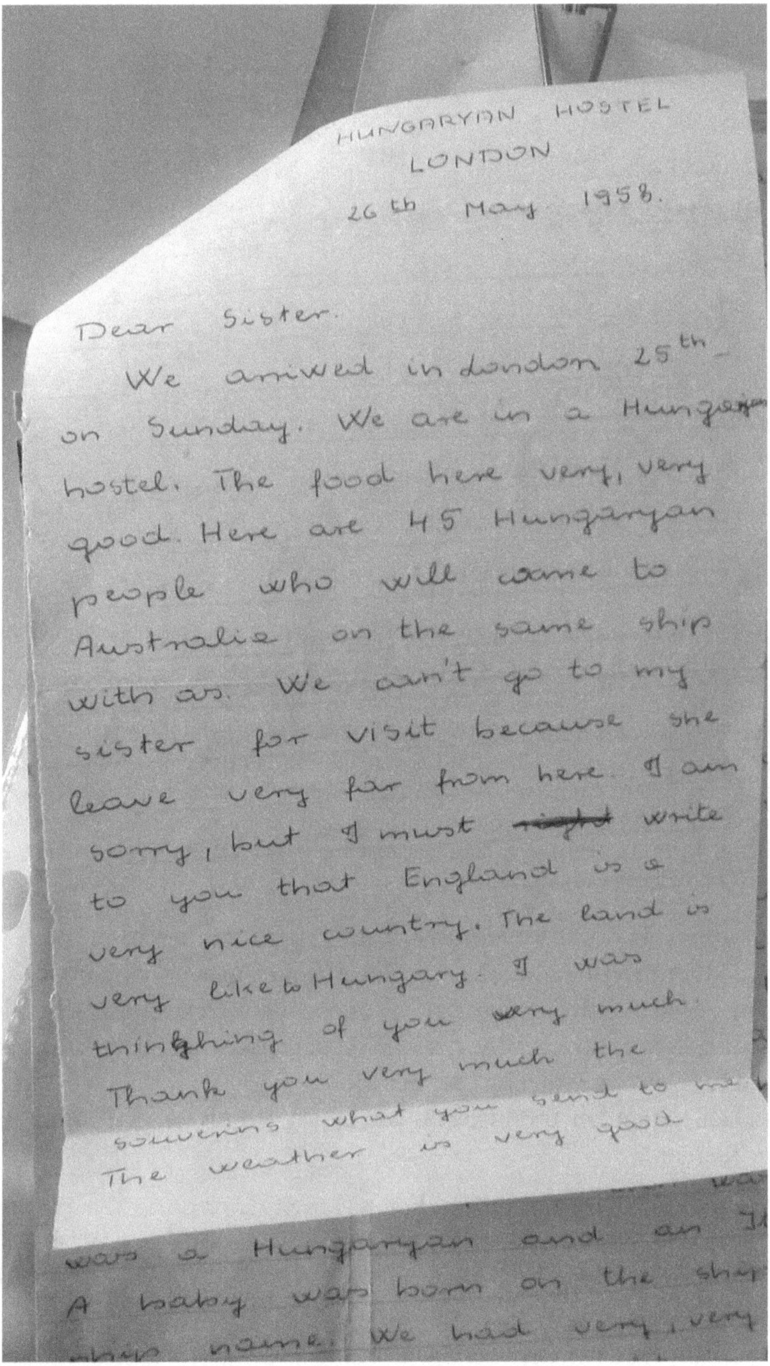

HUNGARYAN HOSTEL
LONDON
26 th May 1958.

Dear Sister.
We arrived in London 25th on Sunday. We are in a Hungary hostel. The food here very, very good. Here are 45 Hungaryan people who will come to Australia on the same ship with us. We can't go to my sister for visit because she leave very far from here. I am sorry, but I must write to you that England is a very nice country. The land is very like to Hungary. I was thinking of you very much. Thank you very much the souvenirs what you send to me. The weather is very good.

was a Hungaryan and an I
A baby was born on the ship
name. We had very, very

Fig. 6.2. A letter from London to Sister Immaculata. Source: Sister Immaculata Collection MCA.

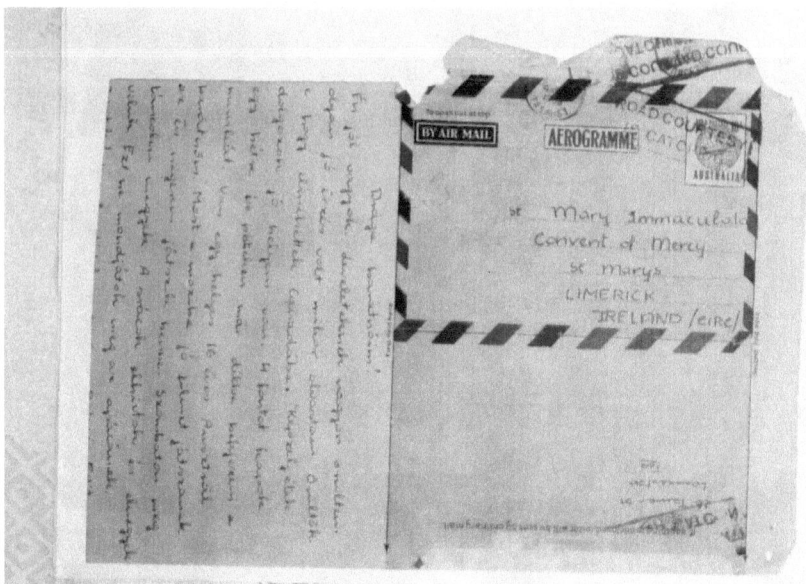

Fig. 6.3. Letter to friends via Sister Immaculata. Source: Sister Immaculata Collection MCA.

> she leave very far from here. I am sorry, buét I must write to you that England is a very nice country. The land is very like to Hungary. I was thinghing of you very much. Thank you very much the souverins what you send to me. The weather is very good here the sun shining and the rain is not raining. I should like to be in Australia very soon because the journey is long. . . . I will write to you again from the ship.[49]

Sister Immaculata was an admirer of de Valera, and her admiration grew stronger after meeting him; she must have spoken to her young pupils about the evil English and the fight for an independent Ireland. Erzsébet, however, felt free to contradict the nationalist narrative that Sister Immaculata cleaved to so strongly throughout her life.[50]

Erzsébet kept her promise and wrote two months later from Launceston in Tasmania:

> We arrived in Tasmania on the 3th July. The city is very nice where we leaw. Near to our house is a very nice park and a river. My mother is still at home, because she can't get work. Here is winter now and to much people can't get work at this time. The journey was very long, but very nice. The ship was nice and clean. The food was not the best. Every day was something on the ship, one night danc and the other night cinema. I was going every day to school

> on the ship. I had two very nice Hungarian girl friend. About 200 people was Hungaryan on the ship. Yugoslav, English, Italian, Finn, German and Hungaryan was on the ship. We were 1600. Oh I forgot to write about the mass. Every morning at half past seven was mass. On the ship was a Hungaryan and an Italyan priest. A baby was born on the ship. She got the ship name. We had very, very hot time too, and I was swimming. We bought in Aden a very nice and a very big carpet for £5. We were sick and we were in bed for 1 week. The Indian ocean was very cross. It was terrible we can't eat. I wright for the girls too, and I am waiting for your answer.

Erzsébet then switched to Hungarian in the letter to inform her girlfriends that she had finally arrived in Tasmania, knowing that Sister Immaculata would share the news in Knockalisheen.[51]

This correspondence flowered briefly as Erzsébet wrote about her new life in Australia and reminisced about her friends back in Knockalisheen, her school days in Ballynanty, and her feelings for Ireland:

> When I got your letter I was very happy. I'm glad the Hungaryans can go to Canada. I am very well here, and I am working in a clothing manu factory. I have an electric machin. The first time was very hard when I begen to learn how to sow. I get £4.6 shillings every week. I bought my first shoe with high hill. My mother is working too. She is housekeeper. She has a very good place the lady who is there like her very much. She get 5 pounds for a week. Dear sister how are you? Are you working very hard? I am thinking of you and from the girls very much. I saw a film from Ireland I was very happy when I saw Dublin and the Nelson pillar. I said to the girls I was here. I hear eiris music often in the radio. How the girls? Are they happy because they can go to Canada? I am finishing my letter because I am going to school now. I'm waiting for your letter.

Once again Erzsébet wrote to her friends in Hungarian, sharing other aspects of her young life, which perhaps were not suitable for Sister Immaculata's eyes:

> Drága barátnőim! Én jól vagyok. Leveleteknek nagyon örültem olyan jó érzés volt mikor olvastam Önűltők e hogy elmehettek Canadábe. Képzeljétek dolgozok jó helyem van. 4 fontot kapok egy hétre és pénteken már délbe befejezem a munkámat. Van egy helyes 16 éves Ausztrál barátnőm. . . . Szombaton meg táncolni megyek. A srácok elhivtak és elmegyek velúk. Ezt ne mondjátok meg az apácának. [My dear (girl) friends! I'm well. I was so pleased to get your letters, and it was such a wonderful feeling when I read that you could all go to Canada. Just imagine, I'm working in a good place. I earn four pounds a week, and I've already finished my work by midday on Fridays. I'm friendly with a nice sixteen-year-old Australian girl. I'm going dancing on Saturday. The lads invited me, and I'm going with them. Don't tell this to the nun.]

3

I wright for the girls too, and I am waiting for your answer.

God bless you with love from
your student who will never
forget you.

Erzsébet Szatmáry.

Drága barátnőim!

Hála Istennek szerencsésen megérkeztünk Tasmániába. Én jól vagyok és szeretek itt a lányok akikhez jöttünk nagyon kedvesek hozzám. Most lemezeket rakok fel és úgy írom a levelet. Drága Babykám és drága Editkém hozzátok szólok először. Nektek majd írok külön olyan sok ujságom van a számotokra. Lesz miről írni. Drága Edithém hogy vagy hogy vannak a szüleid. Sokat gondoltam rátok az uton. Csak itt lennél lenne egy jó barátnőm. Itt nincs magyar lány csak mi. Fiú az van elég. Drága Babykám hogy vagy? Irt-e már neked a Gizi? Mi az ujság a táborba? Hova jártok szórakozni? Én megyek minden héten 2-szer mozitba. Táncolni nem megyek, megfogadtam, hogy csak akkor megyek, ha a 16 évem betöltöttem. Drága Katikám és Marikám írjatok sokat, mert a hajón lehet fogjuk Én is lefogytam, majd írok addig is maradok. Baby és Edit megkaptátok a lapot amit küldtem.

Milliō csók hű barátnőtök a messze távolból. Zsika!

Fig. 6.4. Letter in Hungarian. Source: Sister Immaculata Collection MCA.

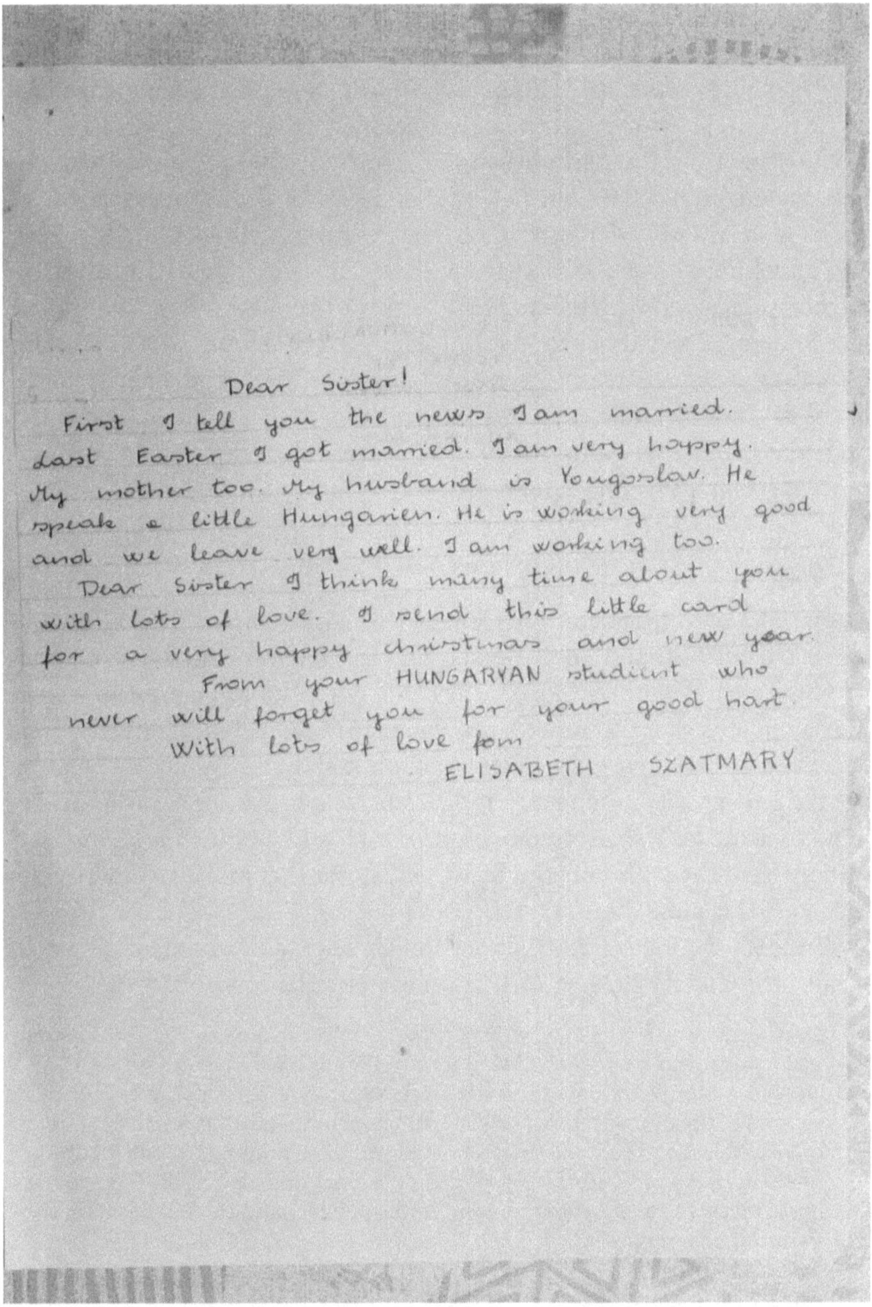

Dear Sister!
First I tell you the news I am married.
Last Easter I got married. I am very happy.
My mother too. My husband is Yougoslav. He
speak a little Hungarien. He is working very good
and we leave very well. I am working too.
    Dear Sister I think many time about you
with lots of love. I send this little card
for a very happy christmas and new year.
        From your HUNGARYAN student who
never will forget you for your good hart.
With lots of love fom
            ELISABETH   SZATMARY

Fig. 6.5. Letter with news of marriage and holiday greetings. Source: Sister Immaculata Collection MCA.

Nuns, therefore, were not privy to all secrets. Erzsébet did write again to tell Sister Immaculata that she was married and that her husband was Yugoslav but spoke a little Hungarian. At this stage, she had anglicized her name to Elisabeth. They settled in East Sydney.[52]

Writing from Canberra, Australia, Annamaria said that they had "settled down completely in our new life" and that "it doesn't seem new at all but as if we always lived just the way we do now. Writing to you is my last and only link with the 10 months we spent in Ireland." She contrasted her memory of Ireland with the different climate of her new home: "Australia is nice but I mean to go back to Ireland if I have a lot of money when I grow up. Here if you want a patch of green grass, you have to live the water sprinkler on all day, not like in Ireland where everything is always green." Here, too, there are strong and positive memories of Ireland, even as life in Australia proceeded smoothly for Annamaria and her family.[53]

Waiting to Set Sail to America

Mária, who corresponded from Canada with Sister Immaculata, also wrote to her friends Kati and Bobby Jónas, who had moved from Knockalisheen to Finglas in Dublin, although they did not plan to stay permanently. Mária updated them on other Hungarian families, including the news that Mr. Venglas had died falling off a roof while fixing a TV aerial. This was not the only fatality among the Hungarians, as another man was murdered in Melbourne for a small sum of money. Mr. Kukk wrote in 1960 that Solű Mihaly "had £25 with him and he was killed for that money. We were very sad to get this news."[54]

In 1960, the Jónas family left for the United States by sea, and Kati described the journey to New York in detail in a letter to Sister Immaculata:

> Dear Sister, we arrived to New York on 5-4-60. Our journey was beautiful and had a great time on the line. We were coming for six days and three of them was quite stormy. In those three days were very sick especially I. We could not go even to the dining room. I was in bed for all day. The other three days were lovely. We used to go up to the deck. I tell you the truth I was a little bit afraid up their. In the night time we went up to the longe and play cards or watch the horse races. In the morning we went to the pictures and in the afternoon the swimming pool is open.
>
> New York is a very big city and it is nice too, especially in the night time when we can hardly see from all the lights that are on the streets. In the first times we were afraid to go anywhere in case we might get lost but now we got use to it. The weather is beautiful here. The highest tempeture was 85% since

we are here, on that day we were to hot that we could not go on the street. They told us that the time will come when it will be 95%.

Kati was not a prolific letter writer, and, like some of her compatriots, she seems to have slipped easily into a new way of life. She did write again to Sister Immaculata to say she had gotten married to another Hungarian and settled in New Jersey. Mária married later as well, also to another Hungarian. Most marriages that were relayed to Sister Immaculata occurred with other Hungarians or Canadians with Hungarian heritage.[55]

Conclusion

Of the original group of 548 Hungarians, just over 140 went to Canada, and over 60 remained in Ireland, some of them waiting to depart elsewhere. Anna Letoha considered that many more Hungarians might have stayed but "*itt nem volt lehetőségek*"—there were no opportunities in Ireland for the many Hungarians with technical skills let alone for the factory workers or miners. She remembered studying English with her husband in the Botanic Gardens, as it was warm in the greenhouses, and watching television for pronunciation. She worked not only to be employed but also to become Irish and was a keen observer of how to do things the Irish way. As a family they strove to give back to Irish society from gratitude and also helped others. For instance, Anna came across a young woman, Gizella Pinter, who was working as a domestic for Lord Moyne and paid for her to study and obtain a qualification at the Grafton Academy. Gizella left the world of cleaning behind and became a qualified junior designer; she also left Ireland and went to the United States, having married an American soldier.

Many of the Hungarians who remained in Ireland thrived and, according to Anna Letoha, were in a position to take advantage of the expansion of the Irish economy in the 1960s. In Dublin, Henrik Spelter worked for Bewleys; Ilona Helfferich found a position with Dr. Robert Collis, the pediatrician who had worked in Belsen at the end of the Second World War. Her two older children, Boglárka and Ibólya, attended the Dominican Convent in Cabra. In Cork, Peter Bora remained with Seafield Fabrics, and in Waterford, Powers Bakery employed László Hudak. Of the separated children, sixteen-year-old István was expelled in April 1958 from Multyfarnham, the agricultural college run by the Franciscans. Two months later, Lady Leitrim employed him in Mulroy, county Donegal.

Mr. Murphy resigned from the Red Cross and issued a lengthy statement concerning his decision:

> I knew that it was the most important assignment of my life and that it would be very difficult. I was not dismayed, because I knew that I could rely on the voluntary workers from Clare and Limerick. There was no organization at all when the refugees arrived except that made by the Army to feed and house them. The voluntary workers were wonderful and it is due to their great sacrifices that records were taken and some order restored. The permanent staff were recruited after some weeks and things put on a business basis. Trouble followed trouble with the refugees as they were all suffering from the after-effects of the revolt in Hungary. Then came the hunger strike, which, in my opinion, could have been avoided if only some person came from headquarters to speak to and reassure the refugees as to their future. During this time of anxiety I found myself alone and although I sent many appeals to Headquarters I received no assistance to end the strike. It was only when I contacted the late Bishop of Limerick, Most Rev Dr O'Neill, that any effort was made to end this unfortunate strike. . . . Misunderstandings between the refugees and Red Cross occurred and orders and counter-orders were given which would not have reflected credit on the Society. The camp is now closed and I truthfully say that it would never have been such a success but for the almost 100 per cent loyalty of the staff, Army, Garda and Red Cross workers. A big debt of gratitude is due to those, and the society should have made some effort to retain some of their services, but they were dismissed with little thanks.[56]

Resigning with Mr. Murphy, and for the same reasons, was Mr. Turton of Greystones, who had acted at times as deputy controller at Knockalisheen.[57]

Following this "bombshell," which was "dropped in Red Cross circles" at their annual social gathering in the Queens Hotel in Ennis, an official of the Ennis branch of the IRC said that a special meeting the following week would call for a full public inquiry into the running of Knockalisheen camp by the IRC executive.[58] While the call for a public inquiry was made, perhaps as a gesture of solidarity with Mr. Murphy, it would have been difficult to realize. The Austrian Red Cross Society had already presented a Medal of Merit to the president of the Irish Red Cross Society, awarded for the outstanding assistance offered by the Irish Red Cross to the Austrian Red Cross Society and to Austria after the 1956 Hungarian Revolution.[59]

In retrospect, Mr. Murphy was drawing one part of his life to a close. He had moved from Wicklow to Ennis in county Clare to find work at the age of twenty-one and secured employment with the post office. He had joined the Irish Red Cross as a part-time interest but by 1956 held the roles of area director of the county Clare branch and membership of the national executive in Dublin so that this part-time interest had clearly developed into something deeper. Mr. Murphy's daughter, Elizabeth, provided a context for the depth of his involvement with the Irish Red Cross and with the 1956 Hungarian refugees in Knockalisheen:

> I was 20 when my father became Camp Commander at Knockalisheen. My mother had died when I was four and my Sister had died when I was 10. Both had contracted TB. These were difficult years for both my father and myself.... I believe that having suffered the loss of his wife and daughter at such an early stage in his life he could empathise very strongly with the Hungarian refugees who were also suffering losses in their lives. I believe he gave his full commitment to looking after the Hungarian Refugees as best he could during their stay in Ireland.

Years later, after the closing of the camp, Sister Immaculata would at times visit Mr. Murphy, as the bond of having worked with the Hungarians endured between these two individuals. Likewise, even as time passed, Mr. Murphy, in his role as a grandfather, would speak to his grandchildren about his time in Knockalisheen.[60]

In contrast, Leslie Bean de Barra, Mrs. Tom Barry, the chair of the Irish Red Cross Society, remained in that role for twenty-three years, having first been appointed in 1950 by president of Ireland Sean T. O'Kelly. She had joined the organization at its establishment in 1939, later becoming prominent in the Cork area leadership. Her leadership style was "professional, perhaps even semi-regimental, as was evident from her habit of wearing the society's uniform," which she wore when representing the Irish Red Cross in public, an affectation not repeated by any other holder of that office. Lehane writes that "within government departmental circles she was considered formidable and formal and known as someone who had an aversion to any interference from civil servants (in Ireland and internationally)." Under her leadership, the Irish Red Cross undertook new initiatives and was a highly respected organization, but she could also be difficult to work with, and despite the success of innovations such as the water safety program, success did not result in greater levels of recruitment to the society. Consequently, as "the leadership appeared to operate with tunnel vision ... the general membership of the society [was] allowed continually to decrease."[61] Eventually, before her term of office ended, Leslie de Barra was removed from her role as chair in 1973 at the age of eighty-one, following the unexplained involvement under her leadership of the Irish Red Cross in the Arms Crisis.[62]

Notes

The epigraphs are from *Commission on Emigration and Other Population Problems 1948–1954* (Dublin: Stationery Office, 1955), 131, and "Statement on Refugees 'Would Be Going to US' Belief," *Irish Press*, January 14, 1957, 3.

1. "Conference on Hungarian Refugees, June 1957," report, 7 and 8, TSCH/3/S11007 E.
2. "Conference on Hungarian Refugees June 1957," report, 9, TSCH/3/S11007 E.
3. "Refugees Unwilling to Move," *Irish Press*, August 1, 1957, 1.
4. Editorial, *Irish Examiner*, August 23, 1957, 6.
5. "Refugees: A New Move," *Irish Press*, August 22, 1957, 7.
6. "Refugees Unwilling to Move," *Irish Press*, August 1, 1957, 1.
7. Camp Committee and Families, July 28, 1957, TSCH/3/S11007 D.
8. Editorial, *Irish Examiner*, August 23, 1957, 6.
9. "Refugees Pay Tribute to Victims of Rising," *Irish Press*, October 24, 1957, 7; "Thoughts on Anniversary," *Evening Herald*, October 23, 1957, 6.
10. "Hungarians Are Still Anxious to Get Away," *Irish Times*, January 2, 1958, 7, ITDA.
11. Mária, letter, April 1958, Sister Immaculata Collection, Mercy Archive, henceforth SICMA.
12. "Canadian Emigration Team for Dublin," *Irish Independent*, March 20, 1958, 2.
13. Ambassador Kiernan, report to the Secretary of the Department of External Affairs, December 3, 1956, DFA/419/33/18.
14. Questionnaire for Canada, DFA/6/419/33/15.
15. "51 Refugees Fail Test for Canada," *Irish Times*, April 1, 1958, 5, ITDA.

    The question of who was a communist is not as easy to disentangle as a simple binary distinction would imply. Some people joined the Communist Party out of conviction; some remained committed to the cause, and others became disillusioned but retained membership; many more joined, if they could, in order to "get on" in life, as being a party member was advantageous.

16. "Knockalisheen Send-Off for Hungarians," *Irish Independent*, August 27, 1958, 9; "Camp Farewell to Refugees," *Irish Press*, August 27, 1958, 5; "Moving Scenes at Farewell Concert to Hungarians," *Limerick Leader*, August 27, 1958, 1.
17. "Farewell to Refugees," *Irish Press*, August 27, 1958, 5.
18. "Hungarians' Final Preparations for Departure," *Limerick Leader*, August 30, 1958, 1.
19. "Hungarians Prepare to Leave," *Evening Herald*, August 29, 1958, 5; "Leaving £25 a Week Job," *Evening Herald*, September 1, 1958, 2.
20. "Camp to Close?" *Irish Press*, April 23, 1958, 7.

    At that point, there were approximately 205 in the camp, with 7 people leaving for Argentina and 13 for Australia under private sponsorship schemes. Approximately 200 had already left unofficially for Britain, gone to other countries through the sponsorship of family or friends, or had returned to Hungary.

21. "Hungarians 'Must Have Own Homes,'" *Irish Press*, November 7, 1958, 7.
22. "Refugees Slow to Take Houses," *Irish Independent*, November 3, 1958, 8; "Houses Offer Turned Down by Refugees," *Irish Press*, November 4, 1958, 1; "Refugees' Flat Refusal to Leave Camp," *Irish Examiner*, November 5, 1958, 9; "Hungarian Refugees in Dublin," *Irish Examiner*, November 8, 1958, 8.
23. "Refugee Camp Hitch," *Irish Independent*, November 15, 1958, 7.

24. "Homes Sought for Refugees," *Irish Independent*, November 13, 1958, 3.
25. "Red Cross Seeks Accommodation for 40 Refugees," *Irish Examiner*, November 17, 1958, 4.
26. "Red Cross Request Council to Provide Housing for Refugees," *Limerick Leader*, November 26, 1958, 4.
27. "Refugees May Live in 150-Year-Old Georgian house," *Irish Examiner*, November 18, 1958, 9.
28. "Refugees Not to Get Georgian House," *Irish Examiner*, November 25, 1958, 9.
29. "Castleconnell and Hungarian Refugees," *Limerick Leader*, November 29, 1958, 1.
30. Cornelius Tobias, a Hungarian physics graduate from the Technical University in Budapest, went to Berkeley in 1939 as a Hungarian American Fellowship recipient. He was a founding member of Berkeley Lab's Donner Laboratory, where he worked for over forty years. He was a pioneer in studying the biological effects of cosmic rays and other ionizing radiation and made major contributions to fundamental radiobiology, space radiation biology, and cancer therapy with heavy ions. His work had major impacts throughout the world. Mr Kozak had clearly been underemployed as a waiter, and there would have been no future for him in 1950s Ireland.
31. "Two Refugee Families Sail for US Today," *Irish Examiner*, December 13, 1958, 9.
32. "Refugee Camp Officially Closed," *Limerick Leader*, December 15, 1958, 1; "Refugee Locks Herself in," *Irish Examiner*, December 19, 1958, 9; "One Family Left at Knockalisheen," *Evening Herald*, December 22, 1958, 3; "Last Hungarians to Leave Camp," *Irish Independent*, January 8, 1959, 3.
33. Lehane, *Irish Red Cross*, 196.
34. "To Audit Accounts of Refugee Camp," *Irish Times*, January 12, 1959, 7, ITDA. "Refugee Camp Property," *Irish Press*, February 5, 1959, 5; "End of the Refugee Camp," *Irish Independent*, February 3, 1959, 4.
35. Quoted in Thomas J. Kiernan, Irish ambassador Ottawa, report, to Department of External Affairs, December 3, 1956, DFA//419/33/18.
  For further background see the historical perspective in Troper "Canada Hungarian Refugees" and for the interaction between politics and the media see Dreisziger, "Biggest Welcome Ever."
36. Thompson and Bangarth, "Transnational Christian Charity," 299–309. The article also mentions rumors concerning religious preference on the part of church organizations, 301.
37. NATO, "Hungarian Refugee Students," 1.
38. Madokoro, "Refugee Ritual," 257.
39. Canada House of Commons debates, fifth session, 22nd parliament, vol. 1, January 8 to February 11, 1957, 25. https://parl.canadiana.ca/view/oop.debates_HOC2205_01/27?r=0&s=1.
40. "Refugees—Only One Got Work," *Sunday Independent*, September 14, 1958, 4.
41. "Remainder of Refugees May Be Housed at Castleconnell," *Limerick Leader*, November 17, 1958, 1.
42. Undated letter, Mr. Kukk, SICMA.
43. Mária, October 26, 1958, SICMA.
44. Mr. Kukk, Christmas greetings, 1966, SICMA.
45. Magdolna, December 1971, SICMA.
46. Undated letter, O family, SICMA.
47. Undated letter, Gabriella, SICMA.

48. Undated letter, Edit, SICMA.

The transformation of Montreal into a primarily French-speaking city occurred during the 1960s and 1970s; prior to this period, the city functioned in English. The majority of Hungarians settled into an English-speaking environment and would, in general, have had little requirement to immerse themselves in French and become proficient. In contrast, the reference here to French occurs in a workplace context, which required some study to gain proficiency in the language.

49. Erzsébet, May 26, 1958, SICMA.
50. This strength of nationalist feeling surfaced during the interview with Sister Immaculata.
51. Erzsébet, July 24, 1958, SICMA.
52. Undated letter, Erzsébet, SICMA.
53. Undated letter, Annamaria, SICMA.
54. Undated letter, Mr. Kukk, 1960, SICMA.
55. Undated letter, Kati, SICMA.
56. "Aftermath of Closing of Hungarian Refugee Camp," *Limerick Leader*, February 4, 1959, 1.
57. "Knockalisheen Camp Controller Resigns from Red Cross," *Irish Independent*, February 4, 1959, 8.
58. "Former Refugee Camp Controller Resigns," *Irish Examiner*, February 4, 1959, 9.
59. "Red Cross Medal for President," *Irish Independent*, October 31, 1958, 14.
60. A note on Mr. Murphy written by Elizabeth K.
61. Lehane, *Irish Red Cross*, 167, 189.
62. The Arms Crisis occurred in 1970 and relates to the dismissal of Finance Minister Charles Haughey and the Minister for Agriculture and Fisheries Neil Blaney. Allegedly, they used state money for the purpose of importing arms for use in Northern Ireland by the IRA. For an in-depth exploration of Leslie de Barra's leadership of the Irish Red Cross, including her links to the Arms Crisis, see Lehane, *Irish Red Cross*, 213–26.

PART III

7

COMPARISONS, LEGACIES, AND CONCLUSION

> Dear Sister Immaculata
> I don't know if you still remember me . . . I remember you quite well from how you taught us in school.
> I'm on my summer holidays and am working as a lifeguard at a nearby pool. As you probably know the 1967 World Exhibit is being held here in Montréal and I'm making good use of it by going there whenever I can.
> I have just turned 16 and am going into my second last year of high school at John F. Kennedy High with fairly good marks. The hardest subject I found was Latin but I think I can struggle through with it for another 2 years. I miss Eirie with its brooks, hills covered with shamrocks and miles of rocky fields. I often think of them and you, so I took the time to write.
> All the family, my mother, father . . . and myself wish you best of health.
>
> —Imre to Sister Immaculata, August 6, 1967

> When we look back in 10 years' time, we may ask ourselves how we allowed the system to exist. The debate sparked by the Tuam mother and baby story should prompt us to reflect on the manner in which all children are treated in Ireland, not merely citizen children.
>
> —Dr. Geoffrey Shannon, quoted in *Children Direct Provision*

Comparisons: Introduction to the International Dimension

From an international perspective, the Hungarian refugee crisis, precipitated by the 1956 revolution, demonstrated that large numbers of people, recognized as refugees, could be resettled effectively without lengthy screening, particularly once states became flexible with their admissions criteria. The scale of the resettlement endeavor, which expanded out of Europe, is seen in the countries of resettlement in table 7.1.[1] The 1956 refugee crisis was also the first major resettlement to occur under the legal framework provided by the 1951 Convention and the Statute of UNHCR.[2] The mandate of the UNHCR ensured international protection for refugees and finding a permanent solution to their predicament by either voluntary repatriation, resettlement in other countries, or integration in their countries of residence. All three solutions occurred in the case of the Hungarians, with 11,273 repatriated voluntarily, 180,000 resettled, and 7,900 integrated in Austria and 675 in Yugoslavia.[3] At the time, UNHCR was a young organization with no high commissioner, but James Read, the deputy commissioner, managed the crisis, which, as UNHCR has commented, began chaotically. Fortunately, there were plenty of empty army camps, complete with barracks, left vacant the previous year by departing British, American, French, and Russian occupying forces in Austria. Austrian Interior Minister Oskar Helmer had requested help from UNHCR and ICEM and the two international bodies; Helmer and his staff and the League of Red Cross Societies and other NGOs formed a committee in Vienna with UNHCR as the lead agency. Auguste Lindt's appointment came in December 1956, and he was determined to clear the camps containing Hungarian refugees. He had been horrified at the sight of two or even three generations of postwar refugees, where adults and children had not known a normal life apart from the refugee camps in Austria.

The United States of America received the greatest number of refugees. By May 1, 1957, the United States had received 32,075 Hungarian refugees, and the Joyce Kilmer Reception Center in New Jersey, a former army camp, closed just over a week later. Like Knockalisheen, it had been a disused army camp, and like Knockalisheen it had multiple administrative layers. Unlike Knockalisheen, the camp was technically not in the United States, so "the army and the US border patrol guarded the outside perimeters to be sure that no one entered the US illegally." Hungarian refugees had arrived "relatively unprocessed and unscreened according to US immigration law. Therefore the legal fiction was that the camp was 'outside' of the country." Consequently, the first impression was of a "camp surrounded by armed guards," which created anxiety among the refugee arrivals until "they became comfortable with the camp environment."[4] The other significant difference was that many Hungarians desired to resettle or join relatives in the United States, which became the beneficiary of the skills brought by academics, highly trained technicians, and students, many of whom made

Table 7.1. Hungarian refugee numbers, May 1, 1958

	Arrivals from Austria, Yugoslavia	Other countries	Departures	Repatriation	
Argentina	930	230	–	–	1,200
Australia	10,990	2,360	50	–	13,300
Austria	380a	179,670b	154,370	7,730	18,200c
Belgium	5,910d	100	270	340	5,400
Brazil	1,560	60	–	–	1,600
Canada	26,320	10,620	–	130	36,800
Chile	270	10	–	–	300
Colombia	210	20	–	–	200
Costa Rica	20	–	–	–	20
Cuba	10	–	–	–	10
Denmark	1,390	–	260	70	1,100
Dominican Republic	580	–	400	–	200
France	12,690	50	3,350	670	8,700
Germany	15,410	160	720	310	14,500
Iceland	50	10	–	–	60
Ireland	540	–	–	–	500
Israel	2,060	30	–	–	2,100
Italy	4,020	10	2,610	160	1,300
Luxembourg	230	20	20	50	200
Netherlands	3,750d	60	220	480	3,200
New Zealand	1,030	20	–	–	1,000
Norway	1,510	10	10	30	1,500
Rhodesia and Nyasaland	60	–	–	–	60
Spain	20	–	–	–	20
Sweden	6,780	20	30	250	6,500
Switzerland	12,720	180	1,310	1,020	10,600
Turkey	510	–	320	20	200
Union of South Africa	1,320	20	–	–	1,300
United Kingdom	21,670g	30	5,790	1,410	14,500
United States of America	37,740	400	90	350	37,700
Uruguay	40	–	–	–	40
Venezuela	640	50	–	–	700

Table 7.1. (*continued*)

	Arrivals from Austria, Yugoslavia	Other countries	Departures	Repatriation	
Yugoslavia	–	19,900h	16,400	2,800	700i
Others	–	–	–	–	500
Total	–	–	–	15,800j	184,300j

Source: UNHCR report, January 1, 1959.
a. Arrivals from Yugoslavia.
b. Of whom an estimated 178,900 directly from Hungary.
c. Including natural increase of about 300.
d. Including an estimated 100 directly from Hungary.
g. Including an estimated 750 directly from Hungary.
h. Arriving from Hungary.
i. Considered to be integrated in Yugoslavia.
j. Totals are rounded.

outstanding contributions to American intellectual, social, and cultural life. NGOs and other services mobilized to absorb the Hungarians as quickly as possible into American society. Tracy Voorhees, the director of the President's Committee for Hungarian Refugee Relief (PCFHRR), considered that all Hungarian refugees "have been permanently resettled," and "no comparable mass movement into America has ever occurred in so short a time—of persons all penniless and few of whom could speak our language."[5]

Given the Cold War context, fears of large-scale communist infiltration did not occur, although a small number were returned to Hungary. President Eisenhower had established the PCFHRR to coordinate the various NGOs and federal and private-sector bodies. Tracy Voorhees ensured acceptance of the Hungarians by organizing positive media stories and advertising campaigns identifying them as "New Americans" who would readily adapt to the American way of life.[6] Overall, the Hungarian refugees integrated well into their countries of settlement. The Hungarian diaspora communities—with those in the United States and Canada being two of the oldest—offered membership to their networks of clubs and societies, which tended to focus on cultural heritage. This focus, relating to individual identity and a sense of belonging, offered individual interpretations of ethnic identification, with its salience depending, for instance, on family ties, language across the generations, evolving political contexts that would permit

Fig. 7.1. Postcard from Hungary to Sister Immaculata. Source: Sister Immaculata Collection MCA.

return to Hungary, and memory. Following the amnesty in 1963, return was to visit family remaining in Hungary and, in later years, for retirement or even higher education for the following generations.[7]

From Contemporaneous to Current Policy

In Ireland, in early December 1956, there was government interest in the steps taken by other countries to deal with the reception and resettlement of Hungarian refugees. Irish legations and embassies in Europe received an inquiry about limits on the number of refugees received and arrangements for "their registration as aliens, maintenance and employment." If the ensuing reports received a significant level of attention in relation to the Hungarians in Knockalisheen, then it remains unclear as to how they contributed to subsequent actions.[8]

The Berne legation responded that Switzerland had reacted swiftly to the crisis, just as Austria had requested, and "because of the speed factor, Swiss immigration formalities in Austria were entirely dispensed with. Anyone who wanted to go to Switzerland was put in a train and, although most of the refugees had papers, these were not necessary for their entry into Switzerland. . . . Instead, the immigration and health formalities were carried out in the reception centres." Four thousand refugees were already in Switzerland and employed by December 1956, and the Swiss labor market was ready to absorb the ten thousand refugees the government had committed to. In a report on the potential impact of the Hungarians, the Office Fédéral de l'Industrie described the position of the labor market and the economy as highly favorable, with the optimistic forecast that by the middle of January 1957 the refugees would all be employed. This was despite factors such as the significant number of intellectuals who had arrived in Switzerland in contrast to manual workers, a noticeable language problem, and the future impact of the Hungarian worker presence on the traditional, seasonal Italian labor supply: "It is thought that the Hungarians, despite the language drawback and the preponderance of intellectuals, can be suitably settled after a period of adaptation and will constitute a much more economic labour force than an equivalent number of Italians who are in the habit of working in Switzerland during the summer months only and sending their earnings home." The Hungarians, therefore, were viewed as a positive addition to the Swiss economy, especially as money would not be leaving the country in the form of remittances sent abroad. One drawback to the lack of original screening was the appearance of a number of Hungarian secret police and communist agents who began to act as agent provocateurs once they began work in a factory or other enterprise. They were, however, considered to be "very naïve in the way they operate" and easily identifiable, particularly as other Hungarians were "eager to cooperate" in handing such individuals over to the police.[9]

The Federal Republic of Germany was in a completely different position as a steady stream of refugees, averaging 25,000 per month, continued to arrive from East Germany; in addition, 186,000 German refugees and 28,000 foreign refugees were also waiting for homes. In accordance with its *Vertriebenen-Gesetz* (refugee law), Germany also had the additional obligation of receiving ethnic Germans from any part of Europe, including Hungary. The government placed no quota limit on Hungarian refugee numbers, and 10,000 Hungarians were already in Germany, of whom 2,000 were of German ethnicity. Three refugee camps, originally used as transit camps for Eastern Zone and other refugees, were used as reception centers solely for the Hungarians. They registered in these camps with a questionnaire used to establish identity; the right of asylum could be granted according to the *Asyl-Verordnung* (asylum regulation) on the grounds of persecution on political, religious, or racial grounds. In general, the Hungarians spent two days in these transit camps before being dispersed to camps throughout the

Länder (administrative regions), in accordance with previously agreed upon ratios. Those with special training or skills, such as miners, went straight from the transit camp to employment while those in the camps in the Länder had another interview where the single and able-bodied were "immediately given work in factories, building and other spheres of employment."[10]

Holland, in contrast, received a mixed group of Hungarian refugees—three thousand for permanent resettlement and two thousand in transit to their final destination in Canada, and the Dutch were making arrangements with the Canadians for a fairly speedy departure. In Holland, use of the word *camp* was contentious because of its connotations, evoking "the atmosphere . . . [and] most unpleasant memories of former concentration camps." Due to such sensitivities, the suggestion to the government was to lodge the two thousand transit refugees, who would be arriving gradually, in private houses; this proposal from local authorities took into account the fact that the waiting period could extend from weeks to months prior to departure for Canada. The refugees who were settling permanently in Holland arrived in Utrecht for screening and after a few days left for recreation centers, buildings placed at the disposal of the government by companies, or the one camp that was in use. Here they formed committees to assist in determining the kind of employment being sought by their compatriots. The Hungarians were kept occupied in the centers with games and organized excursions, and those who liked to keep busy could perform odd jobs as there was no formal employment without official sanction. As the majority of the Hungarians were either skilled or unskilled industrial workers, they presented no employment problems; the contingent of miners had the choice of working in mines in Limburg or being employed in other industries as "there is a shortage of labour in many branches of industry."

Two issues emerged in Holland, one centering on religion and the other being a clash between individual action and authority. Ninety percent of the Hungarians in Holland were Catholics; the other 10 percent were of other faiths or none. The Dutch, as was customary, organized them into four groups—Catholics, Protestants, Jews, and others—with the expectation that, in accordance with Dutch practice, they would form separate communities: "Each group has its spiritual advisers. The members of each group are of course enabled to live as a community in accordance with their religious belief; but this aggregation is alien to the Hungarians and there are signs of discontentment. They would prefer to live as a crowd—as in their own country irrespective of religious persuasion or, indeed, any other differences between them. This is, so far, an unsolved problem; and the authorities fear it may become one with a political complexion."[11] The "political complexion" was straightforward: postwar Hungarian society did not, in general, differentiate according to religion. This social transformation, in contrast to the fascist years and all the horrors of the latter part of the Second World War in Hungary, appears as a significant and positive legacy of the communist state. One of the initial appeals of communism in Hungary had been the emphasis on people rather than race or religion; this attitude remained as a preference and surfaced in Holland.[12]

The second matter related to individual agency and autonomy as opposed to listening to and obeying authorities:

> There is a growing tendency among the refugees to "take matters into their own hands" in some respects. One of them, a professor, is the leader. Under his inspiration, centre committees wish "to dictate" to the authorities how their community life in the Netherlands, etc, shall be regulated. In this respect, there occurred to my mind criticisms I had heard on many occasions of Italian communities in USA. They do not desire to be integrated: separate Italian communities constituting "a piece of Italy abroad." The Dutch authorities are fearing something similar here in the case of the Hungarian refugees.[13]

The Dutch authorities had little to fear about Hungarians not integrating but were not recognizing the effect of the uprising on individuals and on the interpretation of the Dutch attitude to religious freedom. Hungarian refugees had witnessed, and some had participated in, the daring, if spectacularly temporary, transformations wrought up and down Hungarian society by the sudden explosion of free expression and free association instead of the strict prescriptions endured during the Stalinist years. As events had unfolded so swiftly, including flight and resettlement, whether temporary or permanent, there may well have been a temporary safety of staying among compatriots who could understand the psychological toll of these upheavals: Who else could have comprehended this sudden shared history? The Hungarians' interpretation of the Dutch attitude of leaving people to form communities according to religious affiliation could easily have been understood as ghettoizing people, as had occurred with so many Jewish people during the Second World War.[14]

From these embassy reports, it is clear that each country had a slightly different perspective on the Hungarians, and their settlement and integration and the practicalities of resettlement were attended to with urgency and concern. Strikingly evident is the speed with which Hungarians obtained jobs in buoyant, postwar European economies that could readily absorb the sudden inflow of thousands of people. As Hungarians moved swiftly into employment, there was no long-term need for the maintenance systems put in place nationally for Hungarian refugee relief. In France, the government and NGOs supported the Hungarians on arrival. A Hungarian received two thousand francs from the state on arrival, after which the Red Cross supplied pocket money while Secours Catholique (Catholic Aid), the main Protestant organization la Cimade, and Le Service Sociale d'Aide aux Emigrants (Social Service for Emigrant Aid) also made financial contributions. The French government set up a French National Committee for the Reception of Refugees with representation from the Ministries of Foreign Affairs, Interior, Defense, Health, Labor and Social Security as well as trade unions, employers, and the main relief organizations. The state and NGOs combined to arrange for reception and employment and for the "integration into the French community of as many as wish to settle permanently in France."[15]

In contrast, in Ireland, first, planning did not appear to be as coordinated. Though the Irish interdepartmental meetings had taken place, Mrs. Barry had clarified its position of having no decision-making powers during the first meeting. Second, the attitude of leaving everything possible in the hands of the Irish Red Cross exposed the organization's shortcomings in the face of managing a refugee camp long-term, when in fact those same shortcomings could be directly attributed to no direction from government. Third, from the information received, particularly from Holland, it is clear that the Hungarians would neither be gratefully docile nor obey without question and that they had their own views regarding camp activity. This knowledge, coupled with some level of understanding, could have spared the combative attitude that arose between the Irish Red Cross and the inhabitants of Knockalisheen had it been made available to the organization. It would also have made clear that punitive actions would make little contribution to understanding and that disapproval of a democratically chosen representative from the refugee cohort could only arouse suspicion. Furthermore, all this information would have contributed to a different approach to the hunger strike, a serious matter not taken lightly by the Hungarians, who felt all they had left to use as protest was their bodies. Katalin Pálmai Bánki writes that the Hungarians at Knockalisheen lived "in a type of forced separation totally subordinated to the host society," as did the *Victory* voyagers at Rockgrove.[16] It appears inevitable that unhappiness would arise with, for instance, the denial of individual agency, the remoteness of government, and the expectation of docility while waiting in a liminal space. Such problems have surfaced with the arrival of other so-called program refugees who came to Ireland by government invitation, such as the Vietnamese in the 1970s, whose integration did not always progress smoothly.[17] Similarly, lack of communication or placing obstacles in the way of personal effort or agency and disregarding the voices of refugees, even after *appearing* to listen to them, have continued in the policy of Direct Provision, where Knockalisheen continues to serve as a center housing asylum seekers.[18]

Legacies: Children, a Fault-Line in Irish Culture

A question arises as to what legacies remain from the almost two-year Hungarian presence in Knockalisheen, especially as contemporary Irish society, in its diversity, bears little resemblance to 1950s Ireland. These legacies include agency, communication, listening to the voices of refugees, and changes in the position of women and children. As the sojourn for the majority was temporary, the immediate conclusion would appear to be that there is no such legacy. However, this is not the case, as differences remained and continue to the present, are long-term, have policy continuity, and are laced, for example, with the long-lasting effects of the many abuses visited upon children. As with punishment in Daingean and Letterfrack, other Hungarian children experienced the long-standing cruelty of a historical attitude to adoption and, like their counterparts in Ireland, were left to piece together their family backgrounds.

A toxic blend of stigma, prejudice, and righteousness created a legacy of distress for one Hungarian family that had remained in Ireland. Sándor Chikány and Ilona Lukács married in the Presbyterian Church in Limerick on December 17, 1956, and Ilona gave birth to their daughter in 1959. A joyous family occasion soon turned into a long-lasting tragedy as Sándor Chikány had a breakdown resulting in a spell in a mental hospital in Ennis followed by St. Ita's in Portrane, where he remained until 1976. He was eventually repatriated to Hungary into the care of his sister, a nurse. His wife, Ilona, remained behind in Ireland and had to fend for herself, alone, with no family support, in a strange country. Equally, there was no support forthcoming from Knockalisheen Camp due to her situation—namely, being the wife of an ill man at a time when mental health was a deeply stigmatized matter. A record of her as one of the last inhabitants of the camp reads, "Ilona Chikany, nylon stocking repairer, Calvinist: this woman's husband is in the Ennis mental hospital. We cannot give her a good reference." Poverty, with its accompanying lack of status, coupled with prejudice regarding a woman on her own, albeit a married one attempting to provide for herself and her young child, resulted in the eventual loss of her daughter. Elizabeth was placed in the care of "Auntie," who ran an orphanage, Westbank, in Greystones in county Wicklow.[19]

Adeline Mathers, or "Auntie," a former nurse, was a born-again Christian who ran Westbank from 1946 to 1999. Her methods were highly unorthodox. As a private Protestant orphanage, Westbank took no state support, and Auntie kept trustees at arm's length, well away from the thirty to fifty children present in the orphanage at any time. Instead she preferred to procure funding by parading children in her care in Orange Order lodges and churches, mainly in Northern Ireland. She would dress up her charges for their parade through these halls and meeting places in order to collect donations for their upkeep. Children ranged in age from babies of a few months to teenagers, with most leaving when they were age sixteen or seventeen, though some remained well into their twenties, unable to detach themselves from Auntie and her orphanage. Adeline Mathers brought the children up in a strict religious atmosphere, and the children went to school and then returned to the home so that in many ways they remained separated from the outside world. The atmosphere in the home was compounded by fear as Adeline Mathers was happy to beat the children in her care; one example was her use of an electric cord. She played destructive psychological games, setting children against each other; had her favorites, who, in contrast, retained fond memories of the home; constantly demeaned them; and used her power and knowledge to withhold family information from them. Children were malnourished and made to labor within the orphanage.

Illegal adoptions occurred at Westbank, with children being taken illegally from the state to Northern Ireland and even as far away as Scotland. When children asked questions about family, Adeline Mathers could lie with ease, so many children had long-lasting battles later when they wished to ascertain their identities and have knowledge of their families. She would rename the children in her care, altering both first and last names, with all the children bearing one surname: Mathers. However, the children became aware of their family identities when they sat entrance exams for secondary school, particularly Newpark Comprehensive School, which refused to accept children bearing the Mathers surname. As a consequence, children were instructed to complete their application forms by *not* using Mathers but another name, a new surname that they were suddenly confronted with. Some children discovered that they were not the only one with this new surname and realized, for the first time, that this must be their family name, that they had siblings in the home run by Adeline Mathers, and that she had kept these truths from them. Even when some returned as adults, Adeline Mathers could still lie about origins and family relationships. Colm Begley was known as Robin Mathers in Westbank and discovered his family name when he went to Newpark School. Unknowingly, he grew up with a brother, a fact that came out many years later. He said of his years in Westbank, "It's always in my subconscious mind there, it's always in the back of my mind, like, every day goes by, I'd be thinking of it, you know, if things were different, if things were different with my family, with my brother. . . . It'll be a long time before I forgive."[20]

Elizabeth grew up in Westbank as Elizabeth Mathers. She had a very restricted childhood, as "we were very much enclosed, we stayed home" apart from going to school.[21] Part of this childhood included living in fear; Elizabeth said that Auntie "was good with her fists." Adeline Mathers was also good with words. Elizabeth said she could never understand the sense of abandonment she felt when she was told "your mother doesn't want you," though to her "that never rang true," as she remembered her mother visiting:

> I do recall as a teenager, I know Auntie never loved me and Auntie was going "you're just like your mother." I slapped Auntie that day, I was seventeen . . . how dare you! You're blackening her name. . . . It was kind of cathartic. It was my plan to get out of that home, you had to escape. There were older girls (who did not manage to get away). . . . To this day I can honestly say I actually can't blame my mother for leaving me. I do know that what happened behind closed doors, she would not have known what was going on. We were warned to smile when people were coming.

Initially at Westbank and subsequently, after she left the home, Elizabeth made several discoveries about her family. First, while in Westbank, she was taken to sit a school entrance examination and was told her surname: Chikány. While no adult confirmed this fact, she realized that she had grown up with a sister, as there was another girl in the home with the same surname: "Behind that there is a big sorrow. I will never know how others knew their family and siblings, to me that's just beyond cruel. . . .

We were pitted one against the other [and this included her sister] and not encouraged to make attachments. It's amazing my sister and I are so close now, we forged and made that link and it was hard to learn to be a big sister to her. That shouldn't have happened either, being brought up like that behind closed doors." Her second major discovery was her Hungarian heritage and her real name: "I would have been nearly twenty-two when I found out, I've always never felt Irish. . . . I was devastated because growing up at school I had a love of history, European history. We were never allowed to say we were different. I did feel different, when you don't know anything concrete you can't voice it. . . . I didn't know who I was. . . . Having your own name. I grew up as Mathers. Elizabeth Teresa Chikány. . . . I was the daughter of Sándor Chikány." Elizabeth had a Hungarian heritage, long denied, including family in Hungary.

Over time, Elizabeth was able to piece together parts of her story, which included obtaining documentation from Bray Gospel Hall, finding out information through chance encounters, and being helped by strangers. Fortunately, at one point she contacted the Irish Red Cross, who in turn contacted the Hungarian Red Cross on her behalf. This proved to be a life-changing event as her mother's family had lodged a letter searching for Ilona's daughter. At the age of fifty, Elizabeth first went to Hungary, saw photographs of herself as a child, and discovered that Adeline Mathers had received letters for several years from her family. She neither gave those letters to Elizabeth nor replied to them: she returned them unopened to the sender. Elizabeth was never able to find her mother, Ilona, who at one time worked in the kitchen of the school Elizabeth attended; Elizabeth became aware of the presence of Ilona, as her mother was identified to her. Elizabeth was then moved from the school.

For children growing up away from Hungary and away from the social networks forged by family and friends, the desire to understand where they came from and why and to reconnect with their country of birth in a meaningful way can, as with Elizabeth, be the accompaniment of a lifetime. Families keep secrets and make decisions with regard to their children, and yet, regardless of the wisdom of the decision or its intentions, at the time the child may still want to know that secret. In Hungarian families, such secrets can encompass a hidden Jewish heritage and fear of reclaiming that heritage. Other families may retain different secrets to do with past lives. One such secret was kept from H for almost a lifetime. She never knew who her father was, as her mother remarried while she was very young and felt that

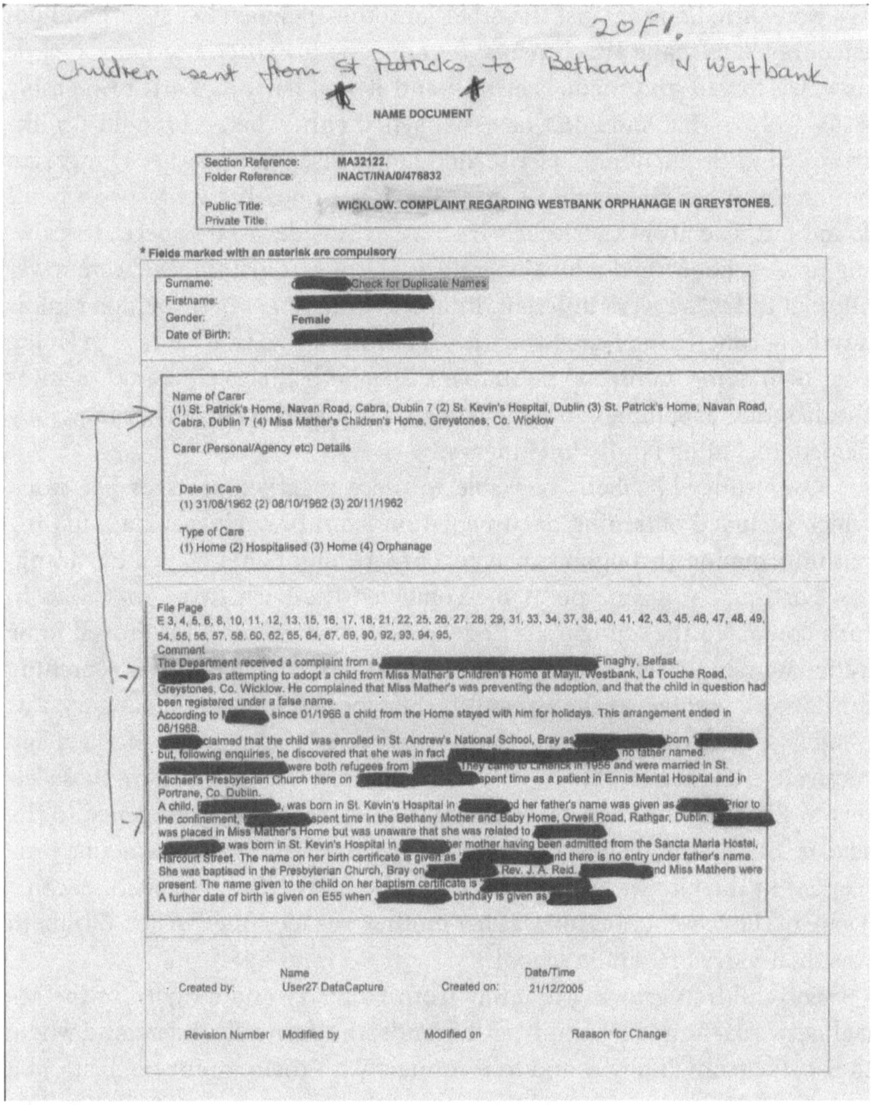

2OF1.

Children sent from St Patricks to Bethany & Westbank

NAME DOCUMENT

Section Reference: MA32122.
Folder Reference: INACT/INA/0/476832

Public Title: WICKLOW. COMPLAINT REGARDING WESTBANK ORPHANAGE IN GREYSTONES.
Private Title:

* Fields marked with an asterisk are compulsory

Surname: [redacted] Check for Duplicate Names
Firstname: [redacted]
Gender: Female
Date of Birth: [redacted]

Name of Carer
(1) St. Patrick's Home, Navan Road, Cabra, Dublin 7 (2) St. Kevin's Hospital, Dublin (3) St. Patrick's Home, Navan Road, Cabra, Dublin 7 (4) Miss Mather's Children's Home, Greystones, Co. Wicklow

Carer (Personal/Agency etc) Details

Date in Care
(1) 31/08/1962 (2) 08/10/1962 (3) 20/11/1962

Type of Care
(1) Home (2) Hospitalised (3) Home (4) Orphanage

File Page
E 3, 4, 5, 6, 8, 10, 11, 12, 13, 15, 16, 17, 18, 21, 22, 25, 26, 27, 28, 29, 31, 33, 34, 37, 38, 40, 41, 42, 43, 45, 46, 47, 48, 49, 54, 55, 56, 57, 58, 60, 62, 65, 64, 67, 69, 90, 92, 93, 94, 95,
Comment
The Department received a complaint from a [redacted] Finaghy, Belfast.
[redacted] as attempting to adopt a child from Miss Mather's Children's Home at Mayil, Westbank, La Touche Road, Greystones, Co. Wicklow. He complained that Miss Mather's was preventing the adoption, and that the child in question had been registered under a false name.
According to [redacted] since 01/1966 a child from the Home stayed with him for holidays. This arrangement ended in 06/1968.
[redacted] claimed that the child was enrolled in St. Andrew's National School, Bray as [redacted] born [redacted] but, following enquiries, he discovered that she was in fact [redacted] no father named.
[redacted] were both refugees from [redacted] They came to Limerick in 1956 and were married in St. Michael's Presbyterian Church there on [redacted] spent time as a patient in Ennis Mental Hospital and in Portrane, Co. Dublin.
A child, [redacted], was born in St. Kevin's Hospital in [redacted] d her father's name was given as [redacted] Prior to the confinement, [redacted] spent time in the Bethany Mother and Baby Home, Orwell Road, Rathgar, Dublin. [redacted] was placed in Miss Mather's Home but was unaware that she was related to [redacted]
[redacted] was born in St. Kevin's Hospital in [redacted] her mother having been admitted from the Sancta Maria Hostel, Harcourt Street. The name on her birth certificate is given as [redacted] nd there is no entry under father's name. She was baptised in the Presbyterian Church, Bray on [redacted] Rev. J. A. Reid. [redacted] nd Miss Mathers were present. The name given to the child on her baptism certificate is [redacted]
A further date of birth is given on E55 when [redacted] birthday is given as [redacted]

	Name		Date/Time
Created by:	User27 DataCapture	Created on:	21/12/2005

Revision Number	Modified by	Modified on	Reason for Change

Fig. 7.2. Complaint about registering a child under a false name. Source: Elizabeth Chikány.

her child should grow up with the knowledge of having one father. While family and friends may have known the secret, it was never divulged, even after the deaths of both her parents so that, for H, it remained an unfulfilled desire. H did not have enough information to enable her to make inquiries in Hungary, and it was only recently that an old family friend finally revealed the secret to H during a visit to Budapest. There was no shocking secret, only information about a man who had loved a young woman working in his laboratory, helped hide her Jewish background during the Second World War, and married her. H was their daughter, a fact she discovered in her seventies. Lost legacies, therefore, are an integral part of the disruption of family life, family ties, and former social networks once a person becomes a refugee. Consequently, a specific focus on children appears integral to any study of refugees. This study has shown how children can both thrive and suffer as refugees as well as carrying the effects of having been a refugee over a lifetime. In the Irish context, too few Hungarians remained to constitute a long-standing ethnic group, as has been the case in countries such as Canada, Australia, and the United States. The 1956 children who came to Ireland would have spoken Hungarian, and families would have enjoyed certain features of Hungarian culture retained in their respective homes. However, children born in Ireland did not speak Hungarian and were assimilated into Irish culture so that, eventually, any Hungarian heritage would have faded away into memory.[22]

The Policy of Direct Provision

There are similarities in the situation of the 1956 Hungarian refugees and the Direct Provision system that the Irish government established in 2000 to cater to the rise in people seeking international protection. Set in the framework of refugees being a problem, the policy was to disperse people so that no particular part of the country would face a burdensome disparity from people accessing state services. At its height Direct Provision served over 7,000 people, in contrast to the one camp at Knockalisheen, where the Irish Red Cross had a mandate to care for 548 Hungarian refugees; these facts may seem disparate, but there are points of similarity that demonstrate how attitudes toward the powerless continue to revert to notions of refugees being a problem, the need to see gratefulness, and the expectation of silence.

Initially, Direct Provision was intended as a short-term measure with people staying in a Direct Provision center for approximately six months while waiting for a judgment on their asylum application. However, this did not become the reality, and people spent years in the system, with the indeterminate nature of their "sentence" seen as the main contributor to its failings. Length of stay in such an environment correlates negatively with personal development or human capital such as learning or improving English; gaining skills, qualifications, or work experience; mental health; and social and cultural integration.[23]

Apart from a small number owned by the state, over twenty private companies have run their centers on a for-profit basis. A few are in urban locations, but most are in rural settings, and there is great variation among them as the buildings were originally hotels, hostels, nursing homes, guesthouses, or convents; a typical center does not exist. Bed occupancy is the accommodation criteria used, and this concept of occupancy results in strangers or family members sharing a bedroom, including children. With communal day rooms being uninviting spaces, bedrooms are multipurpose areas where children do homework or play and where adults also spend time so that there is "no private living space, homework/study space or storage space." Apart from a small allowance for individuals, Direct Provision is a cashless system, so food is served on the premises, and in general there are no individual cooking facilities apart from some communal kitchens where there can be queues waiting to prepare food. There are one or two "showcase" centers with family units and a self-catering option, but overall it is a centralized, institutionalized setting often resulting in apathy, accompanied by adverse mental health impacts and the dread of state-created dependency for those caught in this system.[24]

Over the years, NGOs have commissioned reports, academics have carried out empirical research, and the occasional politician has critiqued the system until, like the 1956 Hungarians, residents of Direct Provision centers began protests in 2014 in an attempt to be heard. Following these demonstrations, they formed the Movement of Asylum Seekers in Ireland, MASI, to create a platform for their voice. That same year, aspects of the Direct Provision service complaints procedure were found to be unlawful, and the government set up a working group chaired by Dr. Bryan McMahon that was to report to the government on improvements to the protection process, Direct Provision, and supports to asylum seekers. The McMahon report's remit was twofold: first, to improve existing arrangements in the processing of protection applications and, second, to show greater respect for the dignity of persons in the system and improve their quality of life by enhancing the support and services currently available, but with no significant increase in costs. As the remit focused on improvement and not on finding alternative solutions to the system, Direct Provision remains in place, though improvements have occurred following implementation of some of the McMahon report's recommendations.[25]

The length of time spent in the system exacerbates all other problems that arise in Direct Provision. McMahon identifies these as the uncertainty overshadowing people's lives; lack of personal autonomy over the most basic aspects of daily life such as cooking; lack of privacy and sharing with strangers; boredom and isolation; unemployment; the impact on children; the impact on families to parent and to live normal lives; the loss of skills and the creation of dependency; and the negative impacts on physical, emotional, and mental health.[26] Many of these themes find an echo in the experience of the 1956 Hungarians in Knockalisheen, where the most significant concern was that they were "being kept far too much in the dark about their own future" and that Ireland was not intended for their permanent settlement.[27] The 1956 Hungarians complained about the food, even though the adults received "full army rations." The camp stocked "all the well-known brands of baby foods, but the mothers will not use them."[28] There was no consideration of other cultural norms regarding what food to offer a child, whether freshly cooked or canned, nor the fact that apart from the communal mess hut, individual huts did not have anywhere to prepare and cook food. The ingenuity of developing homemade electrical appliances so that people had some measure of control over heating water or milk for children created friction with the Irish Red Cross, who turned off the electricity to punish everyone at Knockalisheen. The Hungarians felt the huts were unsuitable for long-term residency, particularly for families with young children. The rejection of this complaint was not born out by the facts: the army had retained the services of the camp doctor, Mr. McCann, as children had developed bronchitis during their first winter in Knockalisheen. Unemployment and boredom were also factors for the Hungarians, and rumor and gossip became daily occurrences at the camp. There was also concern about not admitting certain people to the camp, apparently due to their status as troublemakers. Any visitor had to check in and out of the camp and was not allowed to visit refugees in their huts without an invitation, as the Irish Red Cross did not want "to have people wandering in here and treating this place like a museum. Some people seem to think they have the right to go along and see anything they like."[29] Both sides had their justifiable points of view, but rapprochement became increasingly unlikely as the civilian camp management floundered when faced with refugees criticizing what was being done for them instead of expressing gratitude or remaining silent. The manned barrier at Knockalisheen meant visitors were subject to scrutiny, as has occurred in Direct Provision centers that have security guards manning barriers, with instances of visitor harassment.[30]

Direct Provision centers are open, without the obvious on-site presence of members of the defense forces or gardaí in uniform, as was the case in Knockalisheen. However, both have restrictions on movement: the 1956 Hungarians required a permit if they left the camp for more than twenty-four hours, and Direct Provision house rules restrict visitors to certain communal areas. The Hungarians were ready to go further with their claims as "a collection of one shilling a man was made amongst the refugees remaining in the camp to send two of their leaders on a delegation to bring their grievances to the notice of the government."[31] The dynamic of power relations in Direct Provision centers, however, is not conducive to complaint, as there is no independent process for addressing grievances, and the procedures favor the administration. Residents are effectively silenced. They *fear* making a complaint, especially as one administrative remedy is to label one a "troublemaker," which can result in immediate removal to a potentially more remote and even less agreeable center. Department of Justice officials made such a threat to one group who did not wish to leave their accommodation center.[32] Only a small number of complaints are made annually, and even the government agency working with people seeking international protection acknowledges that this is not evidence of satisfaction with the system. The Hungarians had received refugee status automatically. Today, people seeking international protection have to wait, and the indeterminate sentence creates apathy or worse in crowded Direct Provision centers. Recourse to the law courts has resulted in the ruling that some practices relating to employment, the invasion of privacy, and other aspects of house rules have been unconstitutional.[33]

With regard to children, the first positive note, in contrast with the 1956 Hungarian children, is that access to preschool and primary and secondary education is a right. However, poverty and social exclusion provide obstacles to a child's full enjoyment of all aspects of school life including creating full friendships, as there is no home to invite friends to. The NGO, the Irish Refugee Council, commissioned research that found poverty and social exclusion a year after the introduction of Direct Provision. The report detailed child nutrition concerns; parents buying extra food to supplement the Direct Provision diets of their children; extreme deprivation such as weight loss and even malnutrition in children; inadequate provisions for pregnant women and babies; overcrowding; and effects on psychological well-being and family life, among others. These points find echoes in the McMahon report, which notes that some children "complained of hunger," exacerbated by the fact that, after returning from school, children might have to wait until the prescribed evening meal in order to eat instead of having ready access to a hot meal or at least a snack. A family experiencing overcrowding might be offered better accommodation, usually in a different center, but this would mean uprooting the children from their school and, without having visited the new location, being unable to fully assess the overall benefit of such a move. The 1956 Hungarians could at least reject their proposed removal to McCann Barracks in Templemore as the camp representative had been taken there for a tour of its amenities and had returned unimpressed.[34]

Academic research and reports document the lives of children growing up in Direct Provision; some were born into the system and know no other life, even if they are aware that there are other ways to live, as evidenced by their peers in school. While school can provide a safe haven, it can also be the site of encounters with racism and bullying, with schools having to come to terms with diversity in contrast to a previously perceived homogenous classroom. Like some of the young Hungarians who fell into the industrial school and reformatory system, children in Direct Provision also face dangers, including being in proximity to so many other adults, a cause of concern to parents and child protection agencies.[35] The Faculty of Pediatrics in the Royal College of Physicians of Ireland called for the Direct Provision system to be abolished as "it cannot adequately meet the needs of children and their families in terms of security, family autonomy, nutrition and access to education and health services."[36] MASI has highlighted the fact that even though the government ignores their voice, there is a significant level of research documenting the effects of Direct Provision:

> If the Irish government will not listen to asylum seekers who have consistently called for Direct Provision to be abolished, at least listen to the experts. The Special Rapporteur on Child Protection, the UN's Committee on the

Elimination of Racial Discrimination, and the Faculty of Pediatrics at the Royal College of Physicians of Ireland are among bodies who have recently called on the Irish government to end the system of Direct Provision. Ignoring the plight of asylum seeking children who are trapped in state sponsored poverty that robs them of their childhood is a blatant act of cruelty.[37]

In contrast to 1956, when children were not heard in Irish society, there is recognition that children's experiences of Direct Provision warrant attention. However, this focus on children has come about belatedly. Between 2001 and 2009, there were fifty-eight separated children missing from care, with the state making little effort to trace them. In addition, the differences in care provision for asylum-seeking children in contrast to Irish children in care were considered racist in 2010.[38] Therefore, raising a voice or inclusion in consultations may not be enough to effect systemic change.[39]

Finally, just as there was a housing crisis in parts of Ireland in 1957, when people had to be rehoused from Knockalisheen, an accommodation crisis in contemporary Ireland has resulted in the Department of Justice attempting to procure further Direct Provision centers in rural or small-town settings. Resistance to strangers arriving in a locality occurred in both instances, and in contemporary cases the towns of Tullamore, Rooskey, Oughterard, and Cahersiveen all witnessed citizen protests. Part of these protests was a show of anger at the highhanded nature of the government in Dublin appearing to foist a fait accompli on citizens without going through a consultation process. Another aspect of these demonstrations is evidence of some hijacking of local grievances by people with far-right views. Social media contributed to this amplification of local grievance with the emergence of Facebook pages containing "a stream of racist, anti-immigrant rhetoric and 'Ireland is for the Irish' posts."[40] Evgeny Shtorn, who spent almost two years in Direct Provision, notes that the absence of far-right political parties is seen as a commendable aspect of Irish society. However, as he says, "the 'inexistence' of a far right movement here does not mean the lack of far right thoughts and institutions," as evidenced not only by the protests but by the very existence of the Direct Provision system.[41] In Cahersiveen Direct Provision Centre, some thirty residents began a strike similar to the 1956 Hungarian refugees' hunger strike as protest against conditions at the center. Over one hundred residents had been sent to the center in March 2020, following which some tested positive for COVID-19, so they had to stay inside for significant periods in rooms smaller than standard-size hotel rooms. However, the protest also focused on the lack of suitable nutrition for children, having nowhere to cook, and having "to beg" for basic necessities. As with the 1956 Hungarians, there was a government response, this time occurring within two days from the beginning of the hunger strike and accompanied by intent to immediately close the center. However, with the constant recurrence of the same issues in the same protests, the body of evidence favors neither the system nor the inaction of successive governments.[42]

Conclusion

This study asked the question, Who is a refugee? In the context of the 1956 Hungarian refugee cohort, Tracy Voorhees, appointed by President Eisenhower to lead the PCFHRR, provides an answer: "He is an average guy, about 28 years old, and he attended almost 10 years of school. He wants to go to work as soon as he can and he would like to continue his education. Almost half of the refugees are single males—less than 10% are single females."[43] While there is reasoning provided for this definition, it overlooks women, apart from the 10 percent of single women, who experience a "a double displacement—a physical displacement from the so-called home community and a symbolic and at times violent displacement from agency."[44] UNHCR published its first policy paper on refugee women in 1990. Yet, as this study has shown, the experiences of children and women cannot be ignored by the historical record, as it is precisely the historical context that produces specific experiences including, in the case of Ireland, referral to an industrial school or reformatory, the removal of children from maternal care, and the indulgence of illegal adoptions. Turning to the voices of refugees also reveals, over time, a more complex set of outcomes from the perspective of the 1956 Hungarians who came to Ireland. While most left, and while there had been misunderstanding, mistrust, and acrimony in the camp at Knockalisheen, there were also expressions of gratitude and a long-term fondness for Ireland. The increasingly negative aspects of the 1956 Hungarian refugees' sojourn in Ireland were due in part to perceptions at the time of the Hungarians as Christian warriors escaping the tyranny of communism and as grateful recipients of charity, and the fact that they lived up to neither of those two perceptions. Emma Haddad refers to refugees living in the space between states. The refugee camp at Knockalisheen was in sovereign space and yet, with their refugee status, the Hungarians were set apart so that even within the protection of the border they remained as

Other. The refugees began to live full lives following resettlement in their destination countries or escape from Knockalisheen into the community, to the promise of citizenship and a home. In this context, they remained bound by the concepts of nation and citizen, as indeed they were bound to the solution of integration into the country to which they fled or resettlement as repatriation, which was not a solution: at the time, communism was seen as enduring indefinitely. However, this is not to accept Agamben's assertion of "bare life" at a camp like Knockalisheen. The camp contained people who were creative in their attempts at finding work for themselves and ingenious in their fashioning of homemade electrical devices or illegally distilling a potent alcoholic beverage. Their agency is evident, as are efforts to make themselves heard.[45]

Who, then, are refugees, and what is *refugeeness* apart from a fuzzy and slippery concept, as Peter Nyers argues?[46] There is a historical context for *refugeeness*, as exemplified in this study. The Cold War heightened the relationship between nation, state and citizen; at the same time, the concepts of nation, state, territory, citizenship, and rights are under scrutiny, as are the founding principles of the modern international system with a view to their transformation. Until this transformation occurs, a refugee, as I was, would seek to integrate into existing systems—in other words, to seek citizenship and the enjoyment of mobility rather than long-term endurance of its consequences in a camp or detention center. In a spirit of optimism, I had selected a four-year university course with a mandatory year abroad: to enjoy mobility, I needed a passport, and to obtain a passport I needed citizenship. With my parents too fragile to engage with the state, I navigated those waters on my own. The metaphor of the sea entered chapter 1 of this book in relation to *refugeeness*, which does not end once the movement of refugees is over but rather reverberates over the life course; being or having been a refugee becomes part of one's many identities. Its salience will ebb and flow until it meets coarse discourses such as refugees and migrants being disease carriers, cockroaches, bogus asylum seekers, or economic migrants contrasted with that nebulous concept, the genuine refugee.

To conclude, the Irish government displayed remorse at its offer to take the 1956 Hungarian refugees. Peter Berry received a note for his private information stating that "on the direction of the Government," the Department of External Affairs "was investigating the possibility of dispersing as many as possible Hungarian refugees in Great Britain, Canada, the US and Australia." The Canadian option appeared to be a good one, and "if that came off the problem would be very largely disposed of."⁴⁷ Unfortunately, the Hungarians in Knockalisheen slipped further and further down the list of Canadian priorities, particularly given the decision to take a group of Hungarians in the UK. Another group in Denmark also raised the matter of being in transit with Canada as one of their preferred final destinations. The length of the Hungarians' sojourn in Knockalisheen fomented distrust alongside their hunger strike. Most egregiously, instead of an atmosphere that fostered trust and truth, and despite the Department of External Affairs having received documentation to that effect, there was long-term, constant disbelief of 1956 Hungarian refugees who had been assured of their active role in decision-making via the ICEM information leaflet issued in Austria. This disbelief was coupled with a denial of agency and attempts to silence them.

However, the few refugees who remained in Ireland managed to build lives for themselves, so overall the story of the 1956 Hungarians becomes more a complex portrayal than a black or white depiction. As Yên Lê Espiritu writes, "It is imperative that we always look for the 'something more' in order to see and bring into being what is usually neglected or made invisible."⁴⁸ Consequently, like all refugee stories, the history of the 1956 Hungarians in Ireland—whether remaining as future citizens, departing to other shores, adults or children—deserves to be visible, to be part of the story of the imagined community of the nation. Their inclusion adds to a greater level of diversity than presented in the grand narrative of Irish history; illuminates the treatment of all children in Irish society; and provides a place for refugee voices and experiences, the drama of their telling, and, significantly, their relevance for the present.⁴⁹

Notes

The epigraphs are from Imre to Sister Immaculata, August 6, 1967, SICMA, and Dr. Geoffrey Shannon, special rapporteur on child protection, quoted in *Children Direct Provision*, 2. The reference to Tuam relates to the Bon Secours mother and baby home in Tuam, which gave shelter to orphans and "unmarried mothers" who could give birth in the home. Catherine Corless, a local historian, discovered death certificates for nearly eight hundred babies and children connected to the home but burial notes for only two of them; she uncovered the scandal of the site of a mass burial. While it was the practice to inter the dead in unmarked graves in the grounds of such homes, excavation at the Tuam site in 2019 revealed a large number of human remains, mostly dating from the 1950s. The aim has been to test remains forensically with regard to possible identification followed by respectful burial of the remains.

1. UN High Commissioner for Refugees (UNHCR), *Report of the United Nations High Commissioner for Refugees*, January 1, 1959, A/3828/Rev.1, available at http://www.refworld.org/docid/3ae68c800.html.
2. Zieck, "1956 Hungarian Refugee Emergency," 46.
3. UNHCR Report to General Assembly, 1.
4. Private communication from Gary Filerman, who helped Hungarian refugee students obtain scholarships to study in the United States, January 24, 2020. For a detailed account of the reception of academics and students, see Sheridan, "Support and Surveillance," which acknowledges the work carried out by Gary Filerman. For an in-depth analysis of how the Hungarians entered the United States as parolees, see Bradford, "Utmost Practical Speed."
5. US Information Service, American embassy, London, Thursday, May 16, 1957, 1, DFA/419/33/10/1.
6. Bon Tempo, *Americans at the Gate*, 75–81.
7. There is significant literature on the integration of Hungarian in their countries of settlement. For the United States, see Papp, "Organizational Development"; Papp-Zubrits, "Forgotten Generation"; Papp and Eszterhás, *Hungarian Americans*; Pastor, "American Reception."

> For Canada, see Dreisziger, "Hungarian Revolution," where he notes that "one can safely assert that many of the refugees refrained from participation in Hungarian ethnic life," 204. He considered this to be the case, for instance, because of feeling "ill at ease both among the 'old timers' and in the post-1948 group," 204. For a historical overview, see his chapter "The 1956–1957 Refugee Movement" in *The 1956 Revolution Hungarian Canadian*.

> For Australia: Kunz, *Hungarians Australia*. This is an old text but provides a history of Hungarians in Australia mainly from 1833–1937. With a recent turn towards researching Hungarian Australians, scholarship includes Hungarian language maintenance in Australia and return to Hungary, raising questions of identity and belonging: Tomsic, "Happiness Again"; Andits, "Rethinking Home Belonging"; Kovács, "Hungarian in Australia."

> Settlement in the UK: Czigány, *Just like other students*.

> For a brief reference to the 1956 cohort in Israel see: Surányi, "Complexity Inherent Researching Migrant."

> For Argentina: Némethy, *Szabadságom Lett Börtönöm*.

> Recent literature on diasporas no longer views a static but, instead, a changing relationship between diaspora and homeland. From this perspective regarding 1956 Hungarian refugees, namely the intelligentsia cohort, see Morawska, "Diaspora."

8. Enquiry, December 15, 1956, from the Department of External Affairs directed to embassies and legations in London, Paris, Bonn, Berne, Brussels, The Hague, Stockholm, and Lisbon, DFA/419/33/10/1.
9. Reply from Irish legation, Berne, December 21, 1956, 2–3, 5, 7, DFA/419/33/10/1.
10. Reply, December 20, from Gesandschaft von Irland, Bonn, 2, DFA/419/33/10/1.
11. Reply from Irish legation, The Hague, 2–3, December 21, 1956, DFA/419/33/10/1.
12. For motivating factors in the appeal of communism, see Judt, *Postwar*, 181.
13. Reply from Irish Legation, The Hague, December 21, 1956, 4, DFA/419/33/10/1.
14. For the horrors of the Second World War experienced by Hungary's Jewish communities, see Béla Zsolt's memoir, *Nine Suitcases*, published shortly after the war, and

Sándor's, *Legacy*, which engages with the chaos and cruelty of the closing stages of the war in Hungary. For the experience of children, see Nobel Prize winner Kertész, *Fateless*; Konrád, *A Guest*.

15. Reply from Ambassade d'Irlande, Paris, December 24, 1956, 3, DFA/419/33/10/1.
16. Pálmai Bánki, "Crossing Borders," 134.
17. For Vietnamese refugees, see Maguire and Saris, "Enshrining Vietnamese-Irish Lives"; Sheridan, "With Loneliness and Satisfaction"; Maguire, "Emergent Issues"; Sheridan, "Tuyen Pham"; Sheridan, "Loneliness and Satisfaction"; Fanning, *Migration*.
18. For an account of Direct Provision, see the diary written by Vukašin Nedeljković in Lentin and Nedeljković, *Disavowing Asylum*, 20–37.
19. *Details of Refugees in Knockalisheen Camp* (following its closure in 1958). Undated. Private Collection.
20. Interview with Colm Begley, *Colm Begley on his Westbank Childhood GGTV 18 FEB 17*. Available at https://www.youtube.com/watch?v=mq3OiWOQ-ZQ.

> For the history of Adeline Mathers and her home, see "Inside the Home That 'Auntie' Built," *Wicklow Voice*, March 10, 2017. Also, the RTE programme *Auntie's Family Secrets*, which aired June 4, 2011, with details at https://presspack.rte.ie/2011/06/04/would-you-believe-special.

21. Interview with Elizabeth, May 21, 2018. All quotes from Elizabeth are from this interview.
22. Espiritu, *Body Counts*, 155, draws attention to "unresolved hurts" in refugee families, to secrets and all that people do not want to disclose about their past lives and actions.
23. These are all evidenced in relation to integration in an empirical study that refers to integration as a two-way process in Bakker, Dagevos and Engbersen, "Importance of Resources," 432.

> Integration has been conceptualized theoretically as the beginning of an asylum seeker's journey and not the end, which "implies that early experiences can influence long-term outcomes," 432. This example is used as the two-way process would also appear to be the view in Ireland, as seen in O'Neill, *Integration*, a report to the Minister for Justice, Equality, and Law Reform.

24. McMahon, *Working Group*, 162, 163.
25. For commentary on the illegality of aspects of the complaints procedure, see Thornton "C.A. and T.A.," 116–18. There is discussion at the government level to dismantle the system that, at time of writing, remains in place.
26. McMahon, *Working Group*, 59.
27. "The Refugees and the Red Cross," *Irish Times*, January 17, 1957, 5, ITDA.
28. "'These People Have No Genuine Complaints'—Camp Controller," *Irish Times*, January 14, 1957, 4, ITDA.
29. "The Refugees and the Red Cross," *Irish Times*, January 17, 1957, 5, ITDA.
30. McMahon, *Working Group*, 177.
31. "'These People Have No Genuine Complaints'—Camp Controller," *Irish Times*, January 14, 1957, 4, ITDA.
32. Irish Refugee Council, *Report on Compulsory Transfer of Residence*, 11.
33. In general, people in Direct Provision did not have the right to work, and this was ruled unconstitutional in 2017.
34. McMahon, *Working Group*, 173.

35. See, for instance, Devine, "Welcome to the Celtic Tiger," and repetition of these findings in the Ombudsman for Children's report *Direct Division*. The Ombudsman for Children sought the views of seventy-five children living in Direct Provision centers across Ireland, and their findings present an unsettling picture. Daily life in the centers affected children through management invasion of their privacy and the feeling that they did not live like their Irish peers but was also accompanied by racism in school and the impression that teachers knew "little about what it meant to be an asylum seeker or what living in Direct Provision accommodation is like and the restrictions it placed on the children," in *Direct Division*, 3–4.

    For child protection, see Special Rapporteur Geoffrey Shannon's reports on child protection, which are presented to the Oireachtas and are available at https://www.gov.ie/en/collection/51fc67-special-rapporteur-on-child-protection-reports.

    The Health Information and Quality Authority (HIQA) also flagged children's mental health, the impact of parental mental health on family life, domestic violence, physical abuse, and other protection concerns in Ward and Murphy, *Report on Inspection*, 3.

36. Royal College of Physicians of Ireland, *Children Direct Provision*, 4.

37. Quoted in MASI statement on the HSE and Department of Justice and Equality measures to stop the spread of COVID-19 in Direct Provision, April 24, 2020, https://www.masi.ie/2020/04/24/statement-on-the-hse-and-department-of-justice-and-equality-measures-to-stop-the-spread-of-covid-19-in-direct-provision.

38. Raghallaigh and Thornton, "Vulnerable Childhood," 389.

39. Peter Nyers set out this argument in *Rethinking Refugees*, 123–27.

40. "Protest against Tullamore Direct Provision Centre Scheduled for Weekend," *Irish Times*, February 28, 2020, 3.

41. Evgey Shtorn fled Russia in 2018 and claimed asylum in Ireland. He contributed an opinion piece to RTÉ Brainstorm, an online partnership between RTÉ and Irish third-level institutions. Evgeny Shtorn, "What Is Driving Protests against New Direct Provision Centres?," RTÉ Brainstorm, November 6, 2019, https://www.rte.ie/brainstorm/2019/1106/1089019-what-is-driving-protests-against-new-direct-provision-centres.

42. "Asylum Seekers in Cahersiveen Protest over 'Inhumane Conditions,'" *Irish Times*, July 28, 2020, 3.

43. Voorhees, "Demographics," 1.

44. Soguk. *States and Strangers*, 250. See also Buscher, "Refugee Women"; Edwards, "Transitioning Gender"; Martin, "Gender and the Evolving Refugee Regime."

45. Knockalisheen cannot symbolize all camps; there remains a difference between them, particularly between the Nazi extermination camps and refugee camps, as Owens notes in "Reclaiming 'Bare Life,'" 575–76. In this powerful critique of Agamben's *Homo Sacer*, Owens states that a desperate action, in this instance the act of lip-sewing by people detained in Woomera, Australia, is an act "exposing the unjustifiable actions of the Australian government towards asylum-seekers and refugees. But the politics emerging out of these actions is based on the transcendence of bare life, not its celebration," 579. Agamben does draw attention to the lawlessness in modern camps, and in *No Friend but the Mountains*, Boochani is a witness to the humiliations, horrors, and loss of life, whether murder or suicide, during his years of detention in Australian offshore facilities. However, the very act of writing intermittently with the use of a hidden mobile phone to produce his work is another example of the transcendence of bare life.

46. Nyers, "Rethinking Refugees," xv, 125. For further discussion and critique in relation to omitting the asylum seeker's voice in migration and security studies, see also Innes, *Migration, Citizenship*, which examines security "based in subjectivity and identity," 35.

47. Note to Department of External Affairs, December 8, 1956, DFA/419/33/11.

48. Espiritu, *Body Counts*, 187–88.

49. For the nation as imagined, limited, sovereign, and a community, see Anderson, *Imagined Communities*, 6–7. For a disruptive analysis of the imagined community as displayed in the symbolization of the nation and the nature of *Irishness* in the Irish Constitution, see Hanafin, *Constituting Identity*, and his "question[ing] the fiction of Irish identity," 11. He argues that "an Ireland, uncomplicated, cohesive and immutable," which was rooted in "nationalism and concomitantly religion" and the concept of a "rural Ireland," was not fully inclusive of the nation, 1–2. Note, however, that the Constitution has been amended since Hanafin's publication and that Irish society has experienced a significant level of social change.

BIBLIOGRAPHY

Adam, Christopher, Tibor Egervari, Leslie Laczko, and Judy Young. *The 1956 Hungarian Revolution, Hungarian and Canadian Perspectives*. Ottawa: University of Ottawa Press, 2010.
Agamben, Giorgio. *Homo Sacer, Sovereign Power and Bare Life*. Stanford: Stanford University Press, 1998.
Anderson, Benedict. *Imagined Communities: Reflections on the Origin and Spread of Nationalism*. London: Verso, 1983.
Andits, Petra. "Rethinking Home, Belonging and the Potential of Transnationalism: Australian Hungarians after the Fall of the Berlin Wall." *Ethos* 43, no. 4 (2015): 313–31.
Applebaum, Anne. *Iron Curtain: The Crushing of Eastern Europe 1944–1956*. New York: Doubleday, 2012.
Arendt, Hannah. *The Origins of Totalitarianism*. New York: Harcourt, Brace, Jovanovich, 1973.
Arnold, Bruce. *The Irish Gulag: How the State Betrayed Its Innocent Children*. Dublin: Gill & Macmillan, 2009.
Bakewell, Oliver. "Researching Refugees: Lessons from the Past, Current Challenges and Future Directions." *Refugee Survey Quarterly* 26, no. 3 (2007): 6–14.
Bakhtin, M. M. *The Dialogic Imagination*. Austin: University of Texas Press, 1981.
Bakis, Edward. "The So-Called DP-Apathy in Germany's DP Camps." *Transactions of the Kansas Academy of Science* 55, no. 1 (1952): 62–86.
Bakker, Linda, Jaco Dagevos, and Godfried Engbersen. "The Importance of Resources and Security in the Socio-Economic Integration of Refugees: A Study on the Impact of Length of Stay in Asylum Accommodation and Resident Status on Socio-Economic Integration for the Four Largest Refugee Groups in the Netherlands." *Journal of International Migration and Integration* 15, no. 3 (2014): 431–48.
Balint, Ruth. "Children Left Behind: Family, Refugees and Immigration in Postwar Europe." *History Workshop Journal* 82, no. 1 (2016): 151–72.
Békés, Csaba, Malcolm Byrne, and János M. Rainer. *The 1956 Hungarian Revolution: A History in Documents*. Budapest: Central European University Press, 2002.
Bielenberg, Christabel. *The Past Is Myself and the Road Ahead Omnibus: When I Was a German 1934–1945*. London: Corgi Books, 2011.
Bon Tempo, Carl J. *Americans at the Gate: The United States and Refugees during the Cold War*. Princeton: Princeton University Press, 2008.
Boochani, Behrouz. *No Friend but the Mountains*. Sydney: Picador, 2018.
Bradford, Anita Casavantes. *The Revolution Is for the Children: The Politics of Childhood in Havana and Miami 1959–1962*. Chapel Hill: University of North Carolina Press, 2014.
———. "'With the Utmost Practical Speed': Eisenhower, Hungarian Parolees, and the 'Hidden Hand' Behind US Immigration and Refugee Policy." *Journal of American Ethnic History* 39, 2 (2020): 5–35.

Brandis, Monica. *The Children from Operation Shamrock: German Children in Ireland, Historical Context, Testimonies and Fictionalized Memory Fragments*. Trier: Wissenschaftlicher, 2020.

Brown, Terence. *Ireland a Social and Cultural History 1922–2002*. London: Harper Perennial, 1981.

Buscher, Dale. "Refugee Women: 20 Years On." *Refugee Survey Quarterly* 49, no. 2 (2010): 4–20.

Carruthers, Susan L. *Cold War Captives, Imprisonment, Escape, Brainwashing*. Berkeley: University of California Press, 2009.

CIA. "Section (101) (a) (1) MSA 1951 Escapees, Escapee Program." Accessed on November 2, 2019. https://www.cia.gov/library/readingroom/docs/CIA-RDP80R01731R003300330002-2.pdf.

Clear, Catriona. "Woman's Life Magazine and Women's Lives in Ireland in the 1950s." *Saothar* 38 (2013): 73–81.

Collins, Mark. *Stateless*. Ladywell, Thomastown: Pillar, 2006.

Collis, Robert. *Straight On*. Abingdon: Routledge, 2010.

Commission on Emigration and Other Population Problems 1948–1954. Dublin: Stationery Office, 1955.

Congdon, Lee, Károly Nagy, and Béla Király. *1956: The Hungarian Revolution and War for Independence*. Boulder, CO: Social Science Monographs, 2006.

Connolly, Linda, ed. *Women and the Irish Revolution, Feminism, Activism, Violence*. Newbridge: Irish Academic Press, 2020.

Cox, Terry, ed. *Challenging Communism in Eastern Europe: 1956 and Its Legacy*. London: Routledge, 2009.

Crowe, Catriona. "The Commission and the Survivors." *Dublin Review*. Accessed on September 10, 2021. https://thedublinreview.com/article/the-commission-and-the-survivors/.

Czigány, Magda. *"Just Like Other Students": Reception of the 1956 Hungarian Students in Britain*. Newcastle: Cambridge Scholars, 2009.

Daly, Mary E. "Cultural and Economic Protection and Xenophobia in Independent Ireland, 1920s–1970s." In *Facing the Other: Interdisciplinary Studies on Race, Gender and Social Justice in Ireland*, edited by Borbála Farago and Moynagh Sullivan, 6–18. Newcastle: Cambridge Scholars, 2008.

Department of Children, Equality, Disability, Integration and Youth. *Final Report of the Commission of Investigation into Mother and Baby Homes*. Dublin: Department of Children, Equality, Disability, Integration and Youth, 2021. https://www.gov.ie/en/publication/d4b3d-final-report-of-the-commission-of-investigation-into-mother-and-baby-homes.

Derrida, Jacques. "Hostipitality." *Angelaki, Journal of the Theoretical Humanities* 3 (2000): 3–18.

DeSantis, Alan D. "Caught between Two Worlds: Bakhtin's Dialogism in the Exile Experience." *Journal of Refugee Studies* 14 (2001): 1–19.

Devine, Dympna. "Welcome to the Celtic Tiger? Teacher Responses to Immigration and Increasing Ethnic Diversity in Irish Schools." *International Studies in Sociology of Education* 15, no. 1 (2005): 49–70.

Dreisziger, Nándor F. "The Biggest Welcome Ever: the Toronto Tories, the Ottawa Liberals, and the Admission of Hungarian Refugees to Canada in 1956." *Hungarian Studies Review* 35, no. 1–2 (2008): 41–66.

———. "The Hungarian Revolution of 1956: The Legacy of the Refugees." *Nationalities Papers* 13, no. 2 (1985): 198–208.

———. "The 1956–1957 Refugee Movement in the Context of Hungarian Immigration to Canada since the Late 19th Century." In *The 1956 Hungarian Revolution, Hungarian and Canadian Perspectives*, edited by Christopher Adam, Tibor Egervari, Leslie Laczko, and Judy Young, 194–222. Ottawa: University of Ottawa Press, 2010.

Edwards, Alice. "Transitioning Gender: Feminist Engagement with International Refugee Law and Policy 1950–2010." *Refugee Survey Quarterly* 29, no. 2 (2010): 21–45.

Elie, Jérôme. "Histories of Refugee and Forced Migration Studies." In *The Oxford Handbook of Refugee and Forced Migration Studies*, edited by Elena Fiddian-Qasmiyeh, Gil Loescher, Katy Long, and Nando Sigon, 23–35. Oxford: Oxford University Press, 2016.

Espiritu, Yên Lê. *Body Counts: The Vietnam War and Militarized Refuge(es)*. Oakland: University of California Press, 2014.

Fanning, Bryan. *Migration and the Making of Ireland*. Dublin: University College Dublin Press, 2018.

———. *Racism and Social Change in the Republic of Ireland*. Manchester: Manchester University Press, 2002.

Ferriter, Diarmaid. *Occasions of Sin, Sex and Society in Modern Ireland*. London: Profile, 2009.

———. *The Transformation of Ireland 1900–2000*. London: Profile, 2004.

Foster, R. F. *Modern Ireland, 1600–1972*. London: Penguin, 1988.

Frank, Matthew, and Jessica Rheinisch. "Refugees and the Nation-State in Europe, 1919–1959." *Journal of Contemporary History* 49, no. 3 (2014): 477–90.

Garvin, Tom. *News from a New Republic*. Dublin: Gill and MacMillan, 2010.

Gatrell, Peter. *Free World? The Campaign to Save the World's Refugees 1956–1963*. Cambridge: Cambridge University Press, 2011.

———. *The Making of the Modern Refugee*. Oxford: Oxford University Press, 2013.

———. "Refugees—What's Wrong with History?" *Journal of Refugee Studies* 30, no. 2 (2017): 170–89.

Gatrell, Peter, Anindita Ghoshal, Katarzyna Nowak, and Alex Dowdall. "Reckoning with Refugeedom: Refugee Voices in Modern History." *Social History* (2021): 70–95.

Glynn, Irial. "Famine Commemorations and Asylum Debates in Ireland Conflated." In *History Memory Migration*, edited by J. Olaf Kleist and Irial Glynn, 173–88. Basingstoke: Palgrave Macmillan, 2012.

Goodwin-Gill, Guy S. "The Politics of Refugee Protection." *Refugee Survey Quarterly* 27, no. 1 (2008): 8–23.

Granville, Johanna. *The First Domino: International Decision-Making during the Hungarian Crisis of 1956*. College Station: Texas A&M University Press, 2004.

Griffith, Arthur. *The Resurrection of Hungary: A Parallel for Ireland*. Dublin: University College Dublin, 2004.

Haddad, Emma. *The Refugee in International Society, between Sovereigns*. Cambridge: Cambridge University Press, 2008.

Hanafin, Patrick. *Constituting Identity, Political Identity Formation and the Constitution in Post-Independence Ireland*. Burlington, VT: Ashgate, 2001.

Heil, Alan L. "The Voice of America: A Brief Cold War History." In *Cold War Broadcasting: Impact on the Soviet Union and Eastern Europe*, edited by Ross A. Johnson and Eugene R. Parta, 25–48. Budapest: Central European University Press, 2010.

Hidas, Peter. "Canada and the Hungarian Jewish Refugees 1956–57." *East European Jewish Affairs* 37, no. 1 (2007): 75–89.

———. "The Hungarian Refugee Student Movement of 1956–7 and Canada." *Canadian Ethnic Studies Journal* 30, no. 1 (1998): 19–50.
Hitchcock, William I. *The Bitter Road to Freedom: A New History of the Liberation of Europe*. New York: Free Press, 2008.
Hoblicsek, László, and Sándor Illés. "Az 1956-os kivándorlás népességi hatásai, 85. évfolyam 2. Szám." Budapest: Statisztikai Szemle, 2007. https://www.ksh.hu/statszemle_archive/2007/2007_02/2007_02_157.pdf.
Holfter, Gisela, and Horst Dickel. *An Irish Sanctuary: German-Speaking Refugees in Ireland 1933–1945*. Berlin: Walter de Gruyter, 2018.
Iacovetta, Franca. *Gatekeepers: Reshaping Immigrant Lives in Cold War Canada*. Toronto: Between the Lines, 2006.
Innes, Alexandria J. *Migration, Citizenship and the Challenge for Security: An Ethnographic Approach*. Basingstoke: Palgrave Macmillan, 2015.
Irish Refugee Council. *A Report by the Irish Refugee Council on the Compulsory Transfer of Residence from Mosney Accommodation Centre by the Reception and Integration Agency, Part of the Department of Justice and Law Reform*. Dublin: Irish Refugee Council, 2010.
Judt, Tony. *Postwar: A History of Europe since 1945*. London: Pimlico, 2007.
Kabdebo, Thomas. *Ireland and Hungary: A Study in Parallels, with an Arthur Griffith Bibliography*. Dublin: Four Courts, 2001.
Keogh, Dermot. *Jews in Twentieth-Century Ireland: Refugees, Anti-Semitism and the Holocaust*. Cork: Cork University Press, 1998.
Kertész, Imre. *Fateless*. Translated by Christopher C. Wilson and Katharina M. Wilson. Evanston: Northwestern University Press, 1992.
Kleist, J. Olaf, and Irial Glynn. *History Memory and Migration*. Basingstoke: Palgrave Macmillan, 2012.
Kõll, Anu Mai. "Baltic Refugees and Policy Formation in Sweden 1940–1950." *Journal of Baltic Studies* 46, no. 4 (2015): 427–34.
Konrád, George. *A Guest in my Own Country: A Hungarian Life*. Translated by Jim Tucker. New York: Other Press, 2007.
Kőrösi, Zsuzsanna, and Adrienne Molnár. *Carrying a Secret in My Heart: Children of the Victims of the Reprisals after the Hungarian Revolution in 1956, an Oral History*. Budapest: Central European Press, 2003.
Kovács, Magdolna. "Hungarian in Australia." In *Hungarian Language Contact Outside Hungary*, edited by Anna Fenyvesi, 319–50. Amsterdam: John Benjamins, 2005.
Kunz, Egon F. *The Hungarians in Australia*. Blackburn: AE Australasian Educa Press, 1985.
Kushner, Tony. *Remembering Refugees, Then and Now*. Manchester: Manchester University Press, 2006.
Lee, J. J. "Continuity and Change in Ireland, 1945–70." In *Ireland 1945–70*, edited by J. J. Lee, 166–78. Dublin: Gill and Macmillan, 1979.
———. *Ireland 1912–1985: Politics and Society*. Cambridge: Cambridge University Press, 1989.
Lehane, Shane. *History of the Irish Red Cross*. Dublin: Four Courts, 2019.
Lénárt, András. "Emigration from Hungary in 1956 and the Emigrants as Tourists to Hungary." *Hungarian Historical Review* 1, no. 3–4 (2012): 368–96.
Lentin, Ronit, and Vukašin Nedeljković. *Disavowing Asylum: Documenting Ireland's Asylum Industrial Complex*. London: Rowman and Littlefield, 2021.

Loescher, Gil, and John A. Scanlon. *Calculated Kindness, Refugees and America's Half Open Door, 1945 to the Present.* New York: Free Press, 1986.
Lommax, Bill. *Eye-Witness in Hungary: The Soviet Invasion of 1956.* Nottingham, UK: Spokesman, 1980.
Long, Katy. *Back to Where You Once Belonged: A Historical Review of UNHCR Policy and Practice on Refugee Repatriation.* Geneva: Policy Development and Evaluation Service United Nations High Commissioner for Refugees, 2013.
Lowe, Keith. *Savage Continent: Europe in the Aftermath of World War II.* New York: St. Martin's, 2012.
Luddy, Maria. "Unmarried Mothers in Ireland." *Women's History Review* 20, no. 1 (2011): 109–26.
Madokoro, Laura. "The Refugee Ritual: Sopron Students in Canada." *Journal of the Canadian Historical Association/Revue de la Société Historique du Canada* 19, no. 1 (2008): 253–78.
Maguire, Mark. "Emergent Issues in Ethnic Youth Studies. A Historical and Ethnographic Study of the Vietnamese Irish Experience." *Youth Studies Ireland* 2, no. 2 (2007): 1–34.
Maguire, Mark, and Jamie A. Saris. "Enshrining Vietnamese-Irish Lives." *Anthropology Today* 23, no. 2 (2005): 9–12.
Malkki, Liisa. "National Geographic: The Rooting of Peoples and the Territorialization of National Identity among Scholars and Refugees." *Cultural Anthropology* 7, no. 1 (1992): 24–44.
——. "Refugees and Exile: From 'Refugee Studies' to the National Order of Things." *Annual Review of Anthropology* 24 (1995): 495–523.
Malone, Joe. "The Hungarians in Limerick." Undated cutting, free Limerick newspaper. Sister Immaculata Collection, Mercy Archive.
Mannik, Lynda. *Photography, Memory and Refugee Identity: The Voyage of the SS Walnut, 1948.* Vancouver: University of British Columbia Press, 2013.
Marfleet, Philip. "Refugees and History: Why We Must Address the Past." *Refugee Survey Quarterly* 26, no. 3 (2007): 136–48.
Markowitz, Arthur A. "Humanitarianism versus Restrictionism: The United States and the Hungarian Refugees." *International Migration Review* 7 (1973): 46–59.
Marrus, Michael R. *The Unwanted: European Refugees from the First World War through the Cold War.* Philadelphia: Temple University Press, 2002.
Martin, Susan F. "Gender and the Evolving Refugee Regime." *Refugee Survey Quarterly* 29, no. 2 (2010): 104–21.
McArdle, Dorothy. "The Iron Cage." *Irish Press*, October 26, 1950, 6.
McDowell, Linda. "Workers, Migrants, Aliens or Citizens? State Constructions and Discourses of Identity among Post-War European Labour Migrants in Britain." *Political Geography* 22, no. 8 (2003): 863–86.
McMahon, Bryan. *Working Group to Report to Government on Improvements to the Protection Process, Including Direct Provision and Supports to Asylum Seekers.* Dublin: Department of Justice and Equality, 2015.
Molohan, Cathy. *Germany and Ireland 1945–1955: Two Nations Friendship.* Dublin: Irish Academic Press, 1999.
Morawska, Ewa. "'Diaspora' Diasporas' Representations of their Homelands: Exploring the Polymorphs." *Ethnic and Racial Studies* 34, no. 6 (2011): 1029–48.

NATO. Hungarian Refugee Students, Note by the Canadian Delegation. Unclassified document AC/52-D/275/4, North Atlantic Treaty Organization, 1957. https://archives.nato.int/hungarian-refugee-students-2.

———. *Report on Hungarian Refugees*. Declassified document C-M(57)65, North Atlantic Treaty Organization, 1957. https://www.nato.int/nato_static/assets/pdf/pdf_archives_hungarian_revolution/20130904_C-M_57_65-ENG.PDF.

Némethy, Judith Kesserű. *"Szabadságom Lett a Börtönöm": Az Argentínai Magyar Emigráció Története 1948–1968 ["My Freedom Became My Prison": The History of the Hungarian Emigrés in Argentina, 1948–1968]*. Budapest: A Magyar Nyelv és Kultúra Nemzetközi Társasága, 2003.

Niessen, James P. "God Brought the Hungarians: Emigration and Refugee Relief in the Light of Cold War Religion." *The Hungarian Historical Review* 6, no. 3 (2017): 566–96.

Nyers, Peter. *Rethinking Refugees: Beyond States of Emergency*. New York: Routledge, 2006.

O'Brien, A. N. "Irish Red Cross Develops Water Safety Programme." *The Red Cross World* (October–December 1952): 8–10.

O'Brien, Steve, and Leo Dobbs. "Hungarian Refugee Crisis Presented Ireland with a New Challenge." UNHCR News, November 6, 2006. http://www.unhcr.org/news/latest/2006/11/454f3a95a/hungarian-refugee-crisis-presented-ireland-new-challenge.html.

O'Connor, Siobhán. *Irish Government Policy and Public Opinion towards German-Speaking Refugees 1933–1943*. Newcastle: Cambridge Scholars, 2017.

O'Driscoll, Mervyn. "The 'Half Irish' Herbert Remmel." In *Cultural/Literary Translators: Selected Irish-German Biographies II*, edited by Sabine Egger, 95–116. Trier: Wissenschaftlicher, 2015.

Ombudsman for Children. *Direct Division: Children's Views and Experiences of Living in Direct Provision*. Dublin: Ombudsman for Children, 2020.

O'Neill, Berenice. *Integration: A Two Way Process*. Interdepartmental Working Group on the Integration of Refugees in Ireland. Dublin: Department of Justice, Equality and Law Reform, 1999.

O'Sullivan, Eoin, and Ian O'Donnell. "Coercive Confinement in the Republic of Ireland: The Waning of a Culture of Control." *Punishment and Society* 9, no. 1 (2007): 27–48.

Owens, Patricia. "Reclaiming 'Bare Life?': Against Agamben on Refugees." *International Relations* 23, no. 4 (2009): 567–82.

Pálmai Bánki, Katalin. "Crossing Borders from Hungary to Ireland: The Cross-Cultural Adaptation of Hungarian Refugees from the 1940s and their Compatriots from the 1956 Hungarian Revolution." PhD diss., Dublin City University, 2009.

Papp, Susan M. "Hungarians in Ontario." *Polyphony: Bulletin of the Multicultural History Society of Ontario* 2, no. 2–3 (1979–80): 3–16.

———. "The Organizational Development of the Hungarian Community of Ontario." *Hungarian Studies Review* 8, no. 1 (1981): 85–97.

Papp, Susan M., and Joe Eszterhás. *Hungarian Americans and Their Communities of Cleveland*. Vol. 12. Cleveland Memory, 2010.

Papp-Zubrits, Susan. "The Forgotten Generation: Canada's Hungarian Refugees of 1956 ." *Oral History Forum* 4, no. 2 (1980): 30–34.

Pask, Diane. "Unaccompanied Refugee and Displaced Children: Jurisdiction, Decision-Making and Representation." *International Journal of Refugee Law* 1, no. 2 (1989): 199–219.

Pastor, Peter. "The American Reception and Settlement of Hungarian Refugees in 1956–1957." *Hungarian Cultural Studies* 9 (2016): 197–205. https://doi.org/10.5195/ahea.2016.255.

Perret, Françoise. "ICRC Operations in Hungary and the Middle East in 1956." *International Review of the Red Cross* 313 (1996): unpaginated. https://www.icrc.org/en/doc/resources/documents/article/other/57jn8c.htm.

Pődör, Dora. "Joseph Szövérffy: A Hungarian Scholar in Exile in Ireland." In *The Binding Strength of Irish Studies: Festschrift in Honour of Csilla Bertha and Donald E Morse*, edited by Marianna Gula, Mária Kurd, and István D Rácz, 192–205. Debrecen: Debreceni Egyetem Kiadó, 2011.

Programme for Economic Expansion, Laid by the Government before Each House of the Oireachtas. White Paper, Dublin: Stationery Office, 1958.

Puskás, Julianna. "Hungarian Images of America: The Siren's Song of Tinkling Dollars." In *Distant Magnets: Expectations and Realities in the Immigration Experience, 1840–1930*, edited by Dirk Hoerder and Horst Rössler, 180–98. New York: Holmes and Meier, 1993.

Raftery, Mary, and Eoin O'Sullivan. *Suffer the Little Children*. Dublin: New Island, 1999.

Raghallaigh, Muireann Ní, and Liam Thornton. "Vulnerable Childhood, Vulnerable Adulthood: Direct Provision as After-Care for Aged-Out Separated Children Seeking Asylum in Ireland." *Critical Social Policy* 37, no. 3 (2017): 386–404.

Remmel, Herbert. *From Cologne to Ballinlough: A German and Irish Boyhood in WWII and Post-War Years 1946–1949*. Millstreet: Aubane Historical Society, 2009.

Rév, István. "Just Noise? Impact of Radio Free Europe in Hungary." In *Cold War Broadcasting: Impact on the Soviet Union and Eastern Europe*, edited by Ross A. Johnson and Eugene R. Parta, 239–58. Budapest: Central European University Press, 2010.

Risso, Linda. "Radio Wars: Broadcasting in the Cold War." *Cold War History* 13, no. 2 (2013): 145–52.

Royal College of Physicians of Ireland. *Children in Direct Provision: A Position Paper by the Faculty of Paediatrics*. Dublin: Royal College of Physicians of Ireland, 2019.

Ryan, Des. "Hungarians in Limerick." *Old Limerick Journal* 37 (2001): 55–59.

Ryan, Sean. *Commission to Inquire into Child Abuse*, 5 volumes. Dublin: Stationery Office, 2009.

Salvatici, Silvia. "'Help the People to Help Themselves': UNRRA Relief Workers and European Displaced Persons." *Journal of Refugee Studies* 25, no. 3 (2012): 428–51.

Sándor, Iván. *Legacy*. London: Peter Owen, 2014.

Savage, Roland Burke. "Ireland Tomorrow." *Studies: An Irish Quarterly* 44, no. 173 (1955): 1–4.

Scarlett, Dora. *Window onto Hungary*. Bradford: Broadacre, 1957.

Schmidt, Anna. "'I Know What You're Doing': Reflexivity and Methods in Refugee Studies." *Refugee Survey Quarterly* 26, no. 3 (2007): 82–99.

Sebestyen, Victor. *Twelve Days: The Story of the 1956 Hungarian Revolution*. New York: Vintage, 2007.

Shepherd, Ben. *After Daybreak: The Liberation of Belsen, 1945*. London: Jonathan Cape, 2005.

———. *The Long Road Home: The Aftermath of the Second World War*. London: Bodley Head, 2010.

Sheridan, Vera. "The Inadvertent Cosmopolitan: A Refugee Tale from Hungarian to English." In *The Cause of Cosmopolitanism, Dispositions, Models, Transformations*, edited by Patrick O'Donovan and Laura Rascaroli, 357–74. Bern: Peter Lang, 2011.

———. "Letters of Love and Loss in a Time of Revolution." *History of the Family* 19, no. 2 (2010): 260–71.

———. "Loneliness and Satisfaction: Narratives of Vietnamese Refugee Integration into Irish Society." In *Facing the Other: Interdisciplinary Studies on Race Gender, and Social*

Justice in Ireland, edited by Borbála Faragó and Moynagh Sullivan, 108–22. Newcastle: Cambridge Scholars, 2008.

———. "Support and Surveillance: 1956 Hungarian Refugee Students in Transit to the Joyce Kilmer Reception Centre and to Higher Education Scholarships in the USA." *History of Education* 45, no. 6 (2016): 775–93.

———. "Tuyen Pham: Caught between Two Cultures." In *Integration and Social Change in the Republic of Ireland*, edited by Bryan Fanning, 129–52. Manchester: Manchester University Press, 2007.

———. "With Loneliness and Satisfaction: Tracing the Path of Cross-Cultural Adaptation by Members of the Vietnamese Community in Ireland." Unpublished dissertation, 2005.

Skelly, Joseph Morrison. *Irish Diplomacy at the United Nations 1945–1965: National Interests and the International Order*. Dublin: Irish Academic Press, 1997.

Soguk, Nevzat. *States and Strangers: Refugees and Displacements of Statecraft*. Minneapolis: University of Minnesota Press, 1999.

Stone, Dan. "Refugees Then and Now: Memory, History and Politics in the Long Twentieth Century: An Introduction." *Patterns of Prejudice* 52, no. 2–3 (2018): 101–6.

Surányi, Rachel. "The Complexity Inherent in Researching Migrant Identification: The Case of Hungarian Jews in Israel." *Studies in Ethnicity and Nationalism* 20, no. 1 (2020): 25–50.

Szövérffy, Joseph. "Hungary: Satellite State." *Studies: An Irish Quarterly* 44, no. 175 (1955): 271–80.

Taillon, Ruth. *The Women of 1916*. Dublin: Tatra, 2018.

Taylor, Becky. "'Don't Just Look for a New Pet': The Vietnamese Airlift, Child Refugees and the Dangers of Toxic Humanitarianism." *Patterns of Prejudice* 52, no. 2–3 (2018): 195–209.

———. "Their Only Words of English Were 'Thank You': Rights, Gratitude and 'Deserving' Hungarian Refugees to Britain in 1956." *Journal of British Studies* 55, no. 1 (2016): 120–44.

Thompson, Andrew S., and Stephanie Bangarth. "Transnational Christian Charity: The Canadian Council of Churches, the World Council of Churches, and the Hungarian Refugee Crisis, 1956–1957." *American Review of Canadian Studies* 38, no. 3 (2008): 295–316.

Thompson, E. P. *The Making of the English Working Class*. London: Penguin, 1968.

Thornton, Liam. "C.A. and T.A.: The Direct Provision Case." *Irish Journal of Family Law* 17, no. 4 (2014): 116–18.

Tomsic, Mary. "'Happiness Again': Photographing and Narrating the Arrival of Child Refugees and Their Families 1956–57." *History of the Family* 22, no. 4 (2017): 485–509.

Troper, Harold. "Canada and Hungarian Refugees: The Historical Context." In *The 1956 Hungarian Revolution: Hungarian and Canadian Perspectives*, edited by Christopher Adam, Tibor Egervari, Leslie Laczko, and Judy Young, 176–93. Ottawa: University of Ottawa Press, 2010.

Tyrrell, Peter. *Founded on Fear: Letterfrack Industrial School, War and Exile*. Dublin: Irish Academic Press, 2006.

UNHCR. "Convention and Protocol Relating to the Status of Refugees." Accessed October 2, 2019. http://www.unhcr.org/en-ie/3b66c2aa10.

———. Report of the United Nations High Commissioner for Refugees, January 1, 1959, A/3828/rev.1. Report to General Assembly, United Nations High Commissioner for Refugees. http://www.unhcr.org/3ae68c800.html.

———. *The State of the World's Refugees: Fifty Years of Humanitarian Action*. Oxford: Oxford University Press and UNHCR, 2000.

UNHCR, Policy Unit, Bureau for Europe. "Separated Children in Europe Programme, Statement of Good Practice." Geneva: UNHCR, Policy Unit, Bureau for Europe, 2004. https://www.unhcr.org/4d9474399.pdf.

United Nations. *Report of the Special Committee on the Problem of Hungary*. General Assembly Official Records Eleventh Session supplement no. 18(a/3592), New York, 1957. https://digitallibrary.un.org/record/712474?ln=en.

Vonèche Cardia, Isabelle. *Hungarian October: Between Red Cross and Red Flag: The 1956 Action of the International Committee of the Red Cross*. Geneva: International Committee of the Red Cross, 1999.

Voorhees, Tracy S. "Demographics about the Hungarian Refugees and Stories about Specific Individual Experiences." Folder Joyce Kilmer Reception Center: Story of the Program for Hungarian Refugee Relief. Boxes K and L Hungarian Refugee Relief Files. Rutgers University Library, 1957. https://doi.org/doi:10.7282/T3319V8Q.

Ward, Eilís. "'A Big Show-Off to Show What We Could Do': Ireland and the Hungarian Refugee Crisis of 1956." *Irish Studies in International Affairs* 7 (1996): 131–41.

Ward, Nuala, and Orla Murphy. *Report on Inspection of the Child Protection and Welfare Services Provided to Children Living in Direct Provision Accommodation under the National Standards for the Protection and Welfare of Children, and Section 8(1) (c) of the Health Act 2007*. Dublin: Health Information and Quality Authority, 2015. https://www.rte.ie/documents/news/hiqa-report-on-child-protection-and-welfare-services.pdf.

Webb, Alban. "Cold War Radio and the Hungarian Uprising 1956." *Cold War History* 13, no. 2 (2013): 221–38.

Whitaker, Thomas Kenneth. *Programme for Economic Expansion*. Dublin: Stationery Office, 1958.

Wills, Clair. *That Neutral Island: A Cultural History of Ireland during the Second World War*. London: Faber and Faber, 2007.

Wyman, Mark. *DPs: Europe's Displaced Persons, 1945–1951*. Ithaca: Cornell University Press, 1998.

Zetter, Roger. "Labelling Refugees: Forming and Transforming Bureaucratic Identity." *Journal of Refugee Studies* 4, no. 1 (1991): 39–62.

———. "More Labels, Fewer Refugees: Remaking the Refugee Label in an Era of Globalisation." *Journal of Refugee Studies* 20, no. 2 (2007): 172–92.

Zieck, Marjoleine. "The 1956 Hungarian Refugee Emergency: An Early and Instructive Case of Resettlement." *Amsterdam Law Forum* 2 (2013): 45–63.

Zinn-Collis, Zoltan (with Alicia McCauley). *Final Witness: My Journey from the Holocaust to Ireland*. Dunshaughlin: Maverick House, 2006.

Zsolt, Béla. *Nine Suitcases*. London: Jonathan Cape, 2004.

INDEX

Aarö, Mr., 107
Abbey Theatre, 46
absence in history, refugees, 6–7
abuse, of children, 10–11, 136
administrative regions (*Länder*), 191
adoptions, illegal, 10, 195–96
adult experiences, 5
Advisory Council on Asylum, 125
Aer Lingus, 43–44
Agamben, Giorgio, 210n45
agency, refugee, 27, 192, 194, 205, 206; as decision-making, 38; denial of, 207; as giving back, 52; as work, 48
age profile, *51*
agricultural laborers, 19
Akos, Mr., 113
aliens, wandering, 154
Aliens Act (1935), 23, 70
Aliens Order (1946), 74
Aliens Registration Office, 63
America. *See* United States
amnesty (1963), 3
An Fórsa Cosanta Áitiúil (local defense force), 64
An Garda Síochána (Irish police force), 63, 70, 71, 80, 86
anti-Semitism, 12
apathy, DPs and, 59–61, 88
Appleby, Mr., 52
Arendt, Hannah, 3
Argentina, 4, 75, 108, 113, 157
Arms Crisis, 179, 182n62
Article 12, of Convention Relating to the Status of Refugees (1951), 125
Article 32, of Convention Relating to the Status of Refugees (1951), 64
artifacts, metalwork, 79
artwork, by child, *121*
Arup Ove and Partners, 81

Askalanzi, Stella, 13
assimilation, 112
asylum: countries of first, 54, 105; countries of second, 105; deserving seekers of, 27; seekers, 200. *See also specific topics*
Asyl-Verordnung (asylum regulation), 190
Australia, 4, 12, 75, 103–4, 108; Catholic emigrants to, 158; sailing to, 170–77
Austria, 8, 34–38, 43, 88, 106, 114, 186; Canada and, 54, 159, 165–66; children in, 124–25; IRC and, 44, 91; letters from, 98; *Die Presse* on, 116–17; pressure from, 40–41; refugee burden of, 4; refugee flow to, *37*; statement provided to refugees in, *39*; unaccompanied children in, 127
Austrian Federal Ministry for Social Welfare, 34
authorities, obeying, 192
Az Én Imakönyvem (*My Prayer Book*), 139

B., Mr., 85
Bagnoli Displaced Persons Camp, 13
Ballynanty School, 128, 129, 158, 168
Baltic states, 14, 17, 24, 26
baptism, first, *148*
Barrington's Hospital, 104
Barry, Tom, Mrs., 64, 70, 71, 74, 141, 179
Barth, Mr., 51
BBC, 99
Begley, Colm, 196
Bergen-Belsen concentration camp survivors, 11
Berne legation, 189
Berry, Peter, 63, 107, 206
"between sovereigns," 37
bias: religious, 42; sedentarist analytical, 6
Bielenberg, Christabel, 92n34, 117–18

Index

Bihary, Mr., 128, 156
Bikkes, Sándor, 83, 84
bipolarization, 5
black marketeering, 59
Blaney, Neil, 182n62
boat people, 25
Bodinka, Vilmos, 113
Bolivia, 109
Bora, Peter, 177
Bray Gospel Hall, 197
Brazil, 108
Brennan (Captain), 63, 72
Britain, 35, 106
bronchitis, 155
Browne (Pastor), 24

Cahersiveen Direct Provision Centre, 204
Callaghan (Commander), 69
camp school systems, 60
Canada, 4, 12, 106, 108, 113, 142, 206–7; Austria and, 54, 159, 165–66; Catholic emigrants to, 158; correspondence from, 167–69; Department of External Affairs and, 20, 54; hunger strike and, 99, 102; language in, 169–70; letters from, 98, 167–69; postwar refugees in, 14–16; resettlement in, 70, 165–70; sailing to, 14–22; screening for, 157–59
Canadian Council of Churches, 166
Carcaci, Ernesto Paternò Castello di, 56n28
care, of refugees, 63, 64–66, 75, 91
Caritas (church charity), 11, 41
casual labor, 82
Catholic Aid (Secours Catholique), 193
Catholic Relief Services (CRS), 107, 119n23, 158
Catholics/Catholicism, 23, 48; emigrants to Austria and Canada, 158; freedom fighters for, 61; in Holland, 191. *See also* Roman Catholic Church
Catholic Young Men's Society, 15
charitable organizations, 90
charity to refugees, 17–18; the deserving poor, 88–89, 90; deserving refugees, 27; gratitude, 205
Chief Rabbi's Emergency Appeal for Hungarian Relief, 46

Chikány, Elizabeth, 195–97
Chikány, Sándor, 194–95, 197; wife Ilona, 194
children, 5, 123–26; abuse of, 10–11, 136; artwork by, *121*; in Austria, 124–25; with bronchitis, 155; conclusion to, 147–50; Direct Provision and, 202–4, 210n35; Jewish, 11–12, 25; at Knockalisheen camp, 82; as legacies, 194–205; with pets, *132*; in poverty, 10, 131; registered under false name, *198*; in United Kingdom, 125; in Yugoslavia, 124–25. *See also* unaccompanied children
Children's Act (1908), 137
Christian Brothers, 128, 139, 149
Christians: as freedom fighters, 61; ideals of family life, 34; as warriors against Communism, 90. *See also* Catholics/Catholicism
Christmas, Hungarians in Ireland at, 69
church gate collection, 44
Church of Ireland, 24
Church of Ireland Gazette, 90
Cimade (Protestant organization), la, 193
Cistercian (Trappist) Order, 148
Clancy, Mr., 157
Clancy, Mrs., 68
Clann na Poblachta, 9
Clann na Talmhan, 9
Clare County Council, 75, 137
Clonyn Castle, 12, 25
coarse discourses, refugees, 206
Co. Carlow Resettlement Committee, 118
Cold War, 14, 88, 188, 206; geopolitical context of, 5–6; propaganda wars, 118n5
collections, for IRC, 44–48, 53
collective memory, 7
collective punishment, 86–87
College of Mount Saint Joseph Abbey, 148
College Players, 45–46
Collis, Robert, 11, 40n46
Colombia, 108
Commission on Emigration and Other Population Problems 1948–1954, 154
Commission to Inquire into Child Abuse, 10, 136
communication, lines of, 98–99

Communism/Communists, 5, 92, 129;
  Christians as warriors against, 90;
  "Godless Communism," 46, 71, 149, 157;
  hunger strike and, 111–13
Communist Party, 102
conceptualization, of refugees,
  22–28
concert, at Knockalisheen camp, 160
Congress, US, 109
Congress for Irish Unions, 83
constitutional rights, 82–84
"Continuity and Change in Ireland, 1945–70"
  (Lee), 59
Convention and the Statute of UNHCR
  (1951), 186
Convention Relating to the Status of
  Refugees (1951), 4, 53; Article 12 of, 125;
  Article 32 of, 64
Convent of Mercy, 128
Cook, Don, 5, 29n11
cooking facilities, 156
Córas Iompair Éireann (Irish railway
  company), 69
correspondence. See letters
Costello, John, 9, 44, 89, 91, 120n28
Council of Europe, 13
countries of first asylum, 54, 105
countries of second asylum, 105
COVID-19, 204
crime, 85–88; petty, 10; by unaccompanied
  children, 133–36
CRS. See Catholic Relief Services
Csoka, Josef, 159
cultural differences, 131

Dáil Éireann Debate, 97
Daingean Reformatory, 134–36, 159
de Barra, Leslie Bean, 179, 182n62. See also
  Barry, Tom, Mrs.
deception, in hunger strike, 100–111
Delattre, Simone, 107, 108
Denmark, 207
de Parcher, Mrs., 60
Department of Defense (Ireland), 18, 22, 44,
  48, 70, 91, 163; Knockalisheen camp and,
  62–63

Department of Education (Ireland), 78, 134,
  137
Department of External Affairs (Ireland),
  22, 53, 105, 140–43, 147, 206; Canada and,
  20, 54; Knockalisheen camp and, 66–67,
  102–3; Sweden and, 17
Department of Finance (Ireland), 20
Department of Health and Social Welfare
  (Ireland), 70
Department of Industry and Commerce
  (Ireland), 21, 22, 27, 28, 70, 155; *Victory*
  and, 16–18
Department of Justice (Ireland), 33–34,
  48–49, 63, 66–67, 71, 103, 114; Aliens Act
  and, 70; Canada and, 21; Jewish children
  and, 12; Roman Catholic Church and, 107;
  Victory and, 17–18
Department of the Taoiseach (Ireland), 22
departures, requests for, 144–47
Derrida, Jacques, 28
deserving asylum seekers, 27
deserving refugees, 88–92, 112
de Valera, Éamon, 9, 44, 89, 111, 114, 117,
  120n28, 172
Devlin, Mr., 142
Direct Provision system, 199–205, 210n35
disbelief, of refugees, 118, 207
disinformation: misinformation, 67;
  propaganda wars, 118n5; Soviet, 6
displaced persons (DPs), 7, 12–13, 37; apathy
  and, 59–60, 88. See also specific topics
Dolan (Sergeant), 92
domestic problems, 154–57
domestic services, 19
Donner Laboratory, 181n30
DPs. See displaced persons
drift, in 1950s Ireland, 9, 22
"drink on book," 80
Dublin Trades Union Council, 47
Dundon, Joseph, 165
Dun Laoghaire, 25
Dunne (Superintendent), 85

Economic Development (Whitaker), 30n37
economic migrants, refugees as, 27
Ed Sullivan Show, 35

Index

education: camp school systems, 60; primary school culture, 130; secondary, 147–48. *See also* Department of Education; Immaculata
Eisenhower, Dwight D., 35, 188
Eisenstadt camp, 40–41, 42
election (1954), 9
electricity consumption, 86
Electricity Supply Board (ESB), 52
Elie, Jerôme, 6
Elizabeth (Saint), 47
Emergency, the (1939–45), 11, 24, 61
employment, 19, 21, 34, 112, 155; entrepreneurship and, 78–82, 79, *81*; of Irish nationals, 82; Knockalisheen camp and, 76–84, *77*; unemployment, 25, 111
Enari, Mr., 26
England, 116
English language skills, 78
entrepreneurship, 78–82, 79, *81*
Erzebet (unaccompanied child), 140–41, 144, 145
Erzsébet (pupil), 170, 172–73, *175*
ESB. *See* Electricity Supply Board
Escapee Program, US, 108
Espiritu, Yến Lê, 207
European Economic Community, 10
Evening Herald, 68, 157
expert agitators, 70

Facebook, 204
Faculty of Pediatrics, Royal College of Physicians of Ireland, 203
Fáil, Fianna, 9
family: Christian ideals of, 34; letters to Hungarian family, *161*; searching for, 38–44, *39*, *40*
famine, Irish, 7
Fanning, Bryan, 4
farewell concert, at Knockalisheen camp, 160
Farkas, Béla, 66
Federal Republic of Germany, 190
Ferriter, Diarmaid, 9, 11
Filler, Rezzo (Rezső), 78
finance, 20

financial reserves, 19
first asylum, countries of, 54, 105
First World War, 20
flag, Hungarian, 104
Fogarty, Geraldine, 52, 79, 113
Ford Motor Works, 81
Foster, R. F., 9
France, 23, 193
Francis of Assisi (Saint), 47
freedom fighters, 35, 60–61; "real," 95n78
French National Committee for the Reception of Refugee, 193

Gabriella (pupil), 169
Gallopin, Mr., 141
Galway County Committee of Agriculture, 46
Garda Lowney, 85
Garvin, Tom, 11
Gatrell, Peter, 6, 7, 9
German Lutherans, 21
Germany, 5, 11, 14, 26, 190
Gladstone (ship), 14
"Godless Communism," 46, 71, 149, 157
Goldsmith, Oliver, 45

Haddad, Emma, 22–23, 28, 205
halálig (to the death), 102
Haley, Bill, 47
handicrafts, 78, 86
Hassetts (pub), 80
Haughey, Charles, 182n62
Hayes, Michael, 52
Headen, Michael, 47
Hednesford refugee camp, 8
Helfferich, Ilona, 177
Helmer, Oskar, 186
Herald Tribune, 5
"Heroic Men of Budapest, The" (Kiely), 33
Herzog, Dr., 12
heteroglossia, 8
Higgins, Marguerite, 29n11
historical record, 9; reevaluation of, 6
"history from below," 8
Holland, 191–92
Holy Communion, 149, 153n72

Homo Sacer (Agamben), 210n45
hospitality, 6, 26
hostipitality, 28
housing crisis, 204; shortage of, 163
Hudak, László, 177
Huiré, Huibe, 66, 154
human-interest stories, 5
humanitarianism, 14
human rights violations, 3
Hungarian diaspora community, in Ireland, 29n6
Hungarian language, 129–30
Hungarian Red Cross, 125, 144, 146
Hungarian Refugee Program, 43
"Hungarian Refugees" (Lavan), 97
Hungarian Revolution (1956). *See specific topics*
hunger strike: ambiguous intent in, 101; Canada and, 99, 102; Communists and, 111–13; conclusion to, 114–18; as *halálig*, 102; international and local perspectives on, 116–18; international organizations and representatives and, 105–9, *106*, *108*; liminality and, 97–99; surveillance and deception in, 100–111; women and, 104
huts, Knockalisheen camp, 62, *62*

ICEM. *See* Intergovernmental Committee for European Migration
ICRC. *See* International Committee of the Red Cross
identity, 22–23, 25, 27
illegal adoptions, 195–96
Immaculata (Sister), 129–33, 158, 179; child's artwork for, *121*; letters to, 131–33, 167–69, 170–73, *171*, *172*, *174*, *175*; postcard to, *189*; song book by, 130, *130*
indifference, of government, 143
Industrial Foundries, 76, 78
industrial schools, 134, 137, 139
initial reactions, to crisis, 33–35
interdepartmental meetings, in Knockalisheen camp, 70–76, *71*
Intergovernmental Committee for European Migration (ICEM), 42, 48, 102, 114, 117;

hunger strike and, 105–7; leaflet by, 38, 54; transport costs and, 43
International Committee of the Red Cross (ICRC), 124–26
international dimension, of refugee resettlement, 185–94
international perspective, on hunger strike, 116–18
International Red Cross Committee, 146
International Refugee Organization (IRO), 12
Irish Association of the Sovereign and Military Order of Malta, 45
Irish Ballet Company, 45
Irish Countrywomen's Association, 46
Irish Examiner, 76, 91, 156
Irish Famine, 7
Irish Folklore Commission, 52
Irish Motor Traders Association, 84
Irish Municipal Trades Union, 46
Irish Pictorial, 53
Irish Press, 44, 127, 146, 154
Irish Red Cross (IRC). *See specific topics*
Irish Refugee Council, 203
Irish Shipping Limited, 60
Irish Times, 59, 94n34, 99, 112–13, 115, 123
Irish Transport and General Workers Union (ITGWU), 82
IRO. *See* International Refugee Organization
"Iron Cage, The" (McArdle), 3
Iron Curtain, 37, 107, 139
Israel, 4
Is the Priest at Home? (play), 46
Italy, 13, 105
ITGWU. *See* Irish Transport and General Workers Union

Jewish children, 11–12, 25
Jewish community, 46
Jewish heritage, 197
Jews, 108
John Quins (pub), 80
Jónas, Bobby, 176
Jónas, Kati, 176–77
Joyce Kilmer Reception Center, 186
Judenau camp, 42

Kádár, János, 3
Kádár government, 123, 125
Kaisersteinbruch camp, 42, 43
Kelly, Mr., 143, 144
Keszi-Koch, Janos, 81
Kiely, Benedict, 33
Kilkenny People, 45
Kis (Father), 62, 103, 150
Knockalisheen camp, 4, 28, 34, 48, 51, 61–66, 91, 105–7; bronchitis in, 155; Canadian commission in, 159; children at, 82; closing of, 162–65; daily life in, 5; Department of Defense and, 62–63; Department of External Affairs and, 66–67, 102–3; departure from, 160–62; employment and, 76–84, 77; farewell concert at, 160–62; holidays at, 67–70; huts at, 62, 62; interdepartmental meetings in, 70–76, 71; letter to US from, 109–11; misbehavior at, 85–88; quarantine for, 66–70; as symbol for all camps, 210n45; weddings at, 67–70; weekly menu of, 65; women at, 82. *See also specific topics*
Korean War, 29n11
Kos, Miss, 63
Kotek, Karoly, 81
Kovary, Mrs., 85
Kozak, Mr., 164
Kukk, Mr., 86, 111, 159, 160, 167, 169
Kun, Mr., 164

labor: agricultural laborers, 19; casual, 82; market, 82, 190; shortage, 19; skilled, 166. *See also* employment
Labour Court, 84
Lajos H. (unaccompanied child), 137–39
Lajos R. (unaccompanied child), 164–65
Länder (administrative regions), 191
language: in Canada, 169–70; difficulties, 154–55; English skills, 78; Hungarian, 129–30
larceny, 133
Last Post, 157
Lavan (Superintendent), 72, 74–75, 91, 97–98, 100–101, 127, 133, 155
League of Nations, 10, 57n49
League of Red Cross Societies, 114

Lee, J. J., 9, 59
legacies, children as, 194–205
Legion of Mary, 46
Letoha, Anna, 41, 52, 127, 177
Letoha, János, 79
Letterfrack Industrial School, 139
letters: from Austria, 98; from Canada, 98, 167–69; to Hungarian family, *161*; to Sister Immaculata, 131–33, 167–69, 170–73, *171, 172, 174, 175*; to US from Knockalisheen, 109–11
Levy, Jacob, 12
Limerick Chronicle, 79
Limerick Leader, 164
Limerick Motor Works, 82–83
Limerick Vocational Education Committee, 78
liminality, 97–99, 148
Lindt, Gustav, 140
Lipot, Mr., 145
local perspective, on hunger strike, 116–18
Longford Leader, 25
looking after our own, 7, 25, 117, 163
Lorincz, Mr., 162
Lovas, Laszlo, 53, 79
Lukács, Ilona, 194–95
Lutheran Society of America, 21
Lutheran World Federation (LWF), 21
Lyons, James, 45

MacBride, Seán, 18
MacEoin, Seán, 64, 89
Maev, LÉ (ship), 53
Mahon, George, 113
malaise, 22
malcontents, 75, 90
Maléter, Pál, 3
Malkki, Liisa, 23, 28
Mannik, Lynda, 20, 25
Marfleet, Philip, 7
Mária (pupil), 158, 168, 176–77
MASI. *See* Movement of Asylum Seekers in Ireland
Mathers, Adeline "Auntie," 195–96
McArdle, Dorothy, 3
McCabe, Dr., 134
McCann, Mr., 64, 103, 104, 155

McCann Barracks, 155–56, 157, 203
McCluskey, Mr., 107
McMahon, Bryan, 200–201, 203
McMahon, Mrs., 69
McNeill, Josephine, 55n12, 114, 143
McQuaid, John Charles, 10, 13, 34, 107
media, 8; freedom fighters and, 35; social, 204
medical screening, 49
medical treatment, necessary, 22
memory, collective, 7
metalwork artifacts, 79
Mihaly, Solű, 176
Mihaly B. (unaccompanied child), 140–41, 159
Mills, William, 81
Mindszenty (Cardinal), 46–47, 52
Ministry of Foreign Affairs (Austria), 125
Ministry of Justice (Austria), 125
Ministry of the Interior (Austria), 43, 124, 125
misbehavior, 85–88
misinformation, 67
misunderstanding, 5, 111, 118, 178, 205; as miscommunication, 115
moneymaking enterprises, 78
moral judgments, of women, 24
Mount Melleray College, 148
movement, restriction of, 71
Movement of Asylum Seekers in Ireland (MASI), 200, 203
Multyfarnham Agricultural College, 148
Munster Football Association, 46
Murphy, Mr. (camp controller), 60, 63, 98, 100–101, 137, 145, 178–79; employment and, 78; misbehavior and, 85–86; Pesthy and, 72; photograph of, 71
Murphy, Olga, 35, 62, 102
My Prayer Book (*Az Én Imakönyvem*), 139

Nagy, Imre, 3
National Catholic Resettlement Council, 119n23
National Catholic Welfare Conference (NCWC), 107, 119n23, 158
nationalist perspective, 4, 20, 117, 172, 204
Nationality and Citizenship Act, 23
national self-image, 6–7

NATO. *See* North Atlantic Treaty Organization
Nazi Germany, 11
NCWC. *See* National Catholic Welfare Conference
necessary medical treatment, 22
"New Americans," 188
Newcastle-on-Tyne, England, 116
Newpark Comprehensive School, 195–96
New York Times, 99
NGOs. *See* nongovernmental organizations
Nineteenth International Red Cross Conference, 126, 141
nongovernmental organizations (NGOs), 8, 34, 41–42, 60, 188, 193, 200. *See also specific organizations*
North Atlantic Treaty Organization (NATO), 37, 166
Norway, 26
Nyers, Peter, 206

O'Callaghan (Commandant), 63, 74
O'Ceallaigh, Séan, 89
O'Doherty, Dr., 48
Office Fédéral de l'Industrie, 190
Office of Refugees and Immigration Affairs, 99
Office of the High Commissioner, 124, 143
O'Kelly, Sean T., 179
O'Malley, Mr., 97
O'Neill, Dr. (Reverend), Bishop of Limerick, 69, 72, 115
Operation Shamrock, 11, 23
oral histories, 9
Origins of Totalitarianism (Arendt), 3
orphans. *See* unaccompanied children
O'Shaughnessy, Mrs., 63
O'Shea, Mrs., 80
Ostergren, David, 21
O'Sullivan, (Commandant), 156
O'Sullivan, Mr., 83–84

Page, Barbara, 68, 69
pálinka, 80
Pálmai Bánki, Katalin, 4, 193
Palocz, Mrs., 87, 164
Past Is Myself, The (Bielenberg), 94n34

PCFHRR. *See* President's Committee for Hungarian Refugee Relief
"Peace in the Valley," 35
Pennefather, Heather, 117–18
Penny School of Ballet and Dancing, 160
Pesthy, László, 72–75, 89, 92, 94n34
pets, children with, 132
petty crime, 10
Pickarczyk, Mr., 112, 113
Pickersgill, Mr., 158, 165–66
Pinter, Gizella, 177
Polczer, Tibor (unaccompanied child), 140–41, 150
Polish refugees, 24
postcard, to Sister Immaculata, 189
postwar refugees, 11–13; in Canada, 14–16; on *Victory* (ship), 16–22, 19. *See also specific topics*
poverty, 10, 195; children in, 10, 131
Powers Bakery, 177
practical sympathy, of Irish people, 67–68
prayer meetings, 46
presence, of refugees, 6
President's Committee for Hungarian Refugee Relief (PCFHRR), 188, 205
Presley, Elvis, 35
Presse, Die, 116–17
primary school culture, 130
Probation Act, 25
propaganda wars, in Cold War, 118n5
Protestants, 108
protests: against Direct Provision, 204. *See also* hunger strike
Public Assistance Act (1939), 20
punishment: collective, 86–87; of unaccompanied children, 133–36

quarantine, for Knockalisheen camp, 66–70
Queens Hotel, 178
Quin, Maíre, 80
Quinn, Mr., 84

radio broadcasts, 98–99, 124
Radió Éireann, 47, 48, 81
Radio Free Europe, 99, 118n5
Read, James, 140, 141, 142, 146
"real" freedom fighters, 95n78

"real" refugees, 27
reevaluation, of historical record, 6
referential reflexivity, 8
reformatories, 134
refugee, definition of, 8, 13
refugeedom, 6
refugee flow, 36, 37
refugeeness, 27, 206
refugee numbers, 50, 50–51, 187–88
refugee research, 6–11
refugees. *See specific topics*
"Refugees Abscond to Britain from Knockalisheen," 59
Regan, Miss, 158
rehabilitation, 60, 88–89
rehousing, 162–65
religious bias, 42
Religious Emergency Council, 12
Remenyi, Stephen, 60
Remmel, Herbert, 11, 30n47
repatriation, 147
resettlement, 34, 105; in Canada, 70, 165–70; of DPs, 12–13; in US, 186. *See also specific topics*
Resolution XX, 126
restlessness, 116–17
restriction of movement, 71
returns, requests for, 144–47
revolution (1956), 89
rights: constitutional, 82–84; human rights violations, 3
Road Ahead, The (Bielenberg), 94n34
Rock Around the Clock (film), 47
Rockgrove camp, 18
Roman Catholic Church, 13, 46, 50, 52, 91, 108, 146, 159; Caritas, 11, 41; Department of Justice and, 107; power of, 10, 34
Royal College of Physicians of Ireland, 203
RTÉ Brainstorm, 210n41
Russia, 40, 47

Safari, Paul, 162
Saint Brendan's Cathedral, 46
Saint Conleth's (reformatory), 134, 136
Saint Joseph's Industrial School, 137
Saint Vincent de Paul Society, 15, 90
Sarabande (ship), 15–16

Saunders, Dr., 16
Savage, Roland Burke, 10
school systems, camp, 60
screening: for Canada, 157–59; medical, 49
Seafield Fabrics, 75, 177
secondary education, 147–48
second asylum, countries of, 105
Second World War, 7–8, 10–11, 14, 29n11, 37, 69, 92, 192
Secours Catholique (Catholic Aid), 193
sedentarist analytical bias, 6
self-image, national, 6–7
separated children. *See* unaccompanied children
Service Sociale d'Aide aux Emigrants (Social Service for Emigrant Aid), Le, 193
Shannon, Geoffrey, 185
Shannon airport, 18, 48, 60, 80
Sheehy Skeffington, Owen, 136–39, 151n38
She Stoops to Conquer (Goldsmith), 45
Shtorn, Evgeny, 204, 210n41
silencing, refugees, 73, 199, 202, 207
Singer Company, 61
Siráky, Béla, 78
Sisters of Mercy, 13
skilled labor, 166
skills: English language, 78; technical, 76
Sligo Champion, 15
Smithwick, Walter, 45
social media, 204
Social Service for Emigrant Aid (Le Service Sociale d'Aide aux Emigrants), 193
Somodi, Mr., 112
Somodi family, 69
Somogyi, Mr., 51
Sopron University, 166
Soviet Union (USSR), 3, 12; captured tank of, 1; disinformation in, 6. *See also* Russia
Spain, 23
Spelter, Henrik, 177
sponsorship, 108, 113
Spratzern camp, 42
stagnation, in 1950s Ireland, 9, 10, 22
Stalinism, 54, 192
State Department (US), 99

"Statement on Refugees 'Would Be Going to US' Belief," 154
steelworks, 89
Stewart, Mr., 160
St. John's Church, 24
St. Peter's Lutheran Church, 24–25
Studies (journal), 10, 96n94
surveillance, in hunger strike, 100–111
Sweden, 14, 16–17, 20, 26, 27
Sweeney (Major General), 140, 142
Switzerland, 4, 189–90
sympathy, 90–91; for children in poverty, 10; human-interest stories rousing, 5; practical, 67–68; in Sweden, 26; for *Victory* passengers, 25
Szövérffy, Joseph, 47, 51–52, 88, 92, 96n94, 100, 118, 127

Takács, Ferencz, 79
Takacs, Mr., 53
Taul, Jack, 21
Teachta Dála (TD), 4
technical skills, 76
telegrams, 40
thespians, 45
Third Order of St. Francis, 46
Thompson, E. P., 7
Time (magazine), 35
Tittman, Harold, 43
Tobias, Cornelius, 164, 181n30
to the death (*halálig*), 102
Trades Union Movement, 83
trade unions, 82
Traiskirchen camp, 8, 42
Trappist (Cistercian) Order, 148
treatment, necessary medical, 22
Tunna, Mr., 81–82
Twelfth Infantry S Battalion, 63
Tyrell, Peter, 136–37, 151n38

unaccompanied children, 126–47, *128*, 151n31; crime and punishment of, 133–36; individual cases for, 144–47; international cooperation and, 139–44; offering homes to, 150n15; with pets, *132*; Sister Immaculata and, 129–33; Skeffington and, 136–39

UN Convention on the Rights of the Child, 123
undeserving refugees, 88–92, 112
unemployment, 111
UNHCR. *See* United Nations High Commissioner for Refugees
unions, trade, 82
United Kingdom, 4, 35, 54, 125–26, 159
United Nations, 3, 53, 123
United Nations High Commissioner for Refugees (UNHCR), 105, 125, 140, 143, 186, 205; Caritas and, 41; initial reactions by, 33–34; refugee flow and, 36, *37*
United Nations Relief and Rehabilitation Administration (UNRRA), 12, 60
United States (US), 4, 75, 98, 102, 103–5, 108, 188; Congress, 109; Eisenhower administration in, 35; Escapee Program of, 108; letter from Knockalisheen to, 109–11; resettlement in, 186; sailing to, 176–77; State Department, 99
University College Dublin, 44, 48, 52
University College Dublin Dramatic Society, 45
University College Galway, 47
University of British Columbia, 166
University of Toronto, 166
UNRRA. *See* United Nations Relief and Rehabilitation Administration
US. *See* United States
USSR. *See* Soviet Union

Vanya, Ted, 41
Victory (ship), 16–22, *19*, 24–25, 54, 90
Viking ships, 24
Vincze, Ferencz, 79
Voice of America, 99
Volo (fishing boat), 15
Voorhees, Tracy, 188, 205

Walnut (ship), 14–15, 24, 25
wandering aliens, 154
Ward, Eilís, 4
War Relief Services (WRS), 119n23
weddings, at Knockalisheen camp, 67–70
welfare state: Ireland, 90; Sweden, 26
Whitaker, T. K., 10, 30n37
Williams, Miss, 66
Wills, Clair, 11
Wolf, Josef, 113
women, 10–11, 205; hunger strike and, 104; at Knockalisheen, 82; moral judgments of, 24
Women's Saturday Magazine, 68
World Council of Churches, 108, 164
World War I, 20
World War II, 7–8, 10–11, 14, 29n11, 37, 69, 92, 192
WRS. *See* War Relief Services
Wyrouboff, Mr., 105, 106, 117

Yugoslavia, 4, 91, 114; children in, 124–25
Yugoslav Red Cross, 125

Vera Sheridan is an Associate Member of the School of Applied Language and Intercultural Studies at Dublin City University. She is editor (with Donnacha Ó Beacháin and Sabina Stan) of *Life in Post-Communist Eastern Europe after EU Membership: Happy Ever After*?

www.ingramcontent.com/pod-product-compliance
Lightning Source LLC
Chambersburg PA
CBHW030539230426
43665CB00010B/962